U0144933

97~101年

英文科

指考／學測

等歷屆試題解析

應考破題技巧大公開

等歷屆試題解析

應考破題技巧大公開

市面上，你看不到如此詳細的歷屆試題解題、破題、應考技巧大公開的書。
完整收錄、每題詳細解析──97~101年指考‧學測等歷屆英文科試題。

English

黃惠政 著

序

擔任英文教學工作數十年，尤其在年歲漸長時，更會感到「經驗傳承」的必要。

不論從事任何行業，如果能將所學的菁華重點記錄下來、編輯成冊、出書，可讓讀者「分享好的經驗、少走冤枉路」，那也是美事一椿。

本人在「各層級英語考試教學」與「英語領隊與導遊帶團實務」等兩大專長領域裡，多年來出書多冊。此次，蒙五南圖書出版股份有限公司相邀，撰寫「**英文科**指考‧學測，歷屆試題解析──應考破題技巧大公開」、「**97～100年**，**英文科**統測‧學測，歷屆試題解析──應考破題技巧大公開」二書，希望能在學校一般英語文教學方法之外，提供考生另一種有助得分的解題方式。

作者出版過的英文考試用書，主要目的都是在幫助考生得分過關，本書也不例外。

不論任一層級的英文考試，必包含若干的「試題題型」，包括字彙測驗、語詞測驗……等。所以，考生在準備考試時，必須先了解有哪些試題題型？不同題型的試題怎麼計分？有沒有倒扣？

本書在〈題型分析學測指考篇〉裡，詳細說明了：在不同題型裡有不同的解題技巧與策略、各種題型需注意的地方。

另外，在本書的〈重點文法篇〉裡，也詳列多項文法重點，特別是在不同層級英文試題裡常出現的文法試題。並放入作者的「重點提醒」，請考生一定要多看幾遍「重點提醒」的內容，因為它才是要告訴考生該如何答題的重點。

本書〈附錄〉裡，也收錄了統測、學測、指考等三大考試，考生的必備字彙、俚語＆片語等。請考生在閱讀這些資料時，儘量利用「線上詞典」等的翻譯軟體，快速看出某字當名詞時會有哪些例句，當形容詞時會有哪些例句……等。

當然作者也不忘在此建議考生幾件事：

1. 在做選擇題時，每題的做題時間最好不超過一分鐘。大多數的考生都會為了一個好像會，但一時想不起來的字詞、片語，而浪費太多時間在同一題上，以致延誤了做其他題目的時間。

2. 考試的前一天晚上必須要有充足的睡眠。千萬不要在考前一天的晚上還在熬夜讀書，否則第二天到了考場，就比較會因為睡眠不足，而有忽然間大腦一片空白的情況，那就得不償失了。

3. 到了考場後，要有「一切順其自然」的應考態度，答題時只要憑直覺應答即可。反正考前該準備的都準備了，到了考場後著急也沒有用，所以，你為什麼不以放鬆的心情、愉快應考呢？

最後，在準備相當的字彙量（含片語、俚語）、充分了解各種試題題型的特色，以及應考之道、勤做歷屆考古題、熟練解題技巧與策略等的多管齊下下，想得高分並不難。

作者在此預祝──認真研讀本書的考生，考得高分、金榜題名！

黃惠政

於新北市2011年9月26日

學測、指考，歷屆試題解題技巧

一、詞彙題（15分）

> 說明：第1題至第15題，每題4個選項，其中只有1個是最適當的選項，畫記在答案卡之「選擇題答案區」。各題答對得1分，未作答、答錯、或畫記多於1個選項者，該題以零分計算。

例題1

All the new students were given one minute to _____ introduce themselves to the whole class.

(A) briefly　(B) famously　(C) gradually　(D) obviously

題型解題技巧：

1. 本題屬於一般的「字彙題」題型，在題句裡有一空格，而從 ABCD 四選項擇一作答。

2. 這種「題內有空格」的字彙題，快速答題的關鍵字通常是在空格左、右兩邊各三個字內。如果在這 6 個字內找不到它的關鍵字，不要浪費時間，趕快作下一題，等一下如果有時間再回來看這一題。

3. 以本題為例，關鍵字就在空格左右兩邊的「one minute to _____ introduce themselves」（用一分鐘來_____介紹他們自己），只要考生看懂這幾個關鍵字的中文意思，就可立即判斷 (A) 項的「briefly（簡短地）」才是正確選項。

二、綜合測驗（占15分）

> 說明：第 16 題至第 30 題，每題一個空格，請依文意選出最適當的一個答案，畫記在答案卡之「選擇題答案區」。各題答對得 1 分；未作答、答錯、或畫記多於一個選項者，該題以零分計算。

例題─部分短文

　　When it comes to Egypt, people think of pyramids and mummies, both of which are closely related to Egyptian religious beliefs. The ancient Egyptians believed firmly in life _____16_____ death. When a person died, his or her soul was thought to travel to an underworld, where it _____17_____ a series of judgments before it could progress to a better life in the next world.......

選項

例題16

→(A) for　(B) by　(C) after　(D) into

例題17

→(A) went through　(B) made up　(C) changed into　(D) turned out

題型解題技巧：

1. 「綜合測驗」與「字彙測驗」兩者的解題方法基本上是一樣的，只是字彙題是一題題單獨列出，且兩題之間毫無關聯；而綜合測驗則是在一段短文裡劃分出幾個加註題號的空格，看起來像有了題號的填空題。

2.考生在作答綜合測驗時要特別小心，你在答案紙上的題號與試卷上的題號必須一致。換言之，假設試題卷上的第 16 題你會寫，千萬不要誤用第 17 題的 ABCD 四選項作答。誤用不同題號的四選項作答經常發生，這樣會造成骨牌效應，其後的試題有可能都會答錯。

3.建議考生在作綜合測驗時，與其要看懂整段文章的每一個字，不如重點式的只看每一題的單獨「題句」就好，（其範圍是以「題號空格」為基準，往前與往後，看到「逗點」、「句點」或「連接詞」之處）。以上述第 16、17 題為例，可單獨列出兩題的題句如下：

| 題句16 | The ancient Egyptians believed firmly in life _____16_____ death. |

| 題句17 | where it _____17_____ a series of judgments before ...in the next world |

4.近年來，不同種類英文考試裡的克漏字測驗、文意選填、篇章結構、綜合測驗等，都是同一類的測驗題（即「在文章裡劃有若干標有題號空格」的題型）。建議考生：平常要多多練習，碰到這類型題目時，先快速的將每一題看成單獨題句即可答題。

三、文意選填（10分）

說明：第31題至第40題，每題1個空格。請依文意在文章後所提供的(A)到(J)選項中分別選出最適當者，並將其英文字母代號畫記在答案卡之「選擇題答案區」。各題答對得1分，未作答、答錯、或畫記多於1個選項者，該題以零分計算。

Popcorn is one of the snacks that rarely fail to make watching a movie more fun. However, the modern way of preparing this _____31_____ snack may carry an unhappy secret. Research by the U.S. government now reports that microwave popcorn may contain substances that can cause health _____32_____ .

(A) chemical化學　　(B) amount數量　　(C) popping 突出 爆出　　(D) popular受歡迎的

(E) comes 來　　(F) healthy 健康　　(G) needed 有需要　　(H) responsible負責　　(I) remove 移開

(J) problems 問題

題型解題技巧

1.文意選題的題目與綜合測驗題型幾乎相同，不同的是，文意選填 ABCD 四個選項，都列在該題號，等於是「四選一」作答。綜合測驗，則是從整段文章後的 A～J 10 個選項中擇一作答（有些試題是 A～L 12 個選項，不一定），難度增加。

2.考生在應此類解題法與「二、綜合測驗─題型解題技巧第 3 點」說法一樣，與其看懂整段文章每一個字，倒不如重點式的只看每一題單獨「題句」就好。以上文為例，第 31、32 句的單句範圍如下：

| 題句31 | the modern way of preparing this _____31_____ snack may carry an unhappy secret |

| 題句32 | that microwave popcorn may contain substances that can cause health _____32_____ . |

3.如果考生看懂第 31 題句關鍵字的「preparing this _____31_____ snack」（準備這種 _____ 的點心）中文意思，就知道要選(D)「popular（受歡迎的）」。

四、閱讀測驗（占 32 分）

說明：第 41 題至第 56 題，每題 4 個選項，請分別根據各篇文章之文意選出最適當的一個答案，畫記在答案卡之「選擇題答案區」。各題答對得 2 分；未作答、答錯、或畫記多於一個選項者，該題以零分計算。

There is a long-held belief that when meeting someone, the more eye contact we have with the person, the better. The result is an unfortunate tendency for people making initial contact-in a job interview, for example-to stare fixedly at the other individual. However, this behavior is likely to make the interviewer feel very uncomfortable. Most of us are comfortable with eye contact lasting a few seconds. But eye contact which persists longer than that can make us nervous.

題型解題技巧

1. 閱讀測驗的題型，是在一篇文章後列若干問題，每個問題後也會跟著 ABCD 四個選項，讓考生擇一作答。

2. 這類試題文章長度與內容難易，依不同層級考試不同。但至少每篇文章都需花幾分鐘才看得完，再根據該文內容的了解答題。對字彙量不多的考生是一大考驗。

3. 這類測驗題目，常會問到像「What is the passage mainly about ?」、「What does the word」、「mean ?」、「What is the best title for this passage ?」等。

4. 以第 42 題爲例請見本書 P.174，題目是問「What is true about fixing your eyes on a person when you first meet him/her ?」（與某人第一次見面時就直視對方的後果，下列哪一說法爲眞?）考生從文章裡的「to stare fixedly at the other individual. However, this behavior is likely to make the interviewer feel very uncomfortable」可看出，(C) 才是正確選項。」

第貳部分：非選擇題（占 28 分）

一、中譯英（占 8 分）

說明：1. 請將以下中文句子譯成正確、通順、達意的英文，並將答案寫在「答案卷」上。

2. 請依序作答，並標明題號。每題 4 分，共 8 分。

例題1 臺灣的夜市早已被認爲足以代表我們的在地文化。

題型解題技巧

1. 先將題句內相關字詞寫出中譯。

臺灣的夜市 night markets in Taiwan

早已被認爲 has been long recognized

足以代表 to represent

我們的在地文化 our local culture

整句中譯：The night markets in Taiwan has been long recognized to represent our local culture.

2. 本句主詞 The night markets in Taiwan 是指一件事，一件事是一整體單位，所以其動詞用「has」而非 have。同理，「Five million dollars is a big sum of money」，因 500 萬是一個整體單位，所以必須用單數動詞。

二、英文作文（占 20 分）

說明：1. 依提示在「答案卷」上寫一篇英文作文。

2. 文長約 100 至 120 個單詞（words）。

例題1

提示：請仔細觀察以下三幅連環圖片的內容，並想像第四幅圖片可能的發展，寫出一個涵蓋連環圖片內容並有完整結局的故事。

題型解題技巧：

1.這種「看圖說故事」的作文很容易發揮，它並沒有固定的格式要求考生怎麼寫，只要寫出來的文章不
　離圖意太遠，加上語句通順、文法不要錯，都可得高分。

2.接下來，把每一幅圖畫的細節寫出來，例如：圖1

圖1　那是一場化妝舞會　a boy and a girl were in a costume party

　　　男生帶著眼罩　the boy is wearing a blindfold

　　　女生化妝成選美女王　the girl is playing a role of beauty queen

　　　丘比特愛心之箭射向女生　Cupid's arrow is shooting toward the girl

　　　酒杯裡還剩有酒　there was still some wine left in the glass

100年指考

　　　指考與學測的試題題型幾乎相同，唯一的差別在於：指考試題多了一項「篇章結構」的題
型。與學測相同的題型分析不必重複，在此僅補充篇章結構的題型分析如下：

四、篇章結構（10分）

> 說明：第31題至第35題，每題1個空格。請依文意在文章後所提供的 (A) 到 (F) 選項中分別選出
> 最適當者，填入空格中，使篇章結構清晰有條理，並將其英文字母代號標示在答案卡之「選
> 擇題答案區」。每題答對得2分，未作答、答錯、或畫記多於1個選項者，該題以零分計算。

　　　第31至35題為題組

　　　The effect of bullying can be serious and even lead to tragedy. Unfortunately, it is still a mostly
unresearched area. _____31_____ That year two shotgun-wielding students, both of whom had
been identified as gifted and who had been bullied for years, killed 13 people, wounded 24 and
then committed suicide. A year later an analysis by the US government found that bullying played a
major role in more than two-thirds of the campus violence.

　　　本題型的六個答句選項（請見本書P.79～80）。

題型解題技巧：

1 篇章結構的題型，與上兩種「綜合測驗」、「文意選填」的題型也幾乎相同。三者間的差別在於「綜
　合測驗」是四選一作答、「文意選填」是 10 或 12 選一作答，而「篇章結構」則是從「六個整句」
　裡，選一句放入空格作答，答題難度更高。

2 解題重點是：必須先看懂空格左、右兩句的意思，然後在文章後的六個答案選項句找出某句放入空格
　後，就能有意義地串聯前後兩句，達到完整文意。

3 以第 31 題為例：第 31 題空格左句「Unfortunately....area」，中譯為「不幸的是，這部分至今仍未被調
　查研究過」空格右句「That year....students」，中譯為「那年兩個揮舞獵槍的學生……」。只有 (F) 放入
　空格中，才能有意義地將前後三句串聯起來，達到完整的文意。

目錄

序 (2)
學測、指考、歷屆試題解題技巧 (3)

一、指考（指定考試）（97～100年指考）

97年指考（指定考試） 03
98年指考（指定考試） 25
99年指考（指定考試） 48
100年指考（指定考試） 71

二、學測（學科能力測驗）（97～100年學測）

97年學測（學科能力測驗） 95
98年學測（學科能力測驗） 117
99年學測（學科能力測驗） 140
100年學測（學科能力測驗） 163
101年指考（指定考試） 185
101年指考（解答） 194
101年學測（學科能力測驗） 195
101年學則（解答） 203

附錄

一、統測、學測、指考等之重點文法 204
二、重要片語、俚語之補充（學測、指考、統測） 212
三、重要字彙補充（學測、指考、統測） 214

指考（指定考試）

（97～100年指考）

97 年指考（指定考試）

第壹部分：選擇題（72分）

一、詞彙（10分）

說明：第 1 至10 題，每題選出一個最適當的選項，標示在答案卡之「選擇題答案區」。每題答對得 1 分，答錯或劃記多於一個選項者倒扣 1/3 分，倒扣到本大題之實得分數為零為止。未作答者，不給分亦不扣分。

1. The new stadium was built at a convenient ＿＿＿＿＿＿＿ , close to an MRT station and within walking distance to a popular shopping center.

   新的體育場蓋在方便的 ＿＿＿＿＿＿＿ ，靠近捷運站，到購物中心也走路可到。

   (A) vacancy 空缺　(B) procedure 程序　(C) residence 居住　(D) location 位置

   解析
   (1)答題關鍵在題目空格左、右方的「蓋在方便的」與「靠近捷運站」 ＿＿＿＿＿＿＿ 。
   (2)四個選項中，只有選 (D) 項的「位置」，才可有意義連成「蓋在方便的位置，靠近捷運站……」。

2. The young Taiwanese pianist performed ＿＿＿＿＿＿＿ well and won the first prize in the music contest.

   年輕的臺灣鋼琴家表現 ＿＿＿＿＿＿＿ 好並贏得音樂賽首獎。

   (A) intimately 親密地　(B) remarkably 非常地　(C) potentially 有潛力的　(D) efficiently 有效率地

   解析
   (1)答題關鍵在題目空格左、右方的「表現」與「好」。
   (2)四個選項中，只有選(B)項的「非常地」，才可有意義連成「表現非常地好並贏得……」。

3. As thousands of new ＿＿＿＿＿＿＿ from Southeastern Asia have moved to Taiwan for work or marriage, we should try our best to help them adjust to our society.

   數以千計的新 ＿＿＿＿＿＿＿ 來自於東南亞，來工作或結婚。我們應盡量幫助他們適應我們的社會。

   (A) immigrants 外來的移民　(B) messengers 信差　(C) possessors 持有人　(D) agencies 代理處

解析
(1)答題關鍵在題目空格左、右方的「新」與「來自於東南亞」。
(2)四個選項中，只有選(A)項的「外來移民」，才可有意義連成「新外來移民來自於東南亞」。

4. Although the manager apologized many times for his poor decision, there was nothing he could do to ＿＿＿＿＿＿ his mistake.

雖然經理爲錯誤決定道歉多次，他也無能力 ＿＿＿＿＿＿ 他的錯誤。

(A) resign 辭職　(B) retain 保留　(C) refresh 使……清新　(D) remedy 糾正補救

解析
(1)答題關鍵在題目空格左、右方的「無能力」與「他的錯誤」。
(2)四個選項中，只有選(D)項的「補救」，才可有意義連成「他也無能力補救他的錯誤」。

5. Last winter's snowstorms and freezing temperatures were quite ＿＿＿＿＿＿ for this region where warm and short winters are typical.

去年冬天的大雪及低溫是相當 ＿＿＿＿＿＿ ，對這個典型的溫暖短冬地區來說。

(A) fundamental 基本的　(B) extraordinary 異常的　(C) statistical 統計的　(D) individual 個別的

解析
(1)答題關鍵在題目空格左、右方的「是相當」與「這個溫暖地區來說」。
(2)四個選項中，只有選(B)項的「異常的」，才可有意義連成「是相當異常的，對這個溫暖短冬地區來說」。

6. To overcome budget shortages, some small schools in rural areas have set up ＿＿＿＿＿＿ programs to share their teaching and library resources.

爲克服預算的不足，鄉間的許多小型學校已建立 ＿＿＿＿＿＿ 方案以分享教學與圖書資源。

(A) cooperative 合作的　(B) objective 目的　(C) relative 相對的　(D) infinitive 不定的

解析
(1)答題關鍵在題目空格左、右方的「已建立」與「方案以分享」。
(2)四個選項中，只有選(A)項的「合作的」，才可有意義連成「已建立合作方案以分享……資源」。

7. After spending much time carefully studying the patient's ＿＿＿＿＿＿ , the doctor finally made his diagnosis.

長期且仔細地研究患者的 ＿＿＿＿＿＿ ，醫生最後做出診斷結果。

(A) confessions 承認　(B) symptoms 症狀　(C) protests 抗議　(D) qualifications 資格

解析
(1)答題關鍵在題目空格左、右方的「研究患者的」與「醫生最後」。
(2)四個選項中，只有選 (B) 項的「症狀」，才可有意義連成「研究患者的症狀，醫生最後……」。

8. The universe is full of wonders. Throughout history, people have been _____ by the mystery of what lies beyond our planet.

宇宙充滿美好事物。自古以來人們都被未探索的星球神祕事物所 _____ 。

(A) notified 通知　(B) complicated 複雜　(C) fascinated 著迷　(D) suspended 懸掛；暫停

解析
(1)答題關鍵在題目空格左的「人們都被……」。
(2)四個選項中，只有選(C) 項的「著迷」，才可有意義連成「人們都為……著迷」。

9. The president's speech will be broadcast _____ on television and radio so that more people can listen to it at the time when it is delivered.

總統的演說會在收音機與電視上 _____ 播出，所以人們可在播出時及時收聽。

(A) comparatively 對比的　(B) temporarily 暫時的　(C) simultaneously 同時地　(D) permanently 永久地

解析
(1)答題關鍵在題目空格左、右方的「在收音機與電視上」與「播出」。
(2)四個選項中，只有選(C) 項的「同時地」，才可有意義連成「在收音機與電視上同時播出」。

10. In order to expand its foreign market, the company decided to _____ its products and provide more varieties to the customer.

為了擴展國外市場，該公司決定 _____ 它的產品並為客戶提供多種服務。

(A) exceed 過　(B) dismiss 使……離開　(C) retrieve 收回　(D) diversify 多樣化

解析
(1)答題關鍵在題目空格左、右方的「為了擴展市場，公司決定」與「它的產品」。
(2)四個選項中，只有選 (D) 項的「多樣化」，才可有意義連成「公司決定多樣化它的產品並為客戶提供……」。

二、綜合測驗（20分）

說明：第 11 至 30 題，每題一個空格。請依文意選出一個最適當的選項，標示在答案卡之「選擇題答案區」。每題答對得 1 分，答錯或劃記多於一個選項者倒扣 1/3 分，倒扣到本大題之實得分數為零為止。未作答者，不給分亦不扣分。

第11至15題為題組

　　The telephone is widely considered as the most rapidly evolving technological device today. Many experts in the field believe that future phones will not only look very different—they may not even be ＿＿＿11＿＿＿ . They may be hidden in jewelry or accessories, or even embedded in the body. They will undoubtedly have a lot of additional features and ＿＿＿12＿＿＿ functions, and users may interact with them in new ways, too. ＿＿＿13＿＿＿ they are still called "phones" —a word meaning "voice" in Greek—making voice calls may no longer be their primary function. With advances in contemporary design and technology, the phones may ＿＿＿14＿＿＿ remote controls, house keys, Game Boys, maps, flashlights, health monitors, recorders, handguns, and so on. ＿＿＿15＿＿＿ , they will be "the remote-control for life."

　　電話被廣泛地認為是目前最迅速發展的科技配備。很多在這個領域的專家相信，將來的電話機不僅造型非常不同，它們甚至可能不會被 ＿＿＿11＿＿＿ 。它們可能被隱藏在珠寶或裝飾品內，或者甚至植入人體裡。它們無疑地將有許多特色與 ＿＿＿12＿＿＿ 的功能，並且用戶也可用新的方式與話機互動。 ＿＿＿13＿＿＿ 它們仍然被稱作「電話」── 希臘語意思為「聲音」，打語音電話可能不再是它們的主功能。有了現代化的設計與科技，電話可以 ＿＿＿14＿＿＿ 遙控、房子鑰匙、遊戲電玩、地圖、手電筒、健康顯像器、錄音機、手槍等等。 ＿＿＿15＿＿＿ ，他們將成為「日常生活的遙控器」。

11. 題句：future phones will not only look very different—they may not even be ＿＿＿11＿＿＿
　　　將來的電話機不僅造型非常不同，它們甚至可能會 ＿＿＿11＿＿＿ 。
　　選項：(A) heard 聽到　(B) sold 賣出　(C) changed 交換　(D) seen 看的過去分詞

解析
依題意只有選 (D) 項的「被看見」才是正確選項。 Be seen為「被看見」之意。亦即隱藏而看不到。

12. 題句：They will undoubtedly have a lot of additional features and ＿＿＿12＿＿＿ functions,
　　　它們無疑地將有許多特色與 ＿＿＿12＿＿＿ 的功能，
　　選項：(A) remote 遙遠的　(B) scarce 缺乏的　(C) novel 新奇的　(D) accidental 意外的

解析
依題意，只能選(C)項的「新奇的」才是正確選項。

13. 題句：_____13_____ they are still called "phones"... ─making voice calls may no longer be their primary function.

_____13_____它們仍然被稱作「電話」──打語音電話可能不再是它們的主要功能。

選項：(A) As long as 只要……　(B) Even if 即使　(C) Just as 正當……　(D) Only when 剛好那時

解析

依題意只能選 (B) 項的「即使」，才是正確選項。意即即使仍被稱為電話，但在將來，撥打電話可能不再是電話機的主要功能。

14. 題句：the phones may _____14_____ remote controls, house keys, Game Boys, maps, flashlights,

有了現代化的設計與科技，電話可以 _____14_____ 遙控、房子鑰匙、遊戲男孩……

選項：(A) call for 接人　(B) get over 克服　(C) relate to 有關　(D) serve as 做……服務

解析

依題意只能選 (D) 項的「做……服務」，意即用來當作房屋鑰匙、玩遊戲……等等的遙控服務。

15. 題句：_____15_____ , they will be "the remote-control for life."

_____15_____ ，他們將成為「日常生活的遙控器」。

選項：(A) In short 簡言之　(B) As yet 還沒有　(C) By the way 順便提一下　(D) On the contrary 相反地

解析

依題意只能選 (A) 項的「簡言之」才是正確選項。

第 16 至 20 題為題組

　　The fruits and vegetables we eat often come in distinctive colors. The rich colors, _____16_____ , are not there only to attract attention. They perform another important function for the plants.

　　Research shows that the substances _____17_____ these colors actually protect plants from chemical damage. The colors come mainly from chemicals known as antioxidants. Plants make antioxidants to protect themselves from the sun's ultraviolet (UV) light, _____18_____ may cause harmful elements to form within the plant cells.

　　When we eat colorful fruits and vegetables, the coloring chemicals protect us, too. Typically, an intensely colored plant has _____19_____ of these protective chemicals than a paler one does. Research on how chemicals in blueberries affect brain function even suggests that these chemicals may help our own brains work more _____20_____ . In other words, eating richly colored fruits and vegetables makes us both healthier and smarter.

　　我們吃的蔬果常會有特有的顏色。鮮豔的色彩　　16　　，不僅是引起注意而已，它爲植物執行另一個重要功能。研究顯示　　17　　這些顏色的物質實際上在保護植物免受化學破壞。顏色主要來自一種稱爲抗氧化物的化學物質。植物釋出抗氧化物保護植物本身防止太陽紫外線，　　18　　會在植物内部細胞形成。

　　當我們吃色彩鮮豔的蔬果時，彩色化學物質也保護我們。通常，一棵深色植物比淺色植物有　　19　　的保護物質。在研究藍莓的化學物質如何影響腦功能的報告中，甚至説明這些化學物質有助於我們腦力運作更　　20　　。換句話説，吃色彩鮮豔的蔬果使我們更健康更聰明。

16. 題句：The rich colors, _____16_____ , are not there only to attract attention.
　　選項：(A) almost 幾乎　(B) rarely 稀少地　(C) however 然而　(D) relatively 相對地
解析
在説完The rich colors後，爲了做語氣轉折，應選 (C) 項的「然而」才是正確選項。

17. 題句：Research shows that the substances _____17_____ these colors actually protect plants from chemical damage.
　　選項：(A) capable of 有……能力　(B) different from 與……不同　(C) inferior to 比……差
　　(D) responsible for 爲……負責
解析
依題意只能選 (D) 項的「responsible for」才是正確選項。在此之「爲……負責」是指「爲某事後果的原因」。

**18.題句：to protect themselves from the sun's ultraviolet (UV) light, _____18_____ may cause harmful elements
　　選項：(A) which 哪一　(B) that 那個　(C) what 什麼　(D) such 如此
解析
(1)本題考關係代名詞的用法。
(2)題句空格左方的名詞light，也叫作前置詞。前置詞後沒有逗點時，稱爲關係代名詞的「限定用法」，反之，其後有逗點時，稱爲補述用法。
(3)本題的 light 字後有逗點，屬補述用法，不可選 that 作關代詞，所以 (A) 項的 which 才是正確選項。

**19.題句：Typically, an intensely colored plant has _____19_____ of these protective chemicals
　　選項：(A) more 更多　(B) less 更少　(C) most 最多　(D) least 最少

解析

⑴依題意只能選(A)項的「more」才是正確選項。意指深色植物比淺色植物有更多的保護物質。

⑵再根據最後句的「換句話說，吃色彩鮮豔的蔬果使我們更健康更聰明」來判斷，(A)項的「更多」才是正確選項。

20. 題句：these chemicals may help our own brains work more ＿＿＿20＿＿＿

選項：(A) obviously 顯然地　(B) diligently 勤勉地　(C) efficiently 有效率地　(D) superficially 淺薄地

解析

依題意只能選(C)項的「efficiently」才是正確選項，意指「大腦會更有效率的工作」。

第 21 至 25 題為題組

Recent studies have shown that alcohol is the leading gateway drug for teenagers. Gateway drugs are substances people take that ＿＿＿21＿＿＿ them to take more drugs. Alcohol works directly on the central nervous system and alters one's moods and limits judgment. Since its way of altering moods (changing one's state of mind) is generally expected and socially acceptable, oftentimes it ＿＿＿22＿＿＿ over drinking. Habitual drinkers may find alcohol not stimulating enough ＿＿＿23＿＿＿ and want to seek other more stimulating substances. ＿＿＿24＿＿＿ a circumstance often preconditions teenagers to the possibility of taking other drugs such as marijuana, cocaine or heroin. Another reason why alcohol is the main gateway drug is that the ＿＿＿25＿＿＿ of teenagers it can affect is very wide. It is easily accessible in most societies and common in popular events such as sports gatherings and dinner parties.

近來的研究顯示酒精是青少年吸毒的的入門毒品。入門毒品是人們服用後會 ＿＿＿21＿＿＿ 他們服用更多的物質。酒精直接影響中樞神經系統並且改變一個人的情緒與最低判斷能力。既然酒精的改變情緒（改變一個人的心態）一般是可預料也是社會可接受的，但常會 ＿＿＿22＿＿＿ 飲酒過量。有酗酒習慣的人，＿＿＿23＿＿＿ 可能會發現酒精已不夠刺激，並且想要尋找其他更刺激的東西。＿＿＿24＿＿＿ 情形下，經常促使青少年有提早使用其他藥物的可能性，像是大麻、古柯鹼或海洛因。酒精是入門毒品的另一原因是，青少年 ＿＿＿25＿＿＿ 受影響的情形非常廣泛。整個社會裡酒精很容易取得，在多數社交場合像是運動聚會、宴會派對等地方，也都有酒類供應。

**21.題句：Gateway drugs are substances people take that ＿＿＿21＿＿＿ them to take more drugs.

選項：(A) lead 現在式　(B) leads 主詞三單的現在式　(C) leading 動名詞　(D) led 過去式

解析

⑴空格左邊的 that 帶出來的是屬從屬子句的「that 子句」。

⑵that 子句後必須用現在式動詞，(A)項才是正確選項。

22. 題句：oftentimes it ＿＿＿22＿＿＿ over drinking.

　　選項：(A) applies to 適用於　(B) arrives at 抵達　(C) results in 導致　(D) plans on 打算

解析

依題意只能選 (C) 項的「results in」才是正確選項，意指「它常會造成飲酒過量」。

23. 題句：Habitual drinkers may find alcohol not stimulating enough ＿＿＿23＿＿＿ and want to seek other more stimulating substances.

　　選項：(A) in advance 預先　(B) after a while 稍後　(C) in the least 最少　(D) at most 最多

解析

依題意只能選 (B) 項的「after a while」才是正確選項，意指「酗酒者常會發現酒精過一會就不夠刺激了」。

**24. 題句：＿＿＿24＿＿＿ a circumstance often preconditions teenagers to the possibility of taking other drugs

　　選項：(A) Since 自從　(B) As 當　(C) All 全部　(D) Such 如此

解析

依題意只能選 (D) 項的「such」才能連成 such a circumstance 的片語用法，才是正確選項。

25. 題句：that the ＿＿＿25＿＿＿ of teenagers it can affect is very wide

　　選項：(A) population 人口　(B) popularity 普及知名度　(C) pollution 污染　(D) possibility 可能性

解析

(1)答題關鍵在空格左右方的 the...of teenagers（青少年的～）。

(2)四個選項中只有選 (A) 項的「人口」，才是符合文法的正確選項。

第 26 至 30 題為題組

　　A new year means a new beginning for most of us. On December 28th last year, the New York City sanitation department offered people a new way ＿＿＿26＿＿＿ farewell to 2007. For one hour on that day, a huge paper-cutting machine was set up in Times Square so people could ＿＿＿27＿＿＿ their lingering bad memories. Everything from photos of ex-lovers to lousy report cards could be cut into small pieces, as the organizers had announced ＿＿＿28＿＿＿ the event. Recycling cans were also provided for items such as ＿＿＿29＿＿＿ CDs and regrettable fashion mistakes. Former schoolteacher Eileen Lawrence won the event's $250 award for the most creative memory destined for ＿＿＿30＿＿＿ . She had created a painting from a photo of her ex-boyfriend, who Lawrence was happy to say goodbye to.

　　對我們多數人來說，新年表示一年的新開始。在去年 12 月 28 日，紐約政府的衛生部門提供人們 ＿＿＿26＿＿＿ 告別 2007 的新方式。在那天的一個小時裡，一台

巨大的碎紙機在時代廣場安置起來，因此人們可 ___27___ 他們徘徊不去的痛苦記憶。從舊情人的照片到糟糕的成績卡，都可被切成碎片，如同主辦單位在活動 ___28___ 所宣布的。回收桶也提供來蒐集 ___29___ 的 CD 和令人遺憾舊衣物之類的東西。前教師愛琳·勞倫斯用很高興與之分手的前男友照片，做了一幅畫。___30___ 因而獲最佳創意獎 250 美元。

**26.題句：the New York City sanitation department offered people a new way ___26___ farewell to 2007

選項：(A) bid 向……表示　(B) to bid 不定詞　(C) bidding 動名詞　(D) bidden 過去分詞

解析

⑴答題關鍵在「offered」一字，它是普通動詞，所以其後要接不定詞。

⑵(B) 選項是不定詞，才是符合文法的正確選項。

27. 題句：a huge paper-cutting machine was set up in Times Square so people could ___27___ their lingering bad memories.

選項：(A) destroy 摧毀　(B) maintain 維持　(C) dislike 不喜歡　(D) create 產生

解析

依題意只能選(A)項的「destroy」，意指「毀去他們不幸事物的回憶」才是正確選項。

**28.題句：as the organizers had announced ___28___ the event.

選項：(A) until 直到……　(B) prior to 在……之前　(C) above all 最重要　(D) beforehand 之前

解析

依題意只能選(B)項的「prior to」，意指在活動前就已經宣布，才是正確選項。

29. 題句：Recycling cans were also provided for items such as ___29___ CDs and regrettable fashion mistakes.

選項：(A) available 可用的　(B) amusing 有趣的　(C) annoying 擾人的　(D) artificial 人工的

解析

依題意只能選(C)項的「annoying」才是正確選項，意指提供回收桶以回收擾人的cd光碟片。

**30.題句："Eileen Lawrence won the event's $250 award for the most creative memory destined for ___30___"

選項：(A) machine 機器　(B) machines 機器　(C) a machine 機器　(D) the machine 機器

解析

⑴題句中的「機器」不是任何一部其他機器，而是現場「特定」的那一部機器。

⑵因此，有定冠詞 the 的 (D) 選項才是符合文法的正確選項。

三、文意選填（10分）

第 31 至 40 題為題組

Athletes and sports competitors compete in organized, officiated sports events to entertain spectators. When playing a game, athletes are required to understand the strategies of their game and ___31___ the rules and regulations of the sport. The events in which they compete include both ___32___ sports, such as baseball, basketball, and soccer, and individual sports, such as golf, tennis, and bowling. The level of play varies from unpaid high school athletics to ___33___ sports, in which the best from around the world compete in events broadcast on international television.

Being an athlete involves more than competing in athletic events. Athletes spend many hours each day practicing skills and improving teamwork under the ___34___ of a coach or a sports instructor. They view videotapes not only to critique their own performances and ___35___ but also to learn their opponents' tendencies and weaknesses to gain a competitive advantage. Some athletes work regularly with strength trainers to gain muscle and to ___36___ injury. Many athletes push their bodies ___37___ during both practice and play, so career-ending injury always is a risk. Even minor injuries may put a player ___38___ of replacement. Because competition at all levels is extremely intense and job security is always unstable, many athletes train year round to maintain ___39___ form and technique and peak physical condition. Athletes also must ___40___ to strictly controlled diets during their sports season to supplement any physical training program.

運動員與競賽參與者參加有組織、有裁判的體育競賽以娛樂觀眾。比賽時，運動員被要求了解他們的比賽策略與並 ___31___ 運動的規章制度。他們比賽的運動項目包括兩項 ___32___ 運動項目，像是棒球、籃球、足球，以及個人運動項目像是高爾夫球、網球和保齡球等。比賽的層級從不必付費的高中運動到 ___33___ 運動，這其中有來自全世界各隊最佳選手參加在國際電視網播出的比賽。運動員不僅是參加比賽而已，在教練的 ___34___ 下，他們每天花數小時練習技能與改進團隊精神。他們觀賞錄影帶不僅在檢討自己的表現與 ___35___ ，也是要了解對手的習慣和弱點，以獲得比賽優勢。有些運動員定期與肌肉訓練師做練習以增進力量，並 ___36___ 受傷。很多運動員在比賽與平日練習，都把體能推到 ___37___ ，所以總是冒著比賽生涯斷送的危機。即使是輕傷，也要冒著被替換的 ___38___ 。因為各種級數的競爭極其強烈，工作保障總是不穩定，很多運動員全年做訓練以保持 ___39___ 狀況與技巧及身體的巔峰狀態。運動員也必須 ___40___ 飲食控制任何物質的培養訓練計畫。

(A) conform 遵守　　(B) prevent 防止　　(C) obey 服從　　(D) guidance 指導
(E) excellent 最優的　(F) techniques 技術　(G) professional 專業的　(H) team 團隊
(I) at risk 有風險　　(J) to the limit 達到極限

31. 題句：athletes are required to understand the strategies of their game and _____31_____ the rules and regulations of the sport.

解析

依題意只能選 (C) 項的「obey」，連成 obey the rules and regulations of the sport 才是正確選項。

32. 題句：The events in which they compete include both _____32_____ sports, such as baseball, basketball,

解析

依題意只能選 (H) 項的「team」，連成 team sport（團隊運動）像是棒球、籃球等，才是正確選項。

33. 題句：The level of play varies from unpaid high school athletics to _____33_____ sports,

解析

依題意只能選 (G) 項的「professional」，連成「從高中生選手到職業選手都有」才是正確選項。

34. 題句：Athletes spend many hours each day practicing skills and improving teamwork under the _____34_____ of a coach or a sports instructor.

解析

依題意只能選 (D) 項的「guidance」，意指「在教練或指導員的指導下……」才是正確選項。

35. 題句：They view videotapes not only to critique their own performances and _____35_____ but also to learn their opponents' tendencies and weaknesses to gain a competitive advantage.

解析

依題意只能選 (F) 項的「techniques」才是正確選項，意指「觀看錄像帶不僅在批評檢討他們自己的表現與技巧……」

36. 題句：Some athletes work regularly with strength trainers to gain muscle and to _____36_____ injury.

解析

依題意只能選 (B) 項的「prevent」，意指「防止傷害」才是正確選項。

37. 題句：Many athletes push their bodies _____37_____ during both practice and play,

解析

依題意只能選(J)項的「to the limit」才是正確選項，意指將體能推到極限。

38. 題句：Even minor injuries may put a player _____38_____ of replacement.

解析

依題意只能選(I)項的「at risk」才是正確選項，意指使球員有被換掉的風險。

39. 題句：many athletes train year round to maintain _____39_____ form and technique and peak physical condition.

解析

依題意只能選(E)項的「excellence」才是正確選項，意指全年做訓練以保持最佳狀況。

40. 題句：Athletes also must _____40_____ to strictly controlled diets during their sports season

解析

依題意只能選(A)項的「conform」才是正確選項，意指嚴格遵守比賽期間的飲食。

四、篇章結構（10分）

說明：第 41 至 45 題，每題一個空格。請依文意在文章後所提供的 (A) 到 (E) 選項中分別選出最適當者，填入空格中，使篇章結構清晰有條理，並將其英文字母代號標示在答案卡之「選擇題答案區」。每題答對得 2 分，答錯或劃記多於一個選項者倒扣 1/2 分，倒扣到本大題之實得分數為零為止。未作答者，不給分亦不扣分。

第 41 至 45 題為題組

It is impossible to imagine Paris without its cafés. The city has some 12,000 cafés varying in size, grandeur, and significance. The cafés are like an extension of the French living room, a place to start and end the day, to gossip and debate.

_____41_____ The oldest café in Paris is Le Procope. It was opened in 1686 by Francesco Procopio dei Coltelli, the man who turned France into a coffee-drinking society. _____42_____ By the end of the 18th century, all of Paris was intoxicated with coffee and the city supported some 700 cafés. _____43_____ By the 1840s the number of cafés had grown to 3,000. The men who gathered in these cafés and set the theme of the times included journalists, playwrights and writers. Around the turn of the 20th century, the sidewalk cafés became the meeting halls for artists and literary figures.

_____44_____ The artists gathered at the café may not be as great as those of the past, but faces worth watching are just the same. _____45_____ You'll see the old men in navy berets; ultra-thin, bronzed women with hair dyed bright orange; and schoolchildren sharing an afternoon chocolate with their mothers. The café in Paris has always been a place for seeing and being seen.

　　很難想像巴黎是一個沒有咖啡館的城市。該市有大約 12,000 家不同大小、規模與重要性的咖啡館。這些咖啡館就像家裡客廳的延伸，是一天開始或結束都會去、並且也是閒話家常與討論事情的地方。

　　＿＿＿＿41＿＿＿＿ 巴黎最古老的咖啡館是 Le Procope。它是 Francesco Procopio 在 1686 年創立的。這個人使法國變成一個喝咖啡的社會。 ＿＿＿＿42＿＿＿＿ 到了十八世紀末，整個巴黎社會陶醉於喝咖啡，城內就有約七百家咖啡館。 ＿＿＿＿43＿＿＿＿ 到了一八四〇年代，咖啡館增加到三千家之多。男人在這些咖啡館見面，而成為當代主流人物包括記者、劇作家和作家。快進入二十世紀前，路邊咖啡館已成為藝文人士見面之處。

　　＿＿＿＿44＿＿＿＿ 藝術家在咖啡館見面也許不像以前那麼風光，但面對值得看的事物還是不變的。 ＿＿＿＿45＿＿＿＿ 你會看到老先生戴著法式貝雷帽；而苗條且有古銅色皮膚的婦女把頭髮染成亮眼的橙色；而學童們則與他們的母親共享下午茶的巧克力。巴黎的咖啡館一直都是人們看見或被看見的地方。

(A) When did the cafes in France start?
　　法國的咖啡館起源於何時呢？

(B) Linger a bit and you will see that the Parisian stereotypes are still alive and well.
　　逗留一會你會看到巴黎人的舊式做法仍然很管用。

(C) Nowadays in Paris cafes still play the role of picture windows for observing contemporary life.
　　當今在巴黎的小餐館在當代生活上仍扮演現代生活的角色。

(D) These were like all-male clubs, with many functioning as centers of political life and discussion.
　　這些幾乎都是男性的俱樂部裡，具有政治生涯中心與議題討論的多種功能。

(E) Le Procope attracted Paris's political and literary elite, and thus played an important part among the upper class. Le Procope
　　餐廳吸引了巴黎的政治文化菁英，在上流社會中占重要地位。

41. 正確答案為 (A) 選項。

解析

根據空格下一句的「巴黎最古老的咖啡館是 Le Procope」就是在說明「法國的咖啡館起源於何時呢？」的句子。因此，(A) 項才是正確選項。

42. 正確答案為 (E) 選項。

解析

因為空格上一句在說明「這個人使法國變成一個喝咖啡的社會」，其後再接著說「Le Procope 餐廳吸引了巴黎的政治文化菁英，在上流社會中占重要地位」，文意就更順暢。因此，(E) 項才是正確選項。

43. 正確答案為 (D) 選項。

解析

根據空格下一句有提到「……男人在這些咖啡館見面……」，就可確定 (D) 項的「這些幾乎都是男性的俱樂部裡，具有政治生涯中心與議題討論的多種功能」才是正確選項。

44. 正確答案為 (C) 項。

解析

根據空格上一句的「路邊咖啡館已成為藝文人士見面之處」，就可確定 (C) 項的「當今在巴黎的小餐館在當代生活上仍扮演現代生活的角色」接在後句才是正確選項。

45. 正確答案為 (B) 項。

解析

根據空格上一句的「藝術家在咖啡館……但面對值得看的事物還是不變的」，就可確定 (B) 項的「逗留一會你會看到巴黎人的舊式做法仍然很管用」才是正確選項。

五、閱讀測驗（22分）

說明：第 46 至 56 題，每題請分別根據各篇文章的文意選出一個最適當的選項，標示在答案卡之「選擇題答案區」。每題答對得 2 分，答錯或劃記多於一個選項者倒扣 2/3 分，倒扣到本大題之實得分數為零為止。未作答者，不給分亦不扣分。

第 46 至 49 題為題組

The Lego Group had a very humble beginning in the workshop of Ole Kirk Christiansen, a carpenter from Denmark. Christiansen began creating wooden toys in 1932. Two years later, he stumbled on the Lego name by putting together the first two letters of the Danish words *Leg* and *Godt*, which mean "play well." The name could be interpreted as "I put together" in Latin; it also corresponds to the Greek verb meaning "gather" or "pick up."

In 1947, the company expanded to making plastic toys. At first, the use of plastic for toy manufacture was not highly regarded by retailers and consumers of the time. Many of the Lego Group's shipments were returned, following poor sales. However, Christiansen's son, Godtfred Kirk Christiansen, saw the immense potential in Lego bricks to become a system for creative play. As the junior managing director of the Lego Group, he spent years trying to improve the "locking" ability of the bricks and made the bricks more versatile. In 1958, the modern interlocking brick design was finally developed and patented.

Today Lego is sold in more than 130 countries. Every minute 33,824 Lego bricks are made, and kids around the world spend 5 billion hours a year playing with Lego. There will be more than 400 million people playing with Lego bricks this year. On average, every person in the world owns 62 Lego bricks, and about seven Lego sets are sold every second.

This year Lego fans all over the world are celebrating the 50th anniversary of the tiny building blocks. Though already 50 years old, Lego is still the same product it was in the 1950s. Bricks bought then are still compatible with current bricks and that is probably the reason the toy has never fallen out of favor.

Lego 集團是從簡陋的克里斯汀森工廠起家，克里斯汀森工廠的木匠於 1932 年開始創立木製玩具。以後二年，他碰巧的把丹麥語的 Leg Godt（玩得很好之意）二字，各取前兩個字母拼成 Lego。這個名字可被解釋為拉丁語的「我裝配」；它也符合希臘語動詞的「蒐集」或者「撿起」。

在 1947 年，公司擴充改做塑膠玩具。一開始，零售商和消費者對塑膠玩具的評價不高，很多樂高產品都遭到退貨。不過，克里斯汀森的兒子高弗列德，看見 Lego 積木可以拼組的創意有無限潛力，身為集團的年輕總經理，他花了多年的努力去改進積木的「組合」功能，也更具多樣化。在 1958 年，新式的相互鎖住的積木塊設計終於完成並獲有專利權。

今天樂高組合玩具有超過 130 個國家代為銷售。每分鐘可生產 33,824 塊樂高積木，全世界的孩子每年花 50 億個小時在組合樂高積木。今年將有超過 4 億人玩樂高積木。平均而言，在世界上每人就擁有 62 塊樂高積木，以及每秒鐘就有 7 組 Lego 積木賣出。

今年全世界的樂高迷慶祝迷你屋組合玩具的五十週年紀念日。雖然已經五十歲了，樂高積木仍與一九五〇年代時期的相同產品相容。以前買的和當今生產的組合積木，其相容性是一致的，那或許是這種玩具組合積木從未退流行的原因。

46. Which of the following is true about the name Lego?

下列哪一項與 Lego 名字描述為真？

(A) It is a combination of Greek and Latin words.

它是希臘語和拉丁語單字的結合。

(B) It was created by Ole Kirk Christiansen's son.

它是克里斯汀森的兒子創辦的。

(C) It was created in 1947 for naming the plastic toys.

它用於命名塑膠玩具在 1947 年被建立。

(D) It came from Danish words meaning "play" and "well".

它來自丹麥字的意義「玩」與「好」。

解析

從答題關鍵的「on the Lego name by putting together the first two letters of the Danish words *Leg* and

Godt, which mean "play well."」可看出，(D) 項的「It came from Danish words meaning "play" and "well"」才是正確選項。

47. When did the Lego brick become as a creative form of toy?

樂高積木什麼時候成為有創意的玩具？

(A) 1958　(B) 1947　(C) 1934　(D) 1932

解析

從答題關鍵的「Lego bricks to become a system for creative play.」及「In 1958, the modern interlocking brick design was finally developed and patented.」兩句內容可看出，(A) 項的「1958」才是正確選項。

48. Which of the following is true in describing the popularity of Lego?

描述 Lego 的流行如下哪一選項為真？

(A) More than 5 billion people in the world own Lego sets.

超過 50 億人擁有樂高組合玩具。

(B) Children spend an average of 62 dollars on Lego bricks each year.

孩子每年平均花 62 美元購買樂高積木。

(C) People in the world spend 400 million hours playing with Lego every year.

世界上人們每年花 4 億個小時玩樂高積木。

(D) The Lego Group now produces more than 30 thousand toy bricks every minute.

樂高集團每分鐘生產超過 3 萬塊玩具積木。

解析

從答題關鍵的「Today Lego is sold in more than 130 countries. Every minute 33,824 Lego bricks are made,」可看出，(D) 項的「The Lego Group now produces more than 30 thousand toy bricks every minute.」才是正確選項。

49. What is most likely the reason why Lego still remains popular?

樂高積木一直受歡迎的原因為何？

(A) Old Lego bricks may still be connected to new ones.

舊樂高積木仍可與新樂高積木共用。

(B) The company hasn't changed its name since 1947.

公司從 1947 年來都沒改變名字。

(C) The material for the bricks has proved to be safe.

積木的材料經證明是安全的。

(D) The price of the toy is relatively reasonable.

玩具積木的價格相對合理。

解析

從答題關鍵的「Though already 50 years old, Lego is still the same product it was in the 1950s. Bricks bought then are still compatible with current bricks and that is probably the reason the toy has never fallen out of favor.」可看出，(A) 項的「Old Lego bricks may still be connected to new ones」才是正確選項。

第 50 至 53 題為題組

During my ninth-grade year, I suffered from **anorexia nervosa**. It was not enough to be thin. I had to be the thinnest. Now, however, fully recovered, I can reflect back and realize that my wishes were more complex than fitting into size five pants. Many of my subconscious emotions were related to my relationship with my father. As I was growing up, his work always came first. Sometimes I would not see him for up to two weeks. Not only did he devote his whole self to his work, but he expected me to do the same ("You cannot get anywhere unless you go to the best universities!"). Though, consciously, I never felt pressure to please him, I began dieting after the first time he told me I looked fat.

At the time, all I knew was that I had to be skinny—skinnier than anyone else. Every month my father went to Europe for a week or so and on the days he left, sorrow and emptiness consumed me: Daddy was leaving. Then, I turned to focus on a mysterious weakness—a helpless childlike emotion that came from starving. I liked to know that I needed to be taken care of; maybe Daddy would take care of me. Now, two years later and thirty-eight pounds heavier, I have come to realize that I cannot alter my father's inability to express his feelings. Instead, I must accept myself. I know that I am a valuable person who strives to achieve and accomplish. But I cannot strive solely for others. By starving, I attempted to gain pride in myself by obtaining my father's approval or acknowledgment of my value as a person. But the primary approval must come from me, and I feel secure now that I can live with that knowledge safely locked in my mind.

在我念九年級的時候，我患有厭食症。光是瘦還不夠，我當時是最瘦的。不過，現在我完全康復了，我回想以前同時也體會到，當時我所要的，比穿得下5號褲子更多。多次我的潛意識情感跟我與父親的關係有關。在我成長過程，他總是工作第一，有時候多達兩個禮拜我都見不到父親。不僅他專心在他的工作，也要求我也跟他一樣（你什麼也做不好，除非你讀最好的大學）。雖然，在意識上，我從未感到有壓力要去使父親滿意，而在他第一次說我看起肥胖之後，我就開始節食。

在那時，我所知道的是，我必須比其他人更瘦。每個月我父親會去歐洲一個禮拜左右，在父親出發後，我頓時感到悲傷與空虛。然後，我轉而變成不可思議的虛弱——是由於饑餓所引起、像無助小孩般的情感。我想知道我需要被照顧什麼；或許爸爸將照顧我。現在，兩年過去了，我也胖了 38 磅，我才了解到我不能改變我父親無法表達他的感情之事；反之，我必須接受自己。我知道我是努力要完成實現的有用之人，但是我不能單為他人努力。經由父親的允許或我對價值的認知，在饑餓時我試圖保有自尊。但是主要的允諾必須來自我自己，而深入我腦海的價值認知，已使我感覺很安全。

50. What is "**anorexia nervosa**" as mentioned in the first paragraph?

　　第一段提到的anorexia nervosa是指何意？

　(A) It is an inability to express one's feelings.

　　　它是一種無法表達自己的感覺。

　(B) It describes a situation of feeling insecure.

　　　它是描述沒有安全感的情形。

　(C) It refers to people who are emotionally unstable.

　　　它指感情上不穩定的人。

　(D) It is an illness that makes one want to stop eating.

　　　它是一種使人不想吃東西的病。

解析

從文章第一、二段內容可看出，(D) 項的「It is an illness that makes one want to stop eating.」才是正確選項。

51. Why did the writer suffer from anorexia nervosa?

　　本文作者為什麼受厭食症之苦？

　(A) She was told by her father to take care of herself.

　　　父親告訴她要照顧自己。

　(B) She wanted to go to the best university.

　　　她想要去最好的大學。

　(C) She wanted her father's attention.

　　　她想引起父親的注意。

　(D) She grew up in a poor family.

　　　她在一個貧窮家庭中長大。

解析

從答題關鍵的「Though, consciously, I never felt pressure to please him, I began dieting after the first time he told me I looked fat.」可看出，(C)項的「She wanted her father's attention.」才是正確選項。

52. Which of the following statements is true about the writer?

　　下列哪一項有關作者的說法是真的？

　(A) She has problems controlling her tempers.

　　　她無法控制自己的脾氣。

　(B) She is proud of herself for working hard to succeed.

　　　她為她自己努力成功感到驕傲。

　(C) She has had great confidence in herself since childhood.

她從小就信心滿滿。

(D) She has changed her father's way of expressing himself.

她改變了她父親表達自己的方式。

解析

從答題關鍵的「I know that I am a valuable person who strives to achieve and accomplish.」可看出，(B) 項的「She is proud of herself for working hard to succeed.」才是正確選項。

53. What's the writer's purpose of writing this passage?

作者寫這段文章的目的是什麼？

(A) To blame her father.

責備她的父親。

(B) To report a case of child abuse.

報告虐待小孩的個案。

(C) To reflect on a stage of growing up.

反應成長過程的某一階段。

(D) To teach people how to lose weight.

教人怎樣減輕體重。

解析

從整段文章內容可看出，(C) 項的「To reflect on a stage of growing up」才是正確選項。因為文章中並未提到其他三選項之事。

第 54 至 56 題為題組

　　Africa is a land of many ethnic groups, but when Europeans carved Africa into colonies, they gave no consideration to the territories of African ethnic groups. Some borderlines were drawn that split same groups into different colonies. Other borders threw different groups together. Sometimes the groups thrown together were enemies.

　　When the colonies became independent nations, these same borderlines were often maintained. Today, the Somali people remain split among Ethiopia, Kenya, Somalia, and Djibouti. On the other hand, almost every African nation is home to more than one ethnic group. In Nigeria, for example, live the Hausa, the Fulani, the Yoruba, the Ibo, and many smaller groups.

　　Conflicts have arisen over the way in which ethnic groups were split apart and thrown together. For example, a war between Somalia and Ethiopia was fought because Somalis wanted all their people to be a part of one nation. A civil war in Nigeria, on the other hand, was triggered partly by conflicts between ethnic groups within that nation. Similar conflicts between ethnic groups arose in Chad, Zaire, and Burundi as well. One principal goal among African nations today, therefore, is to help make it possible for their many ethnic groups to live together in peace.

　　非洲是一塊有很多不同種族的土地，但是當歐洲人把非洲劃入殖民地時，他們沒有考慮到不同種族地區。有些邊界線把同種族劃成兩個不同的殖民區域，其他邊界也把不同種族放在一起，有時候被硬放放在同一殖民地區的兩個不同種族是敵人。

當殖民地成為獨立的國家時，這些相同的邊界還是保持著。今天，索馬利亞人在衣索比亞、肯亞、索馬利亞和吉布的國境內還是分裂的。反之，幾乎每個非洲國家都有不止一個不同種族的人。在奈及利亞內，舉例來說，有豪撒人、夫拉尼人、約魯巴人、Ibo 人，和更多小種族的人。

不論是同種族被分裂在兩個國家，或不同種族被錯放在一個國家，衝突都已發生，例如，在索馬利亞和衣索比亞之間的一次戰爭，是因為索馬利亞人想要把所有的索馬利亞種族的人變成索馬利亞國的人。在奈及利亞的一場內戰，情形正好相反，之所以開打部分原因是，該國境家不同種族間的衝突。類似的種族衝突也發生在查德、薩伊與蒲隆地等國。今天的非洲國家的主要目標，是想幫助不同種族的人可以和平共處。

54. What happened to the territorial lines drawn in Africa by the Europeans?

歐洲人在非洲標出的界線導致什麼後果？

(A) They disappeared as the Europeans no longer ruled the colonies.

歐洲人不再統治非洲的殖民地後，界線就消失了。

(B) They were respected by different ethnic groups.

受到不同民族的尊重。

(C) They became borders between countries.

它們成為國家之間的邊境。

(D) They became war memorials.

它們成為戰爭紀念物。

解析

從答題關鍵的「Some borderlines were drawn that split same groups into different colonies.」可看出，(C) 項的「They became borders between countries.」才是正確選項。

55. What does the author think to be a reason for conflicts among the Africans?

作者認為，非洲的種族衝突原因是什麼？

(A) Most ethnic groups have established their own countries.

大多數種族已經建立他們自己的國家。

(B) One ethnic group is broken up among different countries.

同一個種族被分裂在不同國家。

(C) Some Europeans invaded Africa to increase their colonies.

有些歐洲人侵入非洲以增加殖民地。

(D) African nations fought the Europeans to expand their territories.

非洲國家跟歐洲人作戰以擴大他們的領土。

解析

從答題關鍵的「Other borders threw different groups together. Sometimes the groups thrown together were enemies.」可看出，(B) 項的「One ethnic group is broken up among different countries.」才是正確選項。

56. What is the best title for the passage?

　　本文的最好標題是什麼？

　　(A) War and Peace in Africa

　　　　非洲的戰爭與和平

　　(B) Africa：Borderlines Misplaced

　　　　非洲：邊界被錯放

　　(C) European Colonization of Africa

　　　　非洲的歐洲殖民文化

　　(D) Africa Recovered and Reconstructed

　　　　非洲的恢復與重建

解析

從答題關鍵的在「本文多段篇幅都是說明邊界錯放而產生很多問題」，因此 (B) 項的「Africa：Borderlines Misplaced」才是正確選項。

第貳部分：非選擇題（28分）

一、英文翻譯（8分）

說明：1. 將下列兩句中文翻譯成適當之英文，並將答案寫在「答案卷」上。

　　　 2. 未按題意翻譯者，不予計分。

1. 全球糧食危機已經在世界許多地區造成嚴重的社會問題。

解析

先將題句內相關字詞寫出中譯：

全球的 The global　糧食危機 food crisis　世界 world，world-wide　許多地區 many areas、many regions　造成 bring about　嚴重的 serious　社會問題 social problems

整句英譯

The global food crisis has brought about serious social problems in many regions world-wide

2. 專家警告我們不應該再將食物價格低廉視為理所當然。

解析

先將題句內相關字詞寫出中譯：

專家 The experts　警告 warning　我們 us　不應該 should not　價格低廉 low-priced　將某事視爲理所當然 take it for granted

整句英譯

A warning by the experts say that we should not take low-priced food for granted.

二、英文作文（20分）

> 說明：1. 依提示在「答案卷」上寫一篇英文作文。
> 　　　2. 文長至少 120 個單詞。

提示：廣告在我們生活中隨處可見。請寫一篇大約 120～150 字的短文，介紹一則令你印象深刻的電視或平面廣告。第一段描述該廣告的內容（如：主題、故事情節、音樂、畫面等），第二段說明該廣告令你印象深刻的原因。

解析

(1)日常生活中所看到的廣告千百種，但每一個人對廣告的看法都不會一樣。但主題一定要在：「爲什麼這個廣告令你印象深刻？」選好你要寫的廣告後，就可以循「令你印象深刻」這個方向去自由發揮，但要注意，文句要通順且符合文法。

(2)爲作示範，本文就以廣告標題、相關字詞、整篇作文方式寫出供讀者參考。

廣告標題	停車費招牌　Tricky Parking Advertisement（詭異的停車場廣告牌）
相關字詞	parking lot　parking sign　advertisement　receipt　ticket
整篇作文	I am totally fed up with the way the parking fee signs presented at the private-own parking lot. It was a bad experience I had at one of the parking lots in Taipei about a year ago. I was late already for an important meeting that morning, as you might have been aware that finding a parking space during rush hours could be a terrible nightmare. But some how I spotted a parking lot sign which reads: 80 NTD an hour without any hesitation I pulled in, got the receit and left, Three hours later, I went back to the parking lot to get my car, and I was asked to pay 480 NTD for three-hour parking. That was a rip-off, a daylight robbery I said. But the man replied with a sacastic tone "Can't you read the sign? It says 80NTD per half an hour" the problem is that you can hardly see the tiny-sized "half", and that's the way the parking-lot operator cheats the drivers who do not pay enough attention in distinguishing the barely seen "half" an hour for 80 NTD.（本篇計約 175 字）

98 年指考（指定考試）

第壹部分：選擇題（72分）

一、詞彙（10分）

說明：第 1 至 10 題，每題選出一個最適當的選項，標示在答案卡之「選擇題答案區」。每題答對得 1 分，答錯或劃記多於一個選項者倒扣 1/3 分，倒扣到本大題之實得分數為零為止。未作答者，不給分亦不扣分。

1. You'll need the store ＿＿＿＿＿＿ to show proof of purchase if you want to return any items you bought.

　你需要有商店的 ＿＿＿＿＿＿ ，如果要退貨時才能證明有所購物。

　(A) credit 信用　(B) guide 指導　(C) license 執照　(D) receipt 收據

解析

(1)答題關鍵在題目空格左方的「商店的」。

(2)四個選項中，只有選 (D) 項的「收據」，才可有意義連成「你需要有商店的收據，要退貨時才能證明……」。

2. Spending most of his childhood in Spain, John, a native speaker of English, is also ＿＿＿＿＿＿ in Spanish.

　大部分童年在西班牙度過，約翰，一個以英語為母語的人同時亦可 ＿＿＿＿＿＿ 說西語。

　(A) promising 有希望地　(B) grateful 感謝地　(C) fluent 流利地　(D) definite 明確的

解析

(1)答題關鍵在題目空格右方的「說西語」。

(2)四個選項中，只有選 (C) 項的「流利地」，才可有意義連成「同時亦可流利地說西語」。

3. The mirror slipped out of the little girl's hand, and the broken pieces ＿＿＿＿＿＿ all over the floor.

　鏡子從小女孩手中滑落，其玻璃碎片 ＿＿＿＿＿＿ 滿地。

　(A) scattered 散布　(B) circulated 循環　(C) featured 有特色的　(D) released 釋放

解析

(1)答題關鍵在題目空格右方的「滿地」。

(2)四個選項中，只有選 (A) 項的「散布」，才可有意義連成「……玻璃碎片散布滿地」。

4. No one knows how the fire broke out. The police have started an ＿＿＿＿＿ into the cause of it.

　　沒人知道火勢如何發生。警方已展開 ＿＿＿＿＿ 起火原因。

　　(A) appreciation 感謝　(B) extension 伸展　(C) operation 操作　(D) investigation 調查

解析

(1)答題關鍵在題目空格右方的「起火原因」。

(2)四個選項中，只有選(D)項的「調查」，才可有意義連成「……已展開調查起火原因」。

5. When there is a heavy rain, you have to drive very ＿＿＿＿＿ so as to avoid traffic accidents.

　　下大雨時你必須開車非常 ＿＿＿＿＿ 以免發生車禍。

　　(A) cautiously 小心地　(B) recklessly 粗心地　(C) smoothly 順利地　(D) passively 被動地

解析

(1)答題關鍵在題目空格左方的「開車非常」。

(2)四個選項中，只有選(A)項的「小心地」，才可有意義連成「開車非常小心地以免……」。

6. We decided to buy some ＿＿＿＿＿ for our new apartment, including a refrigerator, a vacuum cleaner, and a dishwasher.

　　我們決定為新屋買些 ＿＿＿＿＿ ，包括電冰箱、吸塵器及洗碗機。

　　(A) utensils 器皿　(B) facilities 設施　(C) appliances 家庭電器　(D) extensions 分機

解析

(1)答題關鍵在題目空格右方的「電冰箱、吸塵器」。

(2)四個選項中，只有選 (C) 項的「家庭電器」，才可有意義連成「買些家庭電器，包括電冰箱、吸塵器……」。

7. This math class is very ＿＿＿＿＿ ; I have to spend at least two hours every day doing the assignments.

　　這門數學課非常 ＿＿＿＿＿ ：我必須每天花兩小時做作業。

　　(A) confidential 機密的　(B) logical 邏輯的　(C) demanding 使人吃力的　(D) resistant 抵抗的

解析

(1)答題關鍵在題目空格右方的「我必須每天花兩小時……」。

(2)四個選項中，只有選 (C) 項的「使人吃力的」，才可有意義連成「我必須每天花兩小時……」。

8. One can generally judge the quality of eggs with the naked eye. ＿＿＿＿＿ , good eggs must be clean, free of cracks, and smooth-shelled.

　　用肉眼通常能判斷蛋的品質。 ＿＿＿＿＿ ，好蛋必須乾淨無裂痕及蛋殼平滑。

　　(A) Agriculturally 農業地　(B) Externally 外表上　(C) Influentially 有影響的

(D) Occasionally 偶爾地

解析

(1)答題關鍵在題目空格右方的「好蛋必須乾淨……」。

(2)四個選項中，只有選(B)項的「外表上」，才可有意義連成「外表上好蛋必須乾淨……」。

9. The scientist ＿＿＿＿＿＿ his speech to make it easier for children to understand the threat of global warming.

科學家 ＿＿＿＿＿＿ 他的演說內容使孩童更容易了解地球暖化的威脅。

(A) estimated 估計的　(B) documented 做成文件　(C) abolished 廢除　(D) modified 修正的

解析

(1)答題關鍵在題目空格右方的「他的演說內容」。

(2)四個選項中，只有選(D)項的「修正」，才可有意義連成「修正他的演說內容使孩童更容易了解……」。

10. The Internet has ＿＿＿＿＿＿ newspapers as a medium of mass communication. It has become the main source for national and international news for people.

以大眾傳播媒體而言，網際網路 ＿＿＿＿＿＿ 報紙。它已經成為人們國內外的新聞來源。

(A) reformed 改革的　(B) surpassed 超越　(C) promoted 推廣　(D) convinced 說服

解析

(1)答題關鍵在題目空格左、右方的「網際網路」與「報紙」。

(2)四個選項中，只有選(B)項的「超越」，才可有意義連成「網際網路超越報紙」。

二、綜合測驗（10分）

說明：第 11 至 20 題，每題一個空格。請依文意選出一個最適當的選項，標示在答案卡之「擇題答案區」。每題答對得1分，答錯或劃記多於一個選項者倒扣 1/3 分，倒扣到本大題之實得分數為零為止。未作答者，不給分亦不扣分。

第 11 至 15 題為題組

　　Keele University in the United Kingdom has developed a "virtual patient," created by a computer, to help train the pharmacists of the future. Students in the university's School of ＿＿＿11＿＿＿ work with the "patient" to gain experience in effective communication and decision-making.

　　Students talk with the "patient" directly or by typing questions into a computer. The "patient" responds verbally or with gestures to indicate ＿＿＿12＿＿＿ such as pain, stress or anxiety. As a result, students are forced to communicate clearly ＿＿＿13＿＿＿ that the "patient" understands them completely. The Virtual Patient can also be used to explore various medical situations. For example, the "patient" can be programmed to be allergic to certain medicine and can ＿＿＿14＿＿＿ serious reactions if student learners are not aware of the situation. This kind of practice allows students to learn from mistakes in a safe environment that would not be _____15_____ with textbooks alone. The unique system can both be used in a classroom setting or for distance learning.

　　英國的基爾大學已經發展一種由電腦創造出來的「虛擬病患」來幫助訓練未來的藥劑師。

　　大學的 _____11_____ 學生與虛擬病患一起工作，以獲有效溝通與做決定的經驗。學生直接與虛擬病患交談，或用電腦裡把問題打出來。虛擬病患會用口語回答，或用手勢指出 _____12_____ 像是痛苦、壓力或憂慮。結果是，學生被迫做清楚的表達，_____13_____ 讓虛擬病患完全理解意思。虛擬病患也能用來探索不同的醫療情況。例如，虛擬病患能被設定對某一藥物過敏些並且也可 _____14_____ 較嚴重的反應如果學習者沒有進入情況的話，它這種實習使學生在安全環境下從錯誤中學習，這是單獨用教科書時不 _____15_____ 做到的。這個獨有的系統，可用於課堂上教學與遠距教學。

11. 題句：Students in the university's School of _____11_____ work with the "patient"

　　　　大學的 _____11_____ 學生與虛擬病患一起工作，以獲有效溝通……

　　選項：(A) Education 教育　(B) Business 商業　(C) Pharmacy 藥學　(D) Humanities 人道

解析

依句後的「work with the patient」判斷，只有選(C)項的「藥學」，才是正確選項。

12. 題句：The "patient" responds verbally or with gestures to indicate _____12_____ such as pain, stress or anxiety....

　　　　或用手勢表示 _____12_____ 像是痛苦、壓力或憂慮。

　　選項：(A) expressions 表情　(B) emotions 情感　(C) elements 元素　(D) events 事件

解析

依句後的 such as pain, stress or anxiety 判斷，只有選(A)項的「情感」才是正確選項。

13. 題句：students are forced to communicate clearly _____13_____ that the "patient" understands them completely.

　　　　學生被迫做清楚的表達，_____13_____ 讓虛擬病患完全理解意思。

　　選項：(A) in order 為了要……　(B) in return 回報　(C) in case 萬一　(D) in addition 另外的

解析

依句後的 that the patient understands them completely 判斷，只有選(A)項的「為了要」才是正確選項。

14. 題句：and can _____14_____ serious reactions if student learners are not aware of the situation

　　　　它也可 _____14_____ 較嚴重的反應，如果學習者沒有進入情況的話。

選項：(A) adapt to 適應於　(B) break into 闖入　(C) provide with 提供　(D) suffer from 承受……之苦

解析

依題意只有選(D)項的「承受」才是正確選項。

15. 題句：allows students to learn from mistakes in a safe environment that would not be _____15_____ with textbooks alone.

這種實習使學生在安全環境下從錯誤中學習，這是單獨用教科書時不 _____15_____ 做到的。

選項：(A) exciting 興奮　(B) necessary 必須　(C) possible 可能的　(D) important 重要的

解析

依題意及句後的 with textbooks alone 判斷，(C) 項的「可能的」才是正確選項。意指這種學習僅用教科書是不可能辦到的。

第 16 至 20 題為題組

In spite of modernization and the increasing role of women in all walks of life, the practice of the dowry in India is still widespread. The dowry system, money or property brought by a bride to he husband at marriage, was started centuries ago with the intention of providing security for a girl _____16_____ difficulties and unexpected circumstances after marriage. For this purpose, the parents gave _____17_____ they could to their daughter, which consequently went to the groom's family. By the beginning of the 21st century, however, the custom had deteriorated to a point whereby the groom and his family had become very _____18_____ . When demands for dowry are not met, the bride is _____19_____ torture, and often even killed. The more educated a man is, the _____20_____ is the expectation for dowry at the time of marriage. Girls who are highly educated are required to have larger dowries because they usually marry more educated men.

不論現代化與婦女行業角色的增加，在印度嫁妝的習俗仍然很流行。嫁妝制度，結婚時新娘帶給丈夫的錢或財物，已有數世紀之久。用意在女方婚後 _____16_____ 有困難或不可預料之事發生時有所保障。基於這個理由，父母親會將 _____17_____ 通通給了女兒，結果是這些東西全部都進了新郎家裡。到了二十一世紀初，這個習俗惡化到新郎與他的家人變得很 _____18_____ 。當嫁妝條件不符要求時，新娘 _____19_____ 拷打，也常常遭殺害。男人的教育程度越高，結婚時要女方嫁妝的期待 _____20_____ 。女人的教育程度高，通常會與教育程度高的男人結婚，會被要求拿出更多嫁妝。

16. 題句：providing security for a girl _____16_____ difficulties and unexpected circumstances after marriage.

用意在女方婚後 _____16_____ 有困難或不可預料之事發生時有所保障。

選項：(A) due to 由於　(B) apart from 不同於　(C) in case of 如果發生　(D) with reference to 參考

解析

依題句後段的「有困難或不可預料之事發生時」判斷，只有選 (C) 項的「如果發生」才是正確選項。

**17.題句：the parents gave ＿＿＿17＿＿＿ they could to their daughter,

父母親會將 ＿＿＿17＿＿＿ 通通給了女兒。

選項：(A) whoever 不論是誰　(B) whenever 不論何時　(C) whatever 不論什麼

(D) whichever 不論哪一個

解析

依題意只有選 (C) 項的「不論什麼」才可有意義連結成「父母親會將不論什麼通通給女兒」才是正確選項。

18. 題句：the custom had deteriorated to a point whereby the groom and his family had become very＿＿＿18＿＿＿.

這個習俗惡化到新郎與他的家人變得很 ＿＿＿18＿＿＿ 。

選項：(A) greedy 貪心　(B) pleasant 愉快　(C) regretful 後悔　(D) sympathetic 同情

解析

依題意只有選 (A) 項的「貪心」才是正確選項。

19. 題句：When demands for dowry are not met, the bride is ＿＿＿19＿＿＿ torture, and often even killed

當嫁妝條件不符要求時，新娘 ＿＿＿19＿＿＿ 拷打，也常常遭殺害。

選項：(A) aware of 知道　(B) required by 被要求　(C) furious with 生氣　(D) subject to 易遭受

解析

依題意只有選 (D) 項的「易遭受」才是正確選項。

**20.題句：The more educated a man is, the ＿＿＿20＿＿＿ is the expectation for dowry at the time of marriage.

男人的教育程度越高，結婚時要女方嫁妝的期待 ＿＿＿20＿＿＿ 。

選項：(A) lower 低一些　(B) higher 高一些　(C) better 好一些　(D) worse 差一些

解析

依題意只有選 (B) 項的「高一些」才可有意義連成「男人的教育程度越高，結婚時要女方嫁妝的期待會高一些」，才是正確選項。

三、文意選填（10分）

第 21 至 30 題為題組

Oniomania is the technical term for the compulsive desire to shop, more commonly referred to as compulsive shopping or shopping addiction. Victims often experience feelings of _____21_____ when they are in the process of purchasing, which seems to give their life meaning while letting them forget about their sorrows. Once _____22_____ the environment where the purchasing occurred, the feeling of a personal reward would be gone. To compensate, the addicted person would go shopping again. Eventually a feeling of suppression will overcome the person. For example, cases have shown that the bought goods will be hidden or destroyed, because the person concerned feels _____23_____ of their addiction and tries to conceal it. He or she is either regretful or depressed. In order to cope with the feelings, the addicted person is prompted to _____24_____ another purchase.

Compulsive shopping often begins at an early age. Children who experienced parental neglect often grew up with low _____25_____ because throughout much of their childhood they felt that they were not important as a person. As a result, they used toys to _____26_____ their feelings of loneliness. Because of the ongoing sentiment of deprivation they endured as children, adults that have depended on materials for emotional _____27_____ when they were much younger are more likely to become addicted to shopping. During adulthood, the purchase, instead of the toy, is substituted for _____28_____. The victims are unable to deal with their everyday problems, especially those that alter their self-esteem. Important issues in their lives are repressed by _____29_____ something. According to studies, as many as 8.9 percent of the American population _____30_____ as compulsive buyers. Research has also found that men and women suffer from this problem at about the same rate.

購物狂是強迫購物的技術名詞，通常稱為被迫購物或購物成癮。在購買過程中受害者經常會體驗到 _____21_____ 感覺，這樣好像使他們生活更有意義也忘記他們的傷心事。一旦 _____22_____ 購物環境，購買發生的地方，個人受到獎勵的感覺消失了。為了補償，上癮的人就再去購物。終有一天，一種抑制的感覺會出現。例如，已購物品已被隱藏或毀損，因為當事人對成癮之事會感到 _____23_____ ，就會設法掩飾不讓人知。這時當事人會後悔或沮喪。為了克服這種感覺，上癮的人就會 _____24_____ 再去購物。

強迫購物常從小時候開始。受父母疏忽的孩子長大後 _____25_____ 較少，因為在童年時他們感到自己不重要。因此，他們用玩具來 _____26_____ 孤獨的感覺。由於童年時不斷被剝奪的情緒，在非常年輕時就會嗜好購物，成年後會依賴物質需求得到感情的 _____27_____ 。在成年時期他們購買的不是玩具，而是 _____28_____ 替代品。那些受害者無法處理他們每天的問題，特別是改變他們自尊的問題。在他們一生當中，

重要的議題卻被 ＿＿＿＿29＿＿＿＿ 所壓抑。根據研究，多達8.9%的美國人 ＿＿＿＿30＿＿＿＿ 強迫購買者。研究同時也發現，受這個問題之苦的男性和女性比率差不多。

(A) support 支持　　(B) qualify 被證明　　(C) affection 情感　　(D) ashamed 羞愧
(E) make up for 補償　(F) leaving 留下　　(G) turn to 轉向　　(H) buying 購買
(I) self-esteem 自尊　(J) contentment 滿足

21. 題句：Victims often experience feelings of ＿＿＿＿21＿＿＿＿ when they are in the process of purchasing,

　　在購買過程中受害者經常會體驗到 ＿＿＿＿21＿＿＿＿ 感覺。

解析

依題意只有選 (J) 項的「滿足」才是正確選項。

22. 題句：Once ＿＿＿＿22＿＿＿＿ the environment where the purchasing occurred, the feeling of a personal reward would be gone.

　　一旦 ＿＿＿＿22＿＿＿＿ 購物環境，購買發生的地方，個人受到獎賞的感覺消失了。

解析

依題意只有選 (F) 項的「離開」才是正確選項。

23. 題句：because the person concerned feels ＿＿＿＿23＿＿＿＿ of their addiction and tries to conceal it

　　因為當事人對成癮之事會感到 ＿＿＿＿23＿＿＿＿ ，就會設法掩飾不讓人知。

解析

依題意只有選 (D) 項的「羞愧」才是正確選項。

24. 題句：In order to cope with the feelings, the addicted person is prompted to ＿＿＿＿24＿＿＿＿ another purchase.

　　為了克服這種感覺，上癮的人就會 ＿＿＿＿24＿＿＿＿ 再去購物。

解析

依題意只有選 (G) 項的「轉向」才是正確選項（轉向表示「再折回去」之意）。

25. 題句：Children who experienced parental neglect often grew up with low ＿＿＿＿25＿＿＿＿
　　受父母疏忽的孩子長大後 ＿＿＿＿25＿＿＿＿ 較少。

解析

依題意只有選 (I) 項的「自尊」才是正確選項。

26. 題句：As a result, they used toys to _____26_____ their feelings of loneliness.

　　　　　他們用玩具來 _____26_____ 孤獨的感覺。

解析

依題意只有選(E)項的「補償」才是正確選項。

27. 題句：adults that have depended on materials for emotional _____27_____ .

　　　　　成年後會依賴物質需求得到感情的 _____27_____ 。

解析

依題意只有選(A)項的「支持」才是正確選項。

28. 題句：During adulthood, the purchase, instead of the toy, is substituted for _____28_____ .

　　　　　在成年時期他們購買的不是玩具，而是 _____28_____ 替代品。

解析

依題意只有選(C)項的「情感」才是正確選項。

29. 題句：Important issues in their lives are repressed by _____29_____ something.

　　　　　在他們一生當中，重要的議題卻被 _____29_____ 所壓抑。

解析

依題意只有選(H)項的「購物時」才是正確選項。

30. 題句：8.9 percent of the American population _____30_____ as compulsive buyers.

　　　　　多達8.9%的美國人 _____30_____ 強迫購買者。

解析

依題意只有選(B)項的「被形容為」才是正確選項。qualified as意為「被稱作、被認為」。

四、篇章結構（10分）

> 說明：第 31 至 35 題，每題一個空格。請依文意在文章後所提供的 (A) 到 (E) 選項中分別
> 　　　選出最適當者，填入空格中，使篇章結構清晰有條理，並將其英文字母代號標示
> 　　　在答案卡之「選擇題答案區」。每題答對得 2 分，答錯或劃記多於一個選項者倒
> 　　　扣 1/2 分，倒扣到本大題之實得分數為零為止。未作答者，不給分亦不扣分。

第 31 至 35 題為題組

　　There was a time when Whitney didn't have a lot of friends. She was a bit shy and reserved. _____31_____ All through high school, though, she wasn't able to make good friends or find companionship.

　　When it was time to go to college, Whitney was quite nervous. She was going to be rooming with someone she didn't know and living in a town 300 miles away from home. There wouldn't be a single person she knew in town. _____32_____

　　The first week of classes, something happened that changed Whitney's life forever. _____33_____ She told everyone where she came from and all of the other ordinary details that students share in such situations. The final question for each student to answer was, "what is your goal for this class?" Most of the students said that they would like to get a good grade, pass the class or something similar. _____34_____ She said that her goal was to make just one good friend.

　　While most of the students sat in silence, one student came to Whitney and held out her hand and introduced herself. She asked if they could be friends. The whole room was silent. All eyes focused on Whitney and the hand extended just in front of her. _____35_____

　　Whitney learned the power of asking for what she wanted and taking action on that day.

　　以前惠特尼沒有很多朋友。她有點怕羞並且個性保守。_____31_____ 在高中求學期間她無法交到好朋友或找到好同伴。要上大學時，惠特相當緊張。她將要與不認識的人同住離家 300 英里的小鎮。在小鎮裡她一個人也不認識。_____32_____

　　開學後的第一週，某事發生而永遠改變惠特尼的一生。_____33_____ 她告訴同學她是哪裡人，及其所發生的事來與同學共享。每個學生都要回答的最後問題是，「你來這班上課的目標是什麼？」大多數學生說他們想得到好分數、不要留級之類的事。_____34_____ 她說她的目標是想交到一個好朋友。

　　當大多數學生靜靜坐著時，一個學生走出來，告訴惠特尼並握住她的手也介紹了自己。她問是否他們可以做朋友。整個房間鴉雀無聲。所有的目光集中在惠特尼，友誼之手已張開在她面前，_____35_____。

　　惠特尼學到她敢開口要求的力量，而就從那天付諸行動。

(A) For some reason, Whitney said something entirely different.
　　為某些原因惠尼說了完全不同的事。

(B) Whitney smiled and stretched her hand out and a friendship was formed.
　　惠特尼笑著伸出手，友誼就此建立了。

(C) She had no idea how she was going to make friends in this new environment.
　　她不知道如何在這個新環境裡交朋友。

(D) In her English Composition class, she was asked to share a little about herself.
　　在她的作文班裡，她被要求分享一些有關自己的事。

(E) She never really wanted to be popular, but she did want to have someone to share secrets and laughs with.
　　她從來不想太有名氣，但她卻想要有人能同享祕密與歡樂。

31. 正確答案為 (E) 選項。

解析

⑴依題號空格前句的「她沒有很多朋友」，以及空格後句的「在高中時也無法找到朋友」來看，都是在敘述交朋友之事。

⑵因此，(E) 項的「她從來不想太有名氣，但她卻想要有人能同享祕密與歡樂」才是連接空格前後兩句的正確選項。

32. 正確答案為 (C) 選項。

解析

空格前句是說，她在小鎮一個人也不認識。而後句是說「開學後的第一週，某事發生」。依此題意，(C) 項的「她不知在這個新環境下如何交朋友」才是放入空格的正確選項。

33. 正確答案為 (D) 選項。

解析

空格前句是說「某事發生⋯⋯，」空格後句是說「在她的作文班裡，她被要求分享一些有關自己的事」。依此題意，只有 (D) 項的「她告訴同學她是哪裡人⋯⋯」才是放入空格的正確選項。

34. 正確答案為 (A) 選項。

解析

先看本題句空格前的「大多數學生說他們想得到好分數、不要留級之類的事」。以及空格後的「她說她的目標是想交到一個好朋友」。依此題意，只有選 (A) 項的「為某些原因惠特尼說了完全不同的事。」才是連接空格前後兩句的正確選項。

35. 正確答案為 (B) 選項。

解析

先看空格前後的兩句「友誼之手已張開在她的前面，＿＿＿35＿＿＿。惠特尼學到她敢開口要求的力量，就從那天付諸行動。」依此題意，只有選 (B) 項的「惠特尼笑著伸出手，友誼就此建立了。」才是放入空格的正確選項。

五、閱讀測驗（32分）

說明：第 36 至 51 題，每題請分別根據各篇文章的文意選出一個最適當的選項，標示在答案卡之「選擇題答案區」。每題答對得 2 分，答錯或劃記多於一個選項者倒扣 2/3 分，倒扣到本大題之實得分數為零為止。未作答者，不給分亦不扣分。

第 36 至 39 題為題組

April 22, 2010 will be the 18th celebration of the annual *Take Our Daughters to Work Day* (*TOD*), a project the National Ms. Foundation for Women of America (NFW) developed to expose girls to expanding opportunities for women in the workplace.

The program offers millions of girls a first-hand view of the many career opportunities available in their futures. Now that women make up 46 percent of the U.S. workforce, girls can find role models in every occupational field—from politics to molecular biology to professional athletics, to name just a few. *TOD* encourages girls to focus on their abilities and opportunities, not just their appearance.

The NFW developed the project more than a decade ago to address the self-esteem problems that many girls experience when they enter adolescence. At school, boys often receive more encouragement in the classroom, especially in math, science and computer science, the academic fields that tend to lead to the highest salaries. Women receive on average only 73 cents for every dollar that men are paid, and remain vastly underrepresented in top executive positions and technology fields. *TOD* aims to give girls the confidence and inspiration they need to develop successful careers, particularly in non-traditional fields.

Perhaps because the program had become so widespread and successful, *TOD* had been criticized for excluding boys, and it was expanded in 2003 to include boys. The program's official website states that the program was changed in order to provide both boys and girls with opportunities to explore careers at an age when they are more flexible in terms of gender stereotyped roles. "We should also show boys that becoming a child care provider is as acceptable a choice as becoming a police officer or CEO," added Sara K. Gould, executive director of the NFW.

2010 年 4 月 22 日將是第 18 屆慶祝「帶我們的女兒去工作」（TOD），的日子。這是為美國女性成立的國家女士基金會，目的在幫助女性擴展職場的工作機會。

　　該計畫提供數百萬女性第一手將來的工作機會。既然女性職場占美國總職場的 46%，女性可找到不同的職場角色，——從政治到生物、職業選手等不勝枚舉。TOD 鼓勵女性專心在她們的能力和機會，並非她們的外表。

　　NFW 發展至今已超過十年，說明有關自尊心的問題，這是女性在進入青少年期會經歷到的。在學校，男孩經常在教室裡獲得更多的鼓勵，特別是數學、科學和電算科學，傾向於高薪水的學術領域。在付給男性每一美元裡，女性平均只獲7角3分，而在高階管理的職位與科技領域裡更是不成比例。TOD 目標是給女性有信心及所需要的啟發，特別是在非傳統的領域。

　　或許因為計畫已經變得如此廣泛和成功，TOD 被批評為排除男性，而在 2003 年也擴展到包括男性在內。該計畫的官網說明計畫已有變更，是為了要提供男女兩性的工作機會，在找工作方面更具彈性，而非拘泥在性別方面的舊規。「我們也應該讓男孩看，成為孩童保母與成為一名警官、或執行長一樣都是可接受的選擇。」

36. The purpose for having a Take Our Daughters to Work Day is ＿＿＿＿＿＿。

TOD 的目的是什麼？

(A) to encourage girls to pursue top paying jobs

鼓勵女孩追求高薪工作。

⒝ to let girls spend more time with their mothers

　　讓女孩跟他們的母親多相處。

⒞ to show girls possibilities for work and careers

　　告訴女生工作與創業的可能性。

⒟ to give girls a chance to visit their mothers' offices

　　給女孩機會訪問她們母親的辦公室。

解析

從答題關鍵的「The program offers millions of girls a first-hand view of the many career opportunities available in their futures.」可看出，⒞ 項的「to show girls possibilities for work and careers」才是正確選項。

37. TOD was criticized because some people ＿＿＿＿＿＿＿＿。

　　TOD 被某些人批評。

⒜ thought it was not fair to boys

　　認為這對男孩不公平。

⒝ did not like having children at work

　　不要喜歡在工作時有孩子。

⒞ did not have daughters to take to work

　　不要帶女兒去工作。

⒟ would rather have their daughters stay at home

　　寧願讓他們的女兒待在家裡。

解析

從答題關鍵的「Perhaps because the program had become so widespread and successful, *TOD* had been criticized for excluding boys, and it was expanded in 2003 to include boys. The program's official」可看出，⒜ 項的「thought it was not fair to boys」才是正確選項。

38. Which of the following is true according to the passage?

　　根據本文下列哪項是真？

⒜ Boys are now included on Take Our Daughters to Work Day.

　　目前男孩已包括在 TOD 內。

⒝ Women and men have always been treated equally at work.

　　婦女和男人在職場都被平等對待。

⒞ Homemaking and rearing children are jobs for girls only.

　　持家和養育孩子只是女性的工作。

⒟ Girls grow up receiving more attention than boys.

女孩長大後得到更多的注意。

解析

從整段文章內容來看，只有 (A) 項的「Boys are now included on Take Our Daughters to Work Day.」才是正確選項。

39. Why are women underrepresented in some fields such as technology?

為什麼在一些技術領域裡女性受聘不成比例？

(A) They are not interested in these fields.

她們對這些領域不感興趣。

(B) They are not encouraged to work in these fields.

她們沒被鼓勵在這些領域工作。

(C) They are not paid the same as men in these fields.

她們在這些領域沒得到與男人相同的報償。

(D) They are not allowed to be educated in these fields.

她們不被允許在這些領域受教育。

解析

從答題關鍵的「At school, boys often receive more encouragement in the classroom, especially in math, science and computer science, the academi」可看出，(B) 項的「They are not encouraged to work in these fields.」才是正確選項。

第 40 至 43 題為題組

In all cultures and throughout history hair has had a special significance. In ancient Egypt, as long ago as 1500 BC, the outward appearance expressed the person's status, role in society and political position. Wigs played an important role in this: they were crafted with great artistry and often sprinkled with powdered gold.

In the 8th century BC, the pre-Roman Celts in Northern Europe wore their hair long. In a man it was the expression of his strength, in a woman of her fertility. The idea of long hair as a symbol of male strength is even mentioned in the Bible, in the story of Samson and Delilah. Samson was a leader of the Israelites. His long hair, which he never cut, gave him superhuman powers. The only person who knew his secret was Delilah. However, she spied for the enemy and betrayed him. One night she cut off his hair and thus robbed him of his strength.

In the classical Greek period, curly hair was not only the fashion, but it also represented an attitude towards life. Curls or locks were the metaphor for change, freedom and the joy of living. The ancient Greek word for curls and locks is related to intriguing and tempting someone.

Hair is also used as a symbol of opposition. The punk protest movement today uses hair as a symbol of disapproval of the "middle-class, conventional lifestyle" by wearing provocative haircuts and shockingly colored hair. A different form of objection could be seen in the women's hairstyles in the 1960s. Women's liberation was expressed in a short-cut, straight and simple hairstyle which underlined equality with men without neglecting female attributes. To this day hair has kept its importance as a symbol of power, youth, vitality and health.

　　在全部文化和整個歷史裡，頭髮有著特別的意義。在古埃及，早在西元前1500年，外表是象徵人的地位、社會與政治位階。假髮在這裡起了重要作用，它們被更高的藝術技巧精心製作，並且經常撒上金粉。

　　在西元前八世紀，在北歐洲的前羅馬凱爾特人都留長頭髮。以男人來說，它是實力的表現，以女性來說，是代表她的生育力。留長髮象徵男性實力的想法，早在《聖經》的薩姆森和 Delilah 的故事裡就已提及，薩姆森是一位古以色列的領導人。他的長頭髮從來不剪，給他超常的力量。 Delilah 是唯一知道他祕密的人，不過，她當了敵人的間諜並且背叛他。有一天晚上她剪下他的頭髮，因此搶走他的力量。

　　在古典希臘時期，捲曲的頭髮不僅是流行，而且也代表對生命的態度。 捲髮或者綹是被隱喻為變化、自由和快樂生活。捲髮和髮綹的古希臘語與陰謀和誘惑他人有關。

　　頭髮也被視為反對的象徵。當前的龐克族抗議運動，把頭髮看成對中產家庭與傳統生活模式的不贊同，並透過挑釁的髮型與髮色來抗議。一個不同的反對形式可在一九六〇年代的女性髮型裡看得到。婦女的解放表現在「剪短髮」上，用簡單剪直的髮型來強調與男行的平等，也沒有忽略女性的本質。直到今天頭髮已經保持它是象徵力量、年輕、活力與健康的重要性。

40. The topic of this passage could best be described as ＿＿＿＿＿＿ .
　　對這段文章的最佳描述是 ＿＿＿＿＿＿ 。
　(A) the scientific study of hairstyles
　　　髮型的科學研究。
　(B) the symbolic meanings of hairstyles
　　　髮型的象徵意義。
　(C) the art of designing different hairstyles
　　　設計不同的髮型藝術。
　(D) the contemporary development of hairstyles
　　　髮型的當代發展。

解析
從答題關鍵的「In all cultures and throughout history hair has had a special significance.」，(B) 項的「the symbolic meanings of hairstyles」才是正確選項。

41. Why did ancient Greeks like to wear curls and locks?
　　古希臘人為什麼喜歡留捲髮和髮綹？
　(A) To attract others.
　　　吸引其他人。

(B) To show off their artistry.

炫耀他們的藝術技巧。

(C) To hide their real identity.

隱藏他們的真正的身分。

(D) To represent power and status.

代表能力和地位。

解析

從答題關鍵的「In the classical Greek period, curly hair was not only the fashion, but it also represented an attitude towards life.」可看出，(A) 項的「To attract others.」才是正確選項。

42. How did women in the 1960s use hair to show objection?

六〇年代的婦女怎樣用頭髮表示異議？

(A) They grew long hair.

她們留長髮。

(B) They dyed their hair.

她們染頭髮。

(C) They cut their hair short.

她們把頭髮理短。

(D) They shaved their heads.

他們留光頭。

解析

從答題關鍵的「Women's liberation was expressed in a short-cut,」可看出，(C) 項的「They cut their hair short.」才是正確選項。

43. What can be inferred from the passage?

從本文可推斷出什麼？

(A) Long curly hair has always been popular since ancient times.

長時期從古老的捲曲頭髮一直很受歡迎。

(B) Ancient Egyptians did not pay much attention to their hairstyles.

古老的埃及人沒太注意他們的髮型。

(C) The punk movement is one of the most successful movements in history.

龐克運動是在歷史上的最成功的運動之一。

(D) Samson might never have been defeated if he had kept the secret to himself.

薩姆森如果對自己保密，就不會被打敗。

解析

從答題關鍵的「Samson was a leader of the Israelites. His long hair, which he never cut, gave him superhuman powers. The only person who knew his secret was Delilah. However, she spied for the enemy and betrayed him. One night she cut off his hair and thus robbed him of his strength.」可看出，(D) 項的「Samson might never have been defeated if he had kept the secret to himself.」才是正確選項。

第 44 至 47 題為題組

Camille Mahlknecht, 9, has some big fun planned for this weekend. She and other residents of Agoura Hills, California, plan to pick up trash during their city's annual cleanup. At the same time, Wissam Raed, 12, will be busy volunteering too. Thousands of miles away in Lebanon, Wissam plans to put on a play at an orphanage and bring potted plants to elderly people at a senior citizen center.

Some other children like Nathan White, 10, have personal reasons for volunteering. Nathan's grandmother died of a heart attack. To help raise money for medical research, Nathan participated in Jump Rope for Heart. He and five other boys took turns jumping rope for two and half hours and collected more than US$1,200 in donations for the American Heart Association.

Millions of children around the globe lend a hand to their communities every year. Schools and parents also contribute to the rise in youth service. For example, many schools offer community service activities for students to join. Teachers either combine volunteer work with classroom lessons or make service work a requirement. Parents, on the other hand, encourage their kids to volunteer and do it with them.

Community service is particularly important in this recession time. As the need for monetary support and other aid has increased, many charitable organizations have experienced a significant drop in donations. Camille and other children who volunteer thousands of hours annually can fill in some of the gaps.

According to research, kids who start volunteering are twice as likely to continue doing good deeds when they are adults. So, grab a paintbrush, a trash bag, or whatever you need to help your community. You'll love how you feel after helping others. Even dirty work can be lots of fun, if it's for a good cause.

卡蜜拉 Mahlknecht，9 歲，訂好了本週末的有趣計畫。她和加州 Agoura 山的其他居民，計畫在他們的城市每年一度的清潔日清理垃圾。同時，Wissam Raed，12 歲，也將忙於志工事務。在數千英里外的黎巴嫩，Wissam 計畫在一個育幼院上演話劇，並把盆栽送給老人中心年長者。

其他小孩像是那丹‧懷特，10 歲，有當志工的個人原因。那丹的祖母死於心臟病發作。為了幫醫學研究籌款，那丹參加跳繩節目。他和其他五男孩輪流跳繩跳了兩個半小時，且募集了 1,200 美元以上的捐款給美國心臟協會。

全世界的數百萬個小孩，每年幫忙他們的社區。學校和父母在青年服務中心也有幫忙募款。舉例來說，很多學校提供社區服務活動讓學生參加。教師則是結合志工服務與教室課程，或者是，把志工服務訂為必修課程。父母們，反過來說，鼓勵他們的孩子參與和父母親一起服務的志工隊。

社區服務在這經濟不景氣時特別重要。財務支援與其他服務不斷增加，很多慈善組織看到捐款也顯著減少。卡蜜拉和其他孩子每年當志工數千小時，也可彌補一些缺口。

根據研究，年小時候當志工，長大成年後，會有兩倍的意願繼續做這個好行為。因此，抓一支漆刷，一個廢料袋，或其他需要的器具幫助你的社區。你會喜歡助人後的那種感覺。如果出自善意，即使清除骯髒的工作也會很開心。

44. What's the writer's purpose of writing this passage?

作者寫本文的目的何在？

(A) To recommend youth service programs to schools.

向學校推薦青年服務方案。

(B) To ask charity organizations to serve the community.

請慈善組織來社區服務。

(C) To urge children to take part in volunteering activities.

呼籲孩子們參加志工活動。

(D) To propose alternatives for doing community services.

為社區服務提出不同的選擇。

解析

從整篇內容可看出，(C) 項的「To urge children to take part in volunteering activities.」才是正確選項。因為其他三選項在文中皆未被提及。

45. What is the main idea of the 3rd paragraph?.

本文第三段的大意是什麼？

(A) Community service is gaining popularity among children.

社區服務越來越受孩子們歡迎。

(B) Families and schools help to make community service popular.

家庭和學校也幫助推廣社區服務。

(C) Children now depend more on their teachers than on their parents.

現在的孩子倚賴老師多於倚賴父母親。

(D) Nathan White had a special reason to raise money for medical research.

那丹・懷特有一個特別原因為醫學研究募款。

解析

從答題關鍵的「Millions of children around the globe lend a hand to their communities every year. Schools and parents also contribute to the rise in youth service.」可看出，(B) 項的「Families and schools help to make community service popular.」才是正確選項。

46. Why is community service important in a time of recession?

為什麼社區服務在不景氣時更重要？

(A) It raises money for school activities.

它為學校活動募款。

(B) It teaches children to take care of the sick.

它教孩子照顧病患。

(C) It gives charity organizations some needed help.

給慈善組織一些必要的幫助。

(D) It encourages parents and teachers to work together.

它鼓勵父母和教師一起工作。

解析

從答題關鍵的「Community service is particularly important in this recession time. As the need for monetary support and other aid has increased, many charitable organizations have experienced a significant drop in donations. Camille and other children who volunteer thousands of hours annually can fill in some of the gaps.」可看出，(C) 項的「It gives charity organizations some needed help.」才是正確選項。

47. What can be inferred from the passage?

從本文可推斷出什麼？

(A) Community service can help prevent juvenile delinquency.

社區服務能幫助防止少年犯罪。

(B) Children will probably leave school and work as volunteers.

孩子或許會離開學校去當志工。

(C) Organizing sports events for the school is a kind of community service.

為學校組織比賽活動也是一種社區服務。

(D) Children who do volunteer work are more likely to grow up to be caring adults.

孩提時代當志工，長成後可能更關心別人。

解析

從答題關鍵的「According to research, kids who start volunteering are twice as likely to continue doing good deeds when they are adults.」可看出，(D) 項的「Children who do volunteer work are more likely to grow up to be caring adults.」才是正確選項。

第 48 至 51 題為題組

　　Downloading music over the Internet is pretty common among high school and college students. However, when students download and share copyrighted music without permission, they are violating the law.

　　A survey of young people's music ownership has found that teenagers and college students have an average of more than 800 illegally copied songs each on their digital music players. Half of those surveyed share all the music on their hard drive, enabling others to copy hundreds of songs at any one time. Some students were found to have randomly linked their personal blogs to music sites, so as to allow free trial listening of copyrighted songs for blog visitors, or adopted some of the songs as the background music for their blogs. Such practices may be easy and free, but there are consequences.

Sandra Dowd, a student of Central Michigan University, was fined US$7,500 for downloading 501 files from LimeWire, a peer-to-peer file sharing program. Sandra claimed that she was unaware that her downloads were illegal until she was contacted by authorities. Similarly, Mike Lewinski paid US$4,000 to settle a lawsuit against him for copyright violation. Mike expressed shock and couldn't believe that this was happening to him. "I just wanted to save some money and I always thought **the threat was just a scare tactic.**" "You know, everyone does it," added Mike.

The RIAA (Recording Industry Association of America), the organization that files lawsuits agains illegal downloaders, states that suing students was by no means their first choice. Unfortunately, without the threat of consequences, students are just not changing their behavior. Education alone is not enough to stop the extraordinary growth of the illegal downloading practice.

透過網際網路下載音樂在中學和大學生之間相當普通。不過，當學生下載並且分享獲有版權的音樂而沒經許可時，他們是違犯法律。

一項年輕人的音樂所有權調查，發現青少年和大學生各自有平均超過 800 首非法拷貝的歌，存在他們的音樂播放器裡。其中為數一半的被調查者，將歌曲存放在他們的硬碟裡，以方便隨時拷貝數以百計的歌。

一些學生被發現隨機把他們的個人部落格和音樂場網站連結起來，以允許點入的訪客免費試聽有版權的音樂，甚至把這些歌作為他們部落格的背景音樂。這樣的慣例可能是容易和免費的，但是會自食其果的。

珊卓・多德，一個中密西根大學的學生，從 LimeWire，一個可點對點檔案分享的節目，下載了 501 個檔案而被罰款 7,500 美元。珊卓聲稱她不知道她的下載是不合法的，直到有關單位通知她。與此類似，麥克 Lewinski 支付 4,000 美元來解決一件違反版權的官司。

麥克表示震驚也不敢相信這事發生在他身上。在「我只想省一些錢，我總是認為威脅只是恐嚇戰術而已」。「你知道，每人都這樣下載」，麥克說。

RIAA（美國的錄音工業協會）對不合法的下載者提出控訴，並說明起訴學生絕不是他們的第一個選擇。遺憾的是，沒有盜拷後果的威脅，學生就不會改變他們的行為。只有教育一項，並沒有足夠力量去停止成長特快的不合法下載。

48. Why is it common for students to download copyrighted music?

為什麼學生的下載版權音樂那麼普遍？

(A) They don't think that they will be caught.

他們認為他們不會被抓。

(B) They want their friends to know that they are smart.

他們想要朋友知道他們多聰明。

(C) They think it is a good way to make some extra money.

他們認為賺些額外的錢是一種好方法。

(D) They are against copyright protection over Internet music.

他們反對網路上的版權保護。

解析

從答題關鍵的「Sandra claimed that she was unaware that her downloads were illegal until she was contacted by authorities. Similarly, Mike Lewinski paid US$4,000 to settle a lawsuit against him for copyright violation.」可看出，(A) 項的「They don't think that they will be caught.」才是正確選項。

49. What does Mike mean by saying that "**the threat was just a scare tactic**"?

麥克說的「威脅只是恐嚇戰術」是什麼意思？

(A) One should not be afraid of threats.

一個人不應該害怕威脅。

(B) A lawsuit will result from the threat.

訴訟起因於威脅。

(C) It is unfair to scare people with a threat.

用威脅嚇人是不公平的。

(D) No serious consequence will follow the threat.

威脅之後沒有嚴重的後果。

解析

從答題關鍵的「"I just wanted to save some money and I always thought the threat was just a scare tactic." "You know, everyone does it,"」可看出，(D) 項的「No serious consequence will follow the threat.」才是正確選項。

50. What is RIAA's attitude towards students' illegal downloading behavior?

RIAA 對學生的非法下載行為的態度是什麼？

(A) They believe that education will help greatly in protecting copyrights.

他們相信教育將會在保護版權過程中幫大忙。

(B) They profit from the fines illegal downloaders pay for copyright violations.

他們靠非法下載的罰款獲利。

(C) They like to sue students for downloading music illegally from the Internet.

他們喜歡起訴在網路上非法下載音樂的學生。

(D) They think that illegal downloading behavior needs tough measures to correct.

他們認為非法下載行為需要嚴屬的方法來改正。

解析

從答題關鍵的「Unfortunately, without the threat of consequences, students are just not changing their behavior.」可看出，(D) 項的「They think that illegal downloading behavior needs tough measures to correct.」才是正確選項。

51. What's the best title for this passage?

本文的最好標題是什麼？

(A) Copyright Violators, Beware!

版權侵犯者，注意！

(B) How to Get Free Music Online?

怎樣在線上獲得免費音樂？

(C) A Survey of Students' Downloading Habits

學生下載習慣的調查。

(D) Eliminate Illegal Music Download!

消除非法的音樂下載！

解析

從整篇題意來看，只有 (A) 項的「Copyright Violators, Beware!」才是最切題的正確選項。

第貳部分：非選擇題（28分）

一、中譯英（8分）

說明：1. 將下列兩句中文翻譯成適當之英文，並將答案寫在「答案卷」上。

2. 請依序作答，並標明題號。每題4分，共8分。

1. 玉山是東亞第一高峰，以生態多樣聞名。

解析

先將題句內相關字詞寫出中譯：

玉山 Mt. Jade　第一高峰 The highest peak　東南亞 South East Asia　以……聞名 be famous for
多樣的 multiple　生態 ecology

整句英譯

Mt. Jade is the highest peak in South East Asia, which is famous for multiple ecology.

2. 大家在網路上投票給它，要讓它成爲世界七大奇觀之一。

解析

先將題句內相關字詞寫出中譯：

在網路上 on line　投票 cast the votes　要讓它成爲 make it ~　世界七大奇觀之一 one of the seven wonders in the world

整句英譯

People cast their votes for Mt. Jade, to make it one of the seven wonders of the world.

二、英文作文（20分）

說明：1. 依提示在「答案卷」上寫一篇英文作文。

　　　2. 文長約 120 至 150 個單詞（words）。

提示：如果你可以不用擔心預算，隨心所欲的度過一天，你會怎麼過？請寫一篇短文，第一段說明你會邀請誰和你一起度過這一天？爲什麼？第二段描述你會去哪裡？做些什麼事？爲什麼？

解析

本作文題是一道假設性的題目，文章的寫法就必須符合假設語氣的文法規定。

另外，整段文章唸起來當然要通順，拼法也不要有錯，那就差不多了。

　　If I were to spend a day without worring about the budget, I would invite my twin brother Kevin to spend the day with me. As you can imagine that Keven and I wear the same-pattern clothes, practically anything my parents bought for us, they always come in pair — because we are twin brothers.

　　On this non-worry-budget date, I would buy a folding bike for Kevin and I , folding bick is something we wanted for years. As a matter of fact, I would take the whole family to an elegant and luxury hotel for an expensive buffet dinner.

　　After dinner, I would take them to the fancy restaurant on the 86th floor of Taipei 101 tower for after-meal dessert. It is said that they serve the best coffee in Taipei. By the way, I wouldn't want to miss this once a life time opportunity to do something for my parents, to show my appreciation for what they have done for my brother and I, would buy a good camera for my mother, and an expensive iphone cell phone and ipod for my father.（約162字）

99 年指考（指定考試）

第壹部分：選擇題（72分）

一、詞彙（10分）

1. Chinese is a language with many _____ differences. People living in different areas often speak different dialects.

   華語是一種有許多 _____ 差異的語言。不同地區的人說著不同的方言。

   (A) sociable 善交際的　(B) legendary 傳奇的　(C) regional 地區的　(D) superior 優越的

   解析

   (1)答題關鍵在題目空格左、右方的「許多」與「差異」。

   (2)四個選項中，只有 (C) 項的「地區性」放入空格，才可有意義地連成「華語是一種有許多地區性差異的語言」，才是正確選項。

2. A menu serves to _____ customers about the varieties and prices of the dishes offered by the restaurant.

   菜單是用來 _____ 顧客，餐廳提供哪些菜餚與其價位。

   (A) appeal 上訴　(B) convey 運送　(C) inform 告知　(D) demand 要求

   解析

   (1)答題關鍵在題目空格左、右方的「用來」與「顧客」。

   (2)四個選項中，只有 (C) 項的「告知」放入空格，才可有意義地連成「菜單是用來告知顧客」，才是正確選項。

3. Mary and Jane often fight over which radio station to listen to. Their _____ arises mainly from their different tastes in music.

   瑪莉與珍常為收聽哪一個電台吵架。她們的 _____ 之形成主要是來自對音樂品味的不同。

   (A) venture 冒險　(B) consent 同意　(C) dispute 爭論　(D) temptation 誘惑

解析

(1)答題關鍵在題目空格左、右方的「她們的」與「形成」。

(2)四個選項中，只有 (C) 項的「爭論」放入空格，才可有意義地連成「她們的爭論之形成主要是來自……」，才是正確選項。

4. The baby polar bear is being ＿＿＿＿＿＿ studied by the scientists. Every move he makes is carefully observed and documented.

小北極熊被科學家們 ＿＿＿＿＿＿ 研究。牠的一舉一動都被小心地觀察與記錄歸檔。

(A) prosperously 繁榮地　(B) intensively 密切地　(C) honorably 容易地　(D) originally 起初

解析

(1)答題關鍵在題目空格右方的「研究」。

(2)四個選項中，只有 (B) 項的「密切地」放入空格，才可有意義地連成「小北極熊被科學家們密切地研究」，才是正確選項。

5. At twelve, Catherine has won several first prizes in international art competitions. Her talent and skills are ＿＿＿＿＿＿ for her age.

12 歲時凱薩琳在國際藝術比賽中獲得多項頭獎。她的才能與技藝以她的年齡來說是 ＿＿＿＿＿＿ 。

(A) comparable 可比較的　(B) exceptional 例外地、不尋常地　(C) indifferent 不關心的

(D) unconvincing 不能信服

解析

(1)答題關鍵在題目空格右方的「以她的年齡來說」。

(2)四個選項中，只有 (B) 項的「不尋常的」放入空格，才可有意義地連成「以她的年齡來說是不尋常的」，才是正確選項。

6. After his superb performance, the musician received a big round of ＿＿＿＿＿＿ from the appreciative audience.

在他優良的表現之後，音樂家獲得觀眾很圓滿結束的 ＿＿＿＿＿＿ 。

(A) vacuum 真空　(B) overflow 溢出　(C) applause 鼓掌　(D) spotlight 聚光照明

解析

(1)答題關鍵在題目空格左方的「很圓滿結束的」。

(2)四個選項中，只有 (C) 項的「鼓掌」放入空格，才可有意義地連成「獲得觀眾很圓滿結束的鼓掌」，才是正確選項。

7. The water company inspects the pipelines and ＿＿＿＿＿＿ the water supply regularly to ensure the safety of our drinking water.

水公司檢查管路並定期地 ＿＿＿＿＿＿ 飲水供應系統以保障飲水安全。

(A) exhibits 展出　(B) monitors 監測　(C) interprets 解釋　(D) converts 轉變

解析

(1)答題關鍵在題目空格右方的「飲水的供應系統」。

(2)四個選項中，只有 (B) 項的「監測」放入空格，才可有意義地連成「定期地監測飲水供應系統以保障飲水安全」，才是正確選項。

8. This year's East Asia Summit meetings will focus on critical _____ such as energy conservation, food shortages, and global warming.

本年的亞洲高峰會主題會聚焦在關鍵性 _____ 就像能源保存、食物儲存及地球暖化等。

(A) issues 議題　(B) remarks 評論　(C) conducts 引導　(D) faculties 機能

解析

(1)答題關鍵在題目空格左方的「關鍵性」。

(2)四個選項中，只有 (A) 項的「議題」放入空格，才可有意義地連成「聚焦在關鍵性議題就像能源保存」，才是正確選項。

9. Having fully recognized Mei-ling's academic ability, Mr. Lin strongly _____ her for admission to the university.

完全體會到美玲的學術能力，林先生強烈 _____ 她進入大學。

(A) assured 確定　(B) promoted 晉升　(C) estimated 估計　(D) recommended 推薦

解析

(1)答題關鍵在題目空格右方的「她進入大學」。

(2)四個選項中，只有 (D) 項的「推薦」放入空格，才可有意義地連成「林先生強烈推薦她進入大學」，才是正確選項。

10. The weatherman has warned about drastic temperature change in the next few days, and suggested that we check the weather on a daily basis and dress _____ .

氣象人員警告過幾天會有氣溫的激烈變化，並建議大家要每天注意氣象報告，也要 _____ 穿著。

(A) necessarily 必定地　(B) significantly 意味深長地　(C) specifically 明確地

(D) accordingly 依照

解析

(1)答題關鍵在題目空格左方的「注意氣象報告」與「穿著」。

(2)四個選項中，只有 (D) 項的「依照」放入空格，才可有意義地連成「要每天注意氣象報告，也要依照氣候穿著」，才是正確選項。

二、綜合測驗（10分）

第 11 至 15 題為題組

　　The sun is an extraordinarily powerful source of energy. In fact, the Earth ＿＿＿11＿＿ 20,000 times more energy from the sun than we currently use. If we used more of this source of heat and light, it ＿＿＿12＿＿ all the power needed throughout the world.

　　We can harness energy from the sun, or solar energy, in many ways. For instance, many satellites in space are equipped with large panels whose solar cells transform sunlight directly ＿＿＿13＿＿ electric power. These panels are covered with glass and are painted black inside to absorb as much heat as possible.

　　Solar energy has a lot to offer. To begin with, it is a clean fuel. In contrast, fossil fuels, such as oil or coal, release ＿＿＿14＿＿ substances into the air when they are burned. ＿＿＿15＿＿ , fossil fuels will run out, but solar energy will continue to reach the Earth long after the last coal has been mined and the last oil well has run dry.

　　太陽是非常強力的能源。實際上，地球從太陽 ＿＿＿11＿＿ 的能量比我們目前所用的多出 20,000 倍。如果我們使用光和熱的更多能源，它就能 ＿＿＿12＿＿ 整個世界需要的電能。

　　我們可以控制這些能量。例如，許多在在太空衛星裝有巨大的太陽能板，可以直接的將陽光 ＿＿＿13＿＿ 電能。這些太陽能板被玻璃所覆而內部被漆成黑色以盡量吸收熱能。

　　太陽能用途太多了。首先，它是一種乾淨的燃料。反之，化石燃料，像是油或煤在燃燒時都會釋放出 ＿＿＿14＿＿ 物質。＿＿＿15＿＿ 它會用盡，但煤在開採殆盡後，太陽能仍會繼續造福地球。

11. 題句：the Earth ＿＿＿11＿＿ 20,000 times more energy from the sun than we currently use.

　　選項：(A) repeats 重複　(B) receives 接收到　(C) rejects 拒絕　(D) reduces 減少

解析

依題意，只有選(B)項的「接收到」才是正確選項。

**12. 題句：it ＿＿＿12＿＿ all the power needed throughout the world.

　　選項：(A) supplies 供應　(B) has supplied（現完式）　(C) was supplying（過去進行式）　(D) could supply 當時可供應

解析

(1)答題關鍵在題句前方的「If we used」。屬假設語氣用法，本題 if 前後兩子句都一致要用過去式

動詞。

⑵四個選項中只有(D)項的「could supplied」是過去式，才是符合文法的正確選項。

**13. 題句：whose solar cells transform sunlight directly ＿＿＿13＿＿＿ electric power.

選項：(A) into 在……之內　(B) from 從　(C) with 有、用　(D) off 關、離開

解析

⑴答題關鍵在空格左邊的「transformed 轉換」，其後固定用介係詞是 into。

⑵四個選項中，只有選(A)項的「into」才是符合文法的正確選項。

14. 題句：release ＿＿＿14＿＿＿ substances into the air when they are burned.

選項：(A) diligent 聰明　(B) harmful 有害的　(C) usable 可用的　(D) changeable 可改變的

解析

依題意，只有選(B)項的「harmful」才是正確選項。意指，燃燒時會釋放出有害物質。

15. 題句：＿＿＿15＿＿＿ , fossil fuels will run out, but solar energy will continue to reach the Earth

選項：(A) Otherwise 否則　(B) Therefore 所以　(C) What's more 還有　(D) In comparison 比較

解析

依題意，只有選(C)項的「還有」才是正確選項。

第 16 至 20 題為題組

　　Signs asking visitors to keep their hands off the art are everywhere in the Louvre Museum, Paris. But one special sculpture gallery invites art lovers to allow their hands to ＿＿＿16＿＿＿ the works. The Louvre's Tactile Gallery, targeted at the blind and visually ＿＿＿17＿＿＿ , is the only space in the museum where visitors can touch the sculptures, with no guards or alarms to stop them. Its latest exhibit is a ＿＿＿18＿＿＿ of sculpted lions, snakes, horses and eagles. The 15 animals exhibited are reproductions of famous works found elsewhere in the Louvre. Called "Animals, Symbols of Power," the exhibit ＿＿＿19＿＿＿ animals that were used by kings and emperors throughout history to symbolize the greatness of their reigns. The exhibit, opened in December 2008, ＿＿＿20＿＿＿ scheduled to run for about three years. During guided tours on the weekends, children can explore the art with blindfolds on.

　　在巴黎的羅浮宮博物館裡，到處都有指示牌，要求來訪者不要用手觸摸藝術品。但有一個特別的雕刻品美術館卻邀請藝術愛好者可用手 ＿＿＿16＿＿＿ 作品。羅浮宮的觸覺美術館，是以盲人和視力 ＿＿＿17＿＿＿ 爲對象，是該博物館唯一來訪者可以觸摸展出的雕刻品，沒有警衛或警報系統會阻止觸摸者。它最新的展覽是一組獅子、蛇、馬和鷹的雕刻的 ＿＿＿18＿＿＿ 。這 15 件動物複製自館內著名作品。被稱爲「動物，力量的象徵」這些 ＿＿＿19＿＿＿ 展品，皆爲是歷史上眾帝王使用過，且象徵他們的偉大統治。這個特展於 2008 年 12 月開始展出， ＿＿＿20＿＿＿ 展出期間大約三年。在週

末有專人導覽期間，孩童可用眼罩蒙住眼睛來體驗藝術。

16. 題句：But one special sculpture gallery invites art lovers to allow their hands to
　　　　_____16_____ the works.
　　　　但有一個特別的雕刻品美術館卻邀請藝術愛好者可用手 _____16_____ 作
　　　　品。
　　選項：(A) fix up 修理　(B) run over 接觸、觸摸　(C) take away 拿開　(D) knock off 敲打
　　　　停止

解析
依題意只有選(B)項的「觸摸」才是正確選項。

**17. 題句：The Louvre's Tactile Gallery, targeted at the blind and visually _____17_____ ,
　　　　是以盲人和視力 _____17_____ 為對象，
　　選項：(A) impair 損傷（原形動詞）　(B) impairs（現在式）　(C) impaired（過去分
　　　　詞）　(D) impairing（動名詞）

解析
依題意只有選(C)項過去分詞當形容詞用的「impaired」才是正確選項。

18. 題句：Its latest exhibit is a _____18_____ of sculpted lions, snakes, horses and eagles.
　　　　它最近的展出是一組獅子、蛇、馬和鷹的雕刻的 _____18_____ 。
　　選項：(A) collection 收藏品　(B) cooperation 合作　(C) completion 完成　(D) contribution
　　　　貢獻

解析
(1) 依題意只有選(A)項的「收藏品」才是正確選項。意即 展出一組……雕刻收藏品。
(2) A collection of……是指「一套、一組……的收藏品」。

19. 題句：the exhibit _____19_____ animals that were used by kings and emperors throughout
　　　　history
　　　　這些 _____19_____ 展品，皆為歷史上眾帝王使用過。
　　選項：(A) examines 測驗　(B) protects 保護　(C) represents 代表　(D) features 具特殊意義

解析
依題意只有選(D)項的「具特殊意義」才是正確選項。

**20. 題句：_____20_____ scheduled to run for about three years.
　　　　預計展出期間大約三年。
　　選項：(A) is（be動詞現在式）　(B) being（現在分詞）　(C) has 有　(D) having（現在

分詞)

解析

(1)依題意只有選(A)項的「is」才是正確選項。

(2)is scheduled 是指「被排定、預定」之意。

三、文意選填（10分）

> 說明：第21題至第30題，每題一個空格。請依文意在文章後所提供的(A)到(J)選項中
> 分別選出最適當者，並將其字母代號標示在答案卡之「選擇題答案區」。每題答
> 對得1分，答錯或劃記多於一個選項者倒扣1/9分，倒扣到本大題之實得分數為
> 零為止。未作答者，不給分亦不扣分。

第21至30題為題組

Textese (also known as chatspeak, texting language, or txt talk) is a term for the abbreviations and slang most commonly used among young people today. The _____21_____ of textese is largely due to the necessary brevity of mobile phone text messaging, though its use is also very common on the Internet, including e-mail and instant messaging.

There are no _____22_____ rules for writing textese. However, the common practice is to use single letters, pictures, or numbers to represent whole words. For example, "i <3 u" uses the picture _____23_____ of a heart "<3" for "love," and the letter "u" to _____24_____ "you." For words which have no common abbreviation, textese users often _____25_____ the vowels from a word, and the reader is forced to interpret a string of consonants by re-adding the vowels. Thus, "dictionary" becomes "dctnry," and "keyboard" becomes "kybrd." The reader must interpret the _____26_____ words depending on the context in which it is used, as there are many examples of words or phrases which use the same abbreviations. So if someone says "ttyl, lol" they probably mean "talk to you later, lots of love" not "talk to you later, laugh out loud," and if someone says "omg, lol" they most _____27_____ mean "oh my god, laugh out loud" not "oh my god, lots of love."

The emergence of textese is clearly due to a desire to type less and to communicate more _____28_____ than one can manage without such shortcuts. Yet it has been severely _____29_____ as "wrecking our language." Some scholars even consider the use of textese as "irritating" and essentially lazy behavior. They're worried that "sloppy" habits gained while using textese will result in students' growing _____30_____ of proper spelling, grammar and punctuation.

簡訊用語（也稱為 chatspeak、texting 語言或者 txt）是當今年輕人通用的縮寫俚語的說話方式。簡訊用語的 _____21_____ 基本上由於行動電話簡訊文字有必要簡短，雖然它的使用在網際網路上也非常普遍，包括電子郵件和即時訊息。

簡訊用語並無 _____22_____ 寫法。不過，慣例是使用單一字母、圖案或數字代表整個單字。例如，「i < 3 u」使用一個心的圖案 _____23_____ 「< 3」為「愛」，

並且字母「u」_____24_____「你」。對於沒有共同縮寫的字來說，使用者經常
_____25_____母音字母，讀者被迫以再加母音字母的方式解讀一連串輔音字母。因此，「dictionary」變成「dctnry」，「keyboard」變得「kybrd」。讀者必須依據文章的上下文來解讀_____26_____的意思，因爲使用相同縮寫的字或片語例子很多。因此某人說「ttyl, lol」，他們最_____27_____是指「talk to you later, lots of love」，而不是指「talk to you later, laugh out loud」，還有，如果某人說「omg, lol」，他們很可能是指「oh my god, laugh out loud」，而不是指「oh my god , lots of love」。

簡訊用語的出現很顯然是由於字少但溝通_____28_____的需求。然而它已經被嚴重_____29_____爲「破壞我們的語言」。有一些學者甚至認爲簡訊用語的使用是使人憤怒的，基本上是偷懶的行爲。他們擔心在使用簡訊用語所養成的邋遢習慣，會導致學生日漸對拼法、語法和標點符號的_____30_____。

(A) quickly 快速地　　(B) criticized 批評的　　(C) likely 可能的　　(D) abbreviated 縮寫的
(E) replace 替代的　　(F) remove 去掉　　(G) standard 標準　　(H) ignorance 無知
(I) popularity 流行　　(J) symbol 象徵

21. 題句：The _____21_____ of textese is largely due to the necessary brevity of mobile phone text messaging,

　　　　簡訊用語的_____21_____基本上由於行動電話簡訊文字有必要簡短。

解析

依題意只有選(I)項的「流行」才是正確選項。

22. 題句：There are no _____22_____ rules for writing textese.

　　　　簡訊用語並無_____22_____寫法。

解析

依題意只有選(G)項的「標準」才是正確選項。

23. 題句：For example, "i <3 u" uses the picture _____23_____ of a heart "<3" for "love,"

　　　　使用一個心的圖案_____23_____「＜3」爲「愛」。

解析

依題意只有選(J)項的「象徵」才是正確選項。

24. 題句：and the letter "u" to _____24_____ "you."

　　　　並且字母「u」_____24_____「你」。

解析

依題意只有選(E)項的「替代」才是正確選項。

25. 題句：textese users often _____25_____ the vowels from a word,

使用者經常 _____25_____ 母音字母。

解析

依題意只有選(F)項的「去除」才是正確選項。

26. 題句：The reader must interpret the _____26_____ words depending on the context in which it is used,

讀者必須依據文章的上下文來解讀 _____26_____ 的意思。

解析

依題意只有選(D)項的「縮寫」才是正確選項。

27. 題句：and if someone says "omg, lol" they most _____27_____ mean "oh my god, laugh out loud" not "oh my god, lots of love."

他們最 _____27_____ 是指「talk to you later, lots of love」

解析

依題意只有選(C)項的「可能的」才是正確選項。

28. 題句：a desire to type less and to communicate more _____28_____ than one can manage without such shortcut.

簡訊用語的出現很顯然是由於字少但溝通 _____28_____ 的需求。

解析

依題意只有選(A)項的「快速的」才是正確選項。

29. 題句：Yet it has been severely _____29_____ as "wrecking our language."

然而它已經被嚴重 _____29_____ 為「破壞我們的語言」。

解析

依題意只有選(B)項的「批評的」才是正確選項。

30. 題句：using textese will result in students' growing _____30_____ of proper spelling, grammar and punctuation.

簡訊用語的使用會導致學生日漸對拼法、語法和標點符號的 _____30_____ 。

解析

依題意只有選(H)項的「無知」才是正確選項。

四、篇章結構（10分）

第 31 至 35 題為題組

題型說明：

　1. 這類篇章結構的題目，和綜合測驗克漏字測驗的題型幾乎一樣，但差別在於前者的
　　　空格內待選的是「字詞」，而後者空格內待選的卻是「一整句」。

　2. 不過，解題的方法還是一樣的。前者解題的關鍵字在於「題目空格左、右方的兩三
　　　個字；而後者解題的關鍵字，在於」題目空格左、右方的「一整句」。

　3. 舉例來說，考生要答第 31 題之前，必須要看懂其空格左方的一整句，與其右方的一
　　　整句。

　4. 請考生注意，本題型的題目每題得分為 2 分，但答錯題或複選作答時，每題倒扣 1/2
　　　分，直到本大題的實得分數（註）扣完為止。如果實在沒有把握就不要作答。因為
　　　倒扣太多，會把你原先答對題的分數扣光。

註：本大題型有 5 題，答對每題 2 分，總分為 10 分。但答錯或複選每題到扣 1/2 分

舉例說明：假設考生 5 題裡答對 2 題 x2 得 4 分，但答錯 3 題 x0.5 分，倒扣 1.5 分本大題
　　　　　實得分數為 2.5 分。

　　　Do you have trouble getting started in the morning? Do you have problems learning early in the day? If you do, you are not alone. _____31_____ They learn better at night than they do in the morning.

　　　To investigate when cockroaches learn best, researchers at Vanderbilt University tested the insects for which odor (peppermint or vanilla) they preferred. Most cockroaches preferred the smell of vanilla to that of peppermint at all times. _____32_____ Therefore, the scientists trained the cockroaches to prefer the peppermint smell by rewarding the insects with a taste of sugar water when they approached a peppermint smell. _____33_____

　　　When the cockroaches were trained at night, they remembered the new associations (peppermint = sugar water; vanilla = salt water) for up to 48 hours. However, if the cockroaches were trained in the morning, they quickly forgot which smell went with which water. _____34_____

　　　So, cockroaches learn better at night than they do in the morning. _____35_____ Because of this, it is likely that information they gather at night will be more useful to them. These experiments provide some clues about the interactions between body rhythms, learning and memory.

　　要開始新的一天你有困難嗎？一大早要你學習新事物有困難嗎？如果有，並不是只有你才是這樣，　　31　　他們在晚上比在白天學習的效果好。什麼時候蟑螂學習得最好呢？汎德大學的研究員測試蟑螂看他們喜歡薄荷或香草口味。不管什麼時候，他們喜歡的是香草而不是薄荷，　　32　　因此，科學家們用糖水獎賞來訓練蟑螂喜歡薄荷味道，　　33　　

　　當這些蟑螂在夜間受訓練時，他們記得新的組合（薄荷＝糖水，香草＝鹽水）最高訓練到48小時。然而，如果這些蟑螂在清晨接受相同的訓練，他們很快就忘記哪一種水是哪種口味。　　34　　

　　所以，蟑螂的學習效果晚上比早晨好。　　35　　正因如此，那表示他們在晚上接受的訊息可能較為管用。這些實驗提供軀體節奏、學習與記憶間的互動的線索。

(A) When these insects moved toward a vanilla smell, on the other hand, they were punished with a taste of salt.

反過來說，當這些昆蟲朝著有香草味的方向前進時，他們會受到嚐鹽味的處罰。

(B) This result thus shows that the time when they were trained decided the effect of their learning.

結果顯示，在受訓練期間，就決定了學習的效果。

(C) They are often more active and tend to search for food during the night.

在晚上，他們比較活躍，也會去找食物。

(D) They were also found to like sugar water, but not salt water.

他們也被發現比較喜歡甜水而不是鹹水。

(E) Cockroaches have the same problem

蟑螂也有同樣的問題。

31. 題句：如果有，並不是只有你才是這樣，　　31　　他們在晚上比在白天學習的效果好。

解析

依題意只有選(E)項的「蟑螂也有同樣的問題」才是連接空格前後兩句的正確選項。

32. 題句：他們喜歡的是香草而不是薄荷，　　32　　因此，科學家們用糖水獎賞來訓練蟑螂喜歡薄荷味道。

解析

依題意只有選(D)項的「他們也被發現比較喜歡甜水而不是鹹水」才是連接空格前後兩句的正確選項。

33. 題句：科學家們用糖水獎賞來訓練蟑螂喜歡薄荷味道，_____33_____ 當這些蟑螂在夜間受訓練時，牠們記得新的組合。

解析

依題意只有選 (A) 項的「反過來說，當這些昆蟲朝著有香草味的方向前進時，牠們會受到嚐鹽味的處罰」才是連接空格前後兩句的正確選項。

34. 題句：如果這些蟑螂在清晨接受相同的訓練，牠們很快就忘記哪一種水是哪種口味。_____34_____ 所以，蟑螂的學習效果晚上比早晨好。

解析

依題意只有選 (B) 項的「結果顯示，在受訓期間就決定了學習的效果。」才是連接空格前後兩句的正確選項。

35. 題句：所以，蟑螂的學習效果晚上比早晨好。_____35_____ 正因如此，那表示牠們在晚上接受的訊息可能較為管用。

解析

依題意只有選 (C) 項的「在晚上牠們比較活躍，也會去找食物。」才是連接空格前後兩句的正確選項。

五、閱讀測驗（32分）

說明：第 36 題至第 51 題，每題請分別根據各篇文章的文意選出一個最適當的選項，標示在答案卡之「選擇題答案區」。每題答對得 2 分，答錯或劃記多於一個選項者倒扣 2/3 分，倒扣到本大題之實得分數為零為止。未作答者，不給分亦不扣分。

第 36 至 39 題為題組

The following report appeared in a newspaper in February 2007.

On February 15, 2007, hundreds of people came to New York City's famous railroad station—Grand Central Terminal—to trade in old dollar bills for the new George Washington presidential US $1 coins. The gold-colored coin is the first in a new series by the U.S. Mint to honor former U.S. presidents. The Mint will issue four presidential US $1 coins a year through 2016. These coins will come out in the order in which each president served. The George Washington coin is the first to be released. John Adams, Thomas Jefferson and James Madison coins will come out later this year.

The presidential US $1 coins have a special design. For the first time since the 1930s, there are words carved into the edge of each coin, including the year in which the coin was issued and traditional mottos. Each coin will show a different president on its face, or heads side. It will also show the president's name. The other side of the coin will show the Statue of Liberty and the inscriptions "United States of America" and "$1."

There are some interesting facts about the coins. First, there will be one presidential US $1 coin for each president, except Grover Cleveland. He will have two! Cleveland is the only U.S. president to have served two nonconsecutive terms. The last president now scheduled to get a coin is Gerald Ford. That's because a president cannot appear on a coin when he is still alive. In addition, a president must have been deceased for two years before he can be on a coin.

下列報告是在 2007 年 2 月刊登在報紙上的。

在 2007 年 2 月 15 日，數百人來紐約市的著名火車站──中央車站──用舊的美元紙鈔兌換新版的喬治・華盛頓總統 1 美元硬幣。金黃色的硬幣是美國鑄幣廠爲紀念前任總統而發行新系列的第一種硬幣。

鑄幣廠將每年發行四種總統的 1 美元硬幣直到 2016 年。這些硬幣將依每位總統任期的前後順序發行。喬治・華盛頓硬幣最先被發行。約翰・亞當斯、湯馬斯・傑佛森和詹姆士・麥迪森硬幣今年年底就會出來。

總統的1美元硬幣有一種特別的設計。三〇年代以來的第一次，每枚硬幣的外緣都刻有文字，包括硬幣的發行年分和傳統的座右銘。每枚硬幣都顯示出不同總統的臉部或頭部，還有總統的名字。硬幣的另一面會有自由女神以及美利堅合眾國、1 美元等刻字。

這裡有一些關於發行硬幣的趣聞。首先，除了格魯佛・克理夫蘭之外，會爲每一位總統發行總統 1 美元硬幣。他會有兩枚！克理夫蘭總統是美國唯一沒有連任的總統，最後一枚要出的總統硬幣是吉羅・福特總統。那是因爲還未過世的美國總統不能發行他的硬幣。此外，過世兩年後的前任總統才可有他的硬幣。

36. According to the report, how many presidential US $1 coins were scheduled to be released by the end of 2007 altogether?

根據報告，在 2007 底之前預定發行多少種的總統 1 美元硬幣？

(A) One.　(B) Two.　(C) Three.　(D) Four.

解析

從答題關鍵的「The Mint will issue four presidential US $1 coins a year through 2016.」可看出，(D) 項的「Four.」才是正確選項。

37. Why did the Mint issue the US $1 coins?

造幣廠爲什麼發行 1 美元硬幣？

(A) In response to U.S. citizens' requests.

由於美國公民的請求。

(B) In memory of the late U.S. presidents.

爲了紀念美國所有的前任總統。

(C) To attract more train commuters.

吸引更多的火車通勤者。

(D) To promote the trading of dollar bills.

促進美元買賣。

解析

從答題關鍵的「The gold-colored coin is the first in a new series by the U.S. Mint to honor former U.S. presidents.」可看出，(B) 項的「In memory of the late U.S. presidents.」才是正確選項。

38. What may you find on the heads side of the new US $1 coin?

你可以在新 1 美元硬幣的頭像那一面看到什麼？

(A) The name of a U.S. president.

美國總統的名字。

(B) The year when the coin was made.

硬幣發行的年分。

(C) The Statue of Liberty.

自由女神像。

(D) English proverbs.

英國諺語。

解析

從答題關鍵的「Each coin will show a different president on its face, or heads side. It will also show the president's name.」可看出，(A) 項的「The name of a U.S. president.」才是正確選項。

39. Which of the following can be inferred about the presidential coins?

下列哪項是有關總統硬幣的推斷？

(A) President Gerald Ford's coin was issued in 2008.

吉羅·福特總統的硬幣在 2008 年發行。

(B) The U.S. Mint has issued all the presidential coins by now.

美國造幣廠至今已發行完全部的總統硬幣。

(C) No presidential coin has been released for President Barack Obama.

歐巴馬總統的硬幣尚未發行。

(D) Every U.S. president had his coin made two years after his term was over.

每位美國總統在卸任兩年後，才可發行他的硬幣。

解析

從答題關鍵「That's because a president cannot appear on a coin when he is still alive.」來看，四個選項中只有 (C) 項的「No presidential coin has been released for President Barack Obama.」才是合理的推論，而其他三個選項內容都不正確。

第 40 至 43 題為題組

Newspapers have tried many things to stop a seemingly nonstop decline in readers. Now France is pushing forward with a novel approach: giving away papers to young readers in an effort to turn them into regular customers. The French government recently detailed plans of a project called "My Free Newspaper," under which 18- to 24-year-olds will be offered a free, year-long subscription to a newspaper of their choice.

Newspaper readership in France has been especially low among young people. According to a government study, only 10 percent of those aged 15 to 24 read a paid-for newspaper daily in 2007, down from 20 percent a decade earlier.

Emmanuel Schwartzenberg, a former media editor of *Le Figaro*, the oldest and second-largest national newspaper in France, said he had strong reservations about the government project. At a time when advertising is in steep decline, he said, newspapers should instead be looking at ways to raise more profits from readers, rather than giving papers away. "This just reinforces the belief that newspapers should be free, which is a very bad idea," Mr. Schwartzenberg said.

French readers, young and old, already have plenty of free options from which to choose, including newspaper websites and the free papers handed out daily in many city centers. Some bloggers said the new program might hold the most appeal to the few young people who do already read, and buy, newspapers.

The French government plans to promote the program with an advertising campaign aimed at young readers and their parents. However, when asked how to attract young readers to the printed press, the government said the primary channel for the ads would be the Internet.

報紙已經嘗試多方法要挽回讀者群不停下降的情況。法國採贈送年輕讀者免費報紙的新策略，試圖使他們成為固定客戶。法國政府最近詳述名為「我的免費報紙」計畫，說明 18～24 歲的人可獲免費贈送他們想看的報紙，為期一年。

法國報紙的年輕讀者一直多不起來。根據一項政府研究，在 2007 年只有 10% 的 15～24 歲族群閱讀非免費報紙，比十年前的 20% 少。

愛曼紐 Schwartzenberg，是《費加羅報紙》的前任主編，該報紙是法國歷史最久、規模第二大的國內報紙，說他對於上述政府計畫有極大的保留。當廣告在急速下降時，他說，報紙應趕快想辦法增加讀者以獲利，而不是贈送免費報紙。這樣做只在加強讀者相信報紙應該是免費的，那是一個糟糕的想法。

法國讀者，老老少少，已經有許多選項可選，包括新聞網站以及在很多市中心每天散發的免費報紙。一些部落客說，新計畫訴求的對象可能只有已經付費買報看的年輕人。

法國政府計畫提出目標是年輕族群及他們的家長的廣告活動。不過，當被問到怎樣吸引對報紙有興趣的年輕讀者時，政府卻說該計畫的廣告主要是在網路播出。

40. Why did the French government decide to launch the free newspaper program?
　　法國政府為什麼決定啟動免費報紙計畫？

(A) To fight economic recession.

　　跟經濟衰退作戰。

(B) To win approval from youngsters.

　　獲取年輕人的認同。

(C) To promote newspaper readership.

　　促進報紙讀者人數。

(D) To improve the literacy rate in France.

　　提升法國人的識字率。

解析

從答題關鍵的「Newspapers have tried many things to stop a seemingly nonstop decline in readers」可看出，(C) 項的「To promote newspaper readership」才是正確選項。

41. Which of the following can be concluded from the passage?

　　下列哪項可作本文的總結？

(A) Everyone considers the government project creative.

　　每人認為政府計畫有創造性。

(B) Newspaper readership is much higher in other countries.

　　報紙讀者人數在其他國家高得多。

(C) Research shows young people have no interest in current affairs.

　　研究顯示年輕人對當今時事不感興趣。

(D) Giving away free papers is not a strong enough incentive to attract readers.

　　贈送免費報紙來吸引讀者的獎勵是不夠的。

解析

從整篇文章內容來看，只有 (D) 項的「Giving away free papers is not a strong enough incentive to attract readers」才是正確選項。

42. What is Mr. Schwartzenberg's attitude toward this program?

　　愛曼紐 Schwartzenberg 對政府計畫的態度如何？

(A) Skeptical. 懷疑。　　(B) Devoted. 奉獻。

(C) Optimistic. 樂觀。　　(D) Indifferent. 中立。

解析

從答題關鍵的「Newspapers have tried many things to stop a seemingly nonstop decline in readers」可看出，(A) 項的「Skeptical.」才是正確選項。

43. According to the passage, where would the information about the free newspaper program in France most likely be seen?

根據本文，關於法國的免費報紙計畫的訊息在哪裡看得到？

(A) In magazines 在雜誌裡。　(B) On blogs 在blogs上。

(C) In newspapers 在報紙裡。　(D) On the Internet 在網際網路上。

解析

從答題關鍵的「the government said the primary channel for the ads would be the Internet.」可看出，(D)項的「On the Internet.」才是正確選項。

第 44 至 47 題為題組

　Coffee experts are willing to pay large sums of money for high-quality coffee beans. The high-end beans, such as Kona or Blue Mountain, are known to cost extraordinary sums of money. Then there is Kopi Lowak (translated as "Civet Coffee"), the world's most expensive coffee, which sells for as much as US $50 per quarter-pound.

　This isn't particularly surprising, given that approximately 500 pounds a year of Kopi Lowak constitute the entire world supply. What is surprising is why this particular coffee is so rare. In fact, it's not the plants that are rare. It's the civet droppings. That's right, the civet droppings—the body waste of the palm civet. Coffee beans aren't Kopi Lowak until they've been digested and come out in the body waste of the palm civet.

　Palm civets are tree-dwelling, raccoon-like little animals, native to Southeast Asia and the Indonesian islands. They also have a love for coffee cherries. According to Kopi Lowak suppliers, palm civets eat the fruit whole, but only digest the outer fruit, leaving the beans intact. While the beans are not destroyed, they undergo a transformation in the animal's body. A chemical substance in the digestive system of the palm civet causes some changes to the beans to give them a unique flavor. However, this is not the only explanation why coffee beans retrieved from civet droppings have a special flavor all their own. Another possible reason is that palm civets have an unfailing instinct for picking the coffee cherries at the peak of their ripeness.

　Kopi Lowak is reported to have a character in taste unlike any other coffee, complex with caramel undertones and an earthy or gamey flavor. Currently, most of the world's supply of Kopi Lowak is sold in Japan, though a few US markets are also starting to stock up on Kopi Lowak.

　專家願意為高品質咖啡豆多付錢。高檔的咖啡豆，例如科那或者藍山，為人所知價錢是昂貴的。然後有麝香咖啡，屬當今最昂貴的咖啡，售價是每四分之一英鎊 50 美元。

　這不太驚奇，令人吃驚的是麝香咖啡一年才有 500 磅的產量。為什麼這種特別的咖啡這麼少？實際上，不是植物本身稀有，而是麝香貓的糞便。沒有錯，就是麝香貓的糞便──麝香貓的排泄物。咖啡豆要先經過麝香貓的消化再排出來才是麝香咖啡。

　麝香貓棲息在樹上，看起來像浣熊的小動物，分布在東南亞和印尼島本地。牠們也喜歡咖啡豆。根據麝香咖啡供應者的說法，麝香貓吃整個的咖啡果，但是只消化外層果肉，內部咖啡豆完整無缺。當咖啡豆沒被破壞時，就會在麝香貓的體內產生變化。麝香貓的消化系統裡的化學物質，使體內的咖啡豆產生一種獨特的味道。不過，這不是咖啡豆來自麝香貓糞便的唯一解釋，另一可能原因是，麝香貓在採咖啡果時，有一種可靠的本能只採熟透的果實。

據說麝香咖啡的特殊口味與任何其他咖啡不同，是一種焦糖與土味或鳥獸味的綜合。目前，雖然少數的美國市場也開始販售麝香咖啡，但世界上最大的供應商還是在日本。

44. What does "**This**" in the second paragraph refer to?

在第二段內容所說的「this」是指什麼？

(A) Civet Coffee.

麝香咖啡。

(B) Blue Mountain coffee.

藍山咖啡。

(C) The high price of Kopi Lowak.

麝香咖啡的高價位。

(D) The unique taste of Kona.

Kona的獨特味道。

解析

從文章第一段內容可看出，(C) 項的「The high price of Kopi Lowak.」才是正確選項。

45. Why is Kopi Lowak expensive?

為什麼麝香咖啡那麼昂貴？

(A) There is a very limited supply of the beans.

咖啡豆的供應非常有限。

(B) The coffee trees that grow the beans are scarce.

種豆的咖啡樹不夠。

(C) It takes a long time for the coffee beans to ripen.

咖啡豆成熟很慢。

(D) Only a few experts know how to produce the beans.

只有少數專家會生產咖啡豆。

解析

從答題關鍵的「why this particular coffee is so rare. In fact, it's not the plants that are rare. It's the civet droppings.」可看出，(A) 項的「There is a very limited supply of the beans...」才是正確選項。

46. What is the main point discussed in the third paragraph?

第三段內容主要在討論什麼？

(A) Why palm civets like the coffee beans.

為什麼麝香貓喜歡咖啡豆。

(B) Where Kopi Lowak is mainly harvested.

麝香咖啡的主要收成區在哪裡。

(C) What chemicals are found in the civet's digestive system.

在麝香貓的消化系統裡發現了什麼化學物質。

(D) How palm civets change coffee fruit to Kopi Lowak beans.

麝香貓怎樣把咖啡果變為麝香咖啡。

解析

從整段文章內容來看，(D) 項的「How palm civets change coffee fruit to Kopi Lowak beans.」才是正確選項。

47. Which of the following statements is true, according to the passage?

依本文內容下列哪一項為真？

(A) Little palm civets eat only the outer layer of the coffee cherries.

麝香貓只吃咖啡豆的外層。

(B) Palm civets somehow know the right time when the coffee fruit ripens.

麝香貓就是知道咖啡果最成熟時的正確時間。

(C) Kopi Lowak is most popular in Southeast Asia and the Indonesian islands.

麝香咖啡在東南亞和印尼島是非常受歡迎。

(D) Kona and Blue Mountain are the most expensive coffees but only of average quality.

科那和藍山是最昂貴的咖啡但品質普通。

解析

從答題關鍵的「Another possible reason is that palm civets have an unfailing instinct for picking the coffee cherries at the peak of their ripeness.」可看出，(B) 項的「Palm civets somehow know the right time when the coffee fruit ripens.」才是正確選項。

第 48 至 51 題為題組

　　Gunter Grass was the winner of the 1999 Nobel Prize in Literature. His talents are revealed in a variety of disciplines: He is not only a novelist, poet and playwright, but also a renowned painter and sculptor. As he himself stresses, his creations are closely related to his unique personal history. His father was a German who joined the Nazi party in World War II, while his mother was Polish. As a result, he constantly suffered contradictory feelings: as a Pole who had been victimized, and as someone guilty of harming the Poles. The torment in his heart led him to denounce the Nazis and his political activism has continued throughout his career. His commitment to the peace movement and the environmental movement as well as his unfailing quest for justice has won him praise as "the conscience of the nation."

　　In the spring of 1996, he was inspired during a trip to Italy to write a poem with his watercolor brush directly on one of his paintings. Before long, a collection of his "water poems" was born. Painting and literature have become his major forms of creativity. For him, painting is a form of creation with concrete, sensual elements, while writing is a hard and abstract process. When he cannot find words to convey his thoughts, painting helps him find the words to express himself. In this way, Grass not only creates simple depictions of the objects he is fond of in life, such as melons, vegetables, fish, and mushrooms, but also uses them as symbols for mental associations of various kinds. For example, to express the complexity of reality, he sometimes places unrelated objects in the same painting, such as a bird and a housefly, or a mushroom and a nail. Grass has depicted a wide variety of natural scenes, animals and plants, and even human artifacts of the German countryside, portraying them in poems, and allowing words to make the paintings rich in literary value.

　　岡特‧格拉斯是 1999 諾貝爾文學獎得主。他的才能展示在多種不同領域。他不但是小説家、詩人和劇作家，而且還是著名的畫家和雕刻師。就像他自己強調的，他的創作與其個人的獨特背景有密切關係。他的父親是德國人，二次大戰時加入納粹，而母親是波蘭人。因此，他經常受矛盾情緒所苦：身爲受過迫害的波蘭人，同時迫害過波蘭人而有罪惡感。他内心的折磨使他譴責納粹份子，他的生涯充滿政治激進作風。他對和平運動、環境運動的承諾，以及他的無止境的尋求正義，贏得他被稱爲「國家的良心」。

　　在 1996 年春天，他在前往義大利途中得到啓示，就直接用他的水彩畫筆寫出一首詩。不久，他的水彩詩集問世。繪畫和文學已成爲他創作的主要形式。對他來説，繪畫是一種具體與感官的形式，而寫作則是一種困難與抽象的過程。當他不能用字句來表達他的想法時，作畫可幫助他找到可以表達自己的字句。如此，格拉斯不僅對他喜歡的物品像是瓜、菜蔬、魚和蘑菇等作出簡單的描述，同時也把這些東西作爲各種不同的精神結合的象徵符號。例如，爲了表示現實的複雜性，他有時把無關的物體放在相同的畫裡，例如一隻鳥和一隻蒼蠅，或者是一個蘑菇和一根釘子。格拉斯已經描繪多種自然景物、動植物，以及德國農村的人工製品，用詩詞字句來形容其涵義，使這些詩詞字句增加畫作的文學價值。

48. What caused Grass to feel confused and troubled when he was young?

　　當他年輕時，什麼事情讓他感到混淆與干擾？

(A) He was the son of a Nazi and a victimized Pole.

　　他是一個納粹份子的兒子，也是受害的波蘭人。

(B) He found himself fighting two opposing political parties.

　　他發現他自己與兩個反對黨抗爭。

(C) He was trained to be an artist though he wanted to be a poet.

　　雖然他想成爲詩人，但是他卻被訓練成藝術家。

(D) He was born with so many talents that he couldn't choose a direction.

　　他出生就有很多才能以至於他無法選擇要走哪一個方向。

解析

從答題關鍵的「As a result, he constantly suffered contradictory feelings as a Pole who had been victimized, and as someone guilty of harming the Poles.」可看出，(A) 項的「He was the son of a Nazi and a victimized Pole.」才是正確選項。

49. Why has Grass been praised as "the conscience of the nation"?

為什麼格拉斯被稱為「國家的良心」？

(A) He victimized the Poles and criticized the Nazis.

他迫害波蘭人並且批評納粹份子。

(B) He has been a strong advocate of peace and justice.

他是一名和平和正義的堅定的倡導者。

(C) He has shown great sympathy for the Poles through his poems.

他已經透過他的詩篇對於波蘭人表示同情。

(D) He joined the Nazi party and showed great loyalty to his country.

他加入納粹份子並對國家表現忠誠。

解析

從答題關鍵的「His commitment to the peace movement and the environmental movement as well as his unfailing quest for justice has won him praise as "the conscience of the nation."」可看出，(B) 項的「He has been a strong advocate of peace and justice.」才是正確選項。

50. Why was Grass's trip to Italy important to him?

為什麼格拉斯的義大利之旅對他很重要？

(A) He was inspired by a fine arts master in Italy.

在義大利受到一位美術大師的鼓舞。

(B) He formed a new interest in painting simple objects there.

在那裡他產生描繪簡單物體的興趣。

(C) He developed a new form for creating his poems during the trip.

在旅行期間他創造了寫詩的新方式。

(D) He found a new way to solve the conflict between the Nazis and the Poles.

他發現新的方法解決納粹份子與波蘭人之間的衝突。

解析

從答題關鍵的「In the spring of 1996, he was inspired during a trip to Italy to write a poem with his watercolor brush directly on one of his paintings.」可看出，(C) 項的「He developed a new form for creating his poems during the trip.」才是正確選項。

51. Which of the following correctly characterizes Grass's poems, according to the passage?

依本文內容，哪一項可正確的表示格拉斯的詩篇？

(A) Most of his poems depict the cruelty of the Nazis.

他的大多數詩篇都在描繪納粹份子的殘忍。

(B) The theme of his poems won him the Nobel Peace Prize.

他的詩篇主題為他贏得諾貝爾和平獎。

(C) The poems on his paintings are often not related to objects in the real world.

他畫作上的詩篇常與現實世界無關。

(D) The ideas in his poems are expressed more thoroughly with the help of his paintings.

他詩裡的想法用畫作才更能完全表達。

解析

從答題關鍵的「Grass has depicted a wide variety of natural scenes, animals and plants, and even human artifacts of the German countryside, portraying them in poems, and allowing words to make the paintings rich in literary value.」可看出，(D) 項的「The ideas in his poems are expressed more thoroughly with the help of his paintings.」才是正確選項。

第貳部分：非選擇題（28分）

一、中譯英（8分）

說明：1. 請將以下中文句子譯成正確、通順、達意的英文，並將答案寫在「答案卷」上。
2. 請依序作答，並標明題號。每題 4 分，共 8 分。

1. 近二十年來我國的出生率快速下滑。

解析

先寫出本句的字彙與片語：

近二十年來 nearly the last 20 years / in the last twenty years　我國的出生率 the birthrate in our country
快速下滑 has been decreasing rapidly / has been decreasing sharply

整句英譯

Nearly the last 20 years, the birthrate in our country has been decreasing sharply.

本句是說，出生率近 20 年來一直在下滑，這就是「現在完成進行式」的句型。因此要譯成 has been decreasing（至今還在下滑之意）。副詞的 rapidly 要放在 decreasing 之前或之後都可以。

2. 這可能導致我們未來人力資源的嚴重不足。

解析

(1) 這＝這件事＝This 或 It ...
(2) 可能導致　＝may result in ...
(3) 未來人力資源＝the future manpower
(4) 嚴重不足　＝severely insufficient

整句英譯

It may result in a severe insufficient of our future manpower.

二、英文作文（20分）

說明：1. 依提示在「答案卷」上寫一篇英文作文。
　　　2. 文長至少 120 個單詞（words）。

提示：在你的記憶中，哪一種氣味（smell）最讓你難忘？請寫一篇英文作文，文長至少 120 字，文分兩段，第一段描述你在何種情境中聞到這種氣味，以及你初聞這種氣味時的感受，第二段描述這個氣味至今仍令你難忘的理由。

解析

(1)先寫出與提示內容相關字詞與英譯：

在我的記憶中 in my memory　氣味臭味 odor　氣味香味 scent　氣味 smell　香味 fragrance
臭氣惡臭 stink

(2)提示要求分兩段寫，第一段考生要說明：在何種情境中聞到這種氣味？以及聞到當時的感受？第二段要說明，為什麼這個氣味至今仍令你難忘？

(3)有了上述的提示之後，接下來就要靠考生的自由發揮，你要掰出任何情景都可以，說不定是在密閉的飛機艙裡，被鄰座女士的髮香薰得飄飄然，或是被鄰座男士的強烈香水薰得難過，趕快到洗手間去嘔吐，或者在電梯間忽然有人放屁，要命的電梯偏偏在這個時候故障了 20 分鐘，好好運用你所會的英文字、句去寫出如何度過這臭氣沖天的 20 分鐘。

(4)盡量用過去式的時態敘述，省得煩惱什麼句用現在式、什麼句用過去式、什麼句用現在完成式等。現在讓我們來看看，本篇作文的範例如下：

　　I got a call from Peter, my best friend one morning, he wanted me to be ready for a luncheon today~and he said he would introduce me a girl friend. I was a little tensed and it took me more than an hour to get ready. Then I dashed to the restaurant by a taxi.

　　As soon as I got into the elevator, there's already a well-dressed nice looking girl and 5 more others in the elevator, she pressed floor 50 where the restaurant was. The most embarrassing part was, as the elevator going up, I couldn't help but fart loudly. (I ate too much garlic last night.) Every one in the elevalor looked at me strangely, and the worst part, at this very embarrassing and critical moment, the elevator came to a sudden stop because something went wrong with the motor, and we all wait there hopelessly for about 20 minutes, and I am the one who suffered the most and being blamed for making the bad air. How can I forget the above mentioned incident？ the well-dressed girl Sue in the elevator is now my wife!

100年指考（指定考試）

第壹部分：選擇題（72分）

一、詞彙詞題（10分）

說明：第 1 題至第 10 題，每題 4 個選項，其中只有 1 個是最適當的選項，畫記在答案卡之「選擇題答案區」。各題答對得 1 分，未作答、答錯、或畫記多於 1 個選項者，該題以零分計算。

1. Many people think cotton is the most comfortable _____ to wear in hot weather.
   許多人認為在熱天時，棉質是穿起來最舒服的 _____ 。
   (A) fabric 織物、布料　(B) coverage 覆蓋　(C) software 軟體　(D) wardrobe 衣櫥

   解析
   (1)答題關鍵在「棉質是穿起來最舒服的 _____ 」。
   (2)只有(A)選項的「織物、布料」放入空格，才是符合整句題意的正確選項。

2. Because of the engine problem in the new vans, the auto company decided to _____ them from the market.
   由於新休旅車的引擎有問題，車公司決定要從市場 _____ 這些車。
   (A) recall 召回　(B) clarify 澄清　(C) transform 使改變　(D) polish 磨光

   解析
   (1)答題關鍵在「車公司決定要從市場 _____ 這些車。」
   (2)只有(A)選項的「召回」放入空格，才是符合整句題意的正確選項。

3. After a day's tiring work, Peter walked _____ back to his house, hungry and sleepy.
   工作累了一天下來，彼得 _____ 走回他的家，又餓又想睡。
   (A) splendidly 壯麗地　(B) thoroughly 徹底地　(C) wearily 疲倦地　(D) vaguely 不清楚地

   解析
   (1)答題關鍵在「彼得 _____ 走回他的家，又餓又想睡」。
   (2)只有 (C) 選項的「彼得 _____ 走回他的家，又餓又想睡。」放入空格，才是符合整句題意的正確選項。

4. In team sports, how all members work as a group is more important than how they perform _____.

在團隊運動裡，團員的團隊精神比他們 _____ 的表現更重要。

(A) frequently 頻繁地　(B) typically 典型地　(C) individually 單獨地　(D) completely 完整地

解析

(1)答題關鍵在「團員的團隊精神比他們 _____ 的表現更重要」。

(2)只有(C)選項的「單獨的」放入空格，才是符合整句題意的正確選項。

5. Despite her physical disability, the young blind pianist managed to overcome all _____ to win the first prize in the international contest.

不顧她的軀體障礙，這位年輕的失明畫家設法克服所有 _____ 要在國際比賽贏得頭獎。

(A) privacy 隱　(B) ambition 有野心　(C) fortunes 財富　(D) obstacles 障礙

解析

(1)答題關鍵在「設法克服所有 _____ 要在國際比賽贏得頭獎」。

(2)只有(D)選項的「障礙」放入空格，才是符合整句題意的正確選項。

6. Each of the planets in the solar system circles around the sun in its own _____ , and this prevents them from colliding with each other.

太陽系的每一行星在它們自己的 _____ 環繞地球。

(A) entry 入口　(B) haste 急速　(C) orbit 運行軌道　(D) range 範圍

解析

(1)答題關鍵在「每一行星在它們自己的 _____ 環繞地球」。

(2)只有(C)選項的「運行軌道」放入空格，才是符合整句題意的正確選項。

7. Professor Wang is well known for his contributions to the field of economics. He has been _____ to help the government with its financial reform programs.

王教授以貢獻經濟領域而出名。他被_____用他的改革方案來幫助政府。

(A) recruited 招募　(B) contradicted 否認　(C) mediated 調解　(D) generated 產生

解析

(1)答題關鍵在「他被 _____ 用他的改革方案來幫助政府」

(2)只有(A)選項的「招募」放入空格，才是符合整句題意的正確選項。

8. Most earthquakes are too small to be noticed; they can only be detected by _____ instruments.

大多數地震太小不能被注意到，它們只能用 _____ 儀器才能偵測到。

(A) manual 手動的　(B) sensitive 敏感的　(C) portable 手提的　(D) dominant 支配的

解析

(1)答題關鍵在經「它們只能用 ＿＿＿＿＿＿ 儀器才能偵測到」。

(2)只有(B)選項的「敏感的」放入空格，才是符合整句題意的正確選項。

9. With Wikileaks releasing secrets about governments around the world, many countries are worried that their national security information might be ＿＿＿＿＿＿ .

維基洩露了許多政府的秘密，這些國家耽心她們的國家安全資訊可能被 ＿＿＿＿＿ 。

(A) relieved 放心的　(B) disclosed 揭露　(C) condensed 濃縮的　(D) provoked 被激怒

解析

(1)答題關鍵在「這些國家耽心她們的國家安全資訊可能被 ＿＿＿＿＿＿ 」。

(2)只有(B)選項的「揭露」放入空格，才是符合整句題意的正確選項。

10. I'm afraid we can't take your word, for the evidence we've collected so far is not ＿＿＿＿＿＿ with what you said.

抱歉，我們不能相信你，因我們獲得的證據與你的説法不 ＿＿＿＿＿＿ 。

(A) familiar 熟悉的　(B) consistent 一致的　(C) durable 耐久的　(D) sympathetic 同情的

解析

(1)答題關鍵在「我們獲得的證據與你的説法不 ＿＿＿＿＿＿ 。」

(2)只有(B)選項的「一致的」放入空格，才是符合整句題意的正確選項。

二、綜合測驗（10分）

説明：第 11 題至第 20 題，每題 1 個空格。請依文意選出最適當的 1 個選項，畫記在答案卡之「選擇題答案區」。各題答對得 1 分，未作答、答錯、或畫記多於 1 個選項者，該題以零分計算。

第 11 至 15 題為題組

Handling customer claims is a common task for most business firms. These claims include requests to exchange merchandise, requests for refunds, requests that work ＿＿＿11＿＿＿ , and other requests for adjustments. Most of these claims are approved because they are legitimate. However, some requests for adjustment must be ＿＿＿12＿＿＿ , and an adjustment refusal message must be sent. Adjustment refusals are negative messages for the customer. They are necessary when the customer is ＿＿＿13＿＿＿ or when the vendor has done all that can reasonably or legally be expected.

An adjustment refusal message requires your best communication skills ＿＿＿14＿＿＿ it is bad news to the receiver. You have to refuse the claim and retain the customer ＿＿＿15＿＿＿ .You may refuse the request for adjustment and even try to sell the customer more merchandise or service. All this is happening when the customer is probably angry, disappointed, or inconvenienced.

對多數公司行號來説，處理客訴是一般性的工作。這些訴求包括換貨、退貨、物品功能 ＿＿＿11＿＿＿ ，及要求調低價格等。由於多數這些客訴是合理的，所以會被允

許所求。不過，一些對調價的要求必須 ＿＿＿ 12 ＿＿＿，且必須寄出拒絕調價的訊息。調價對用戶來說是負面消息。當用戶 ＿＿＿ 13 ＿＿＿，或者賣主已合理或合法盡到該負的責任時，發出拒調低價通知是必要的。

　這個通知需要你的高度溝通技巧 ＿＿＿ 14 ＿＿＿ 這是受方的壞消息。你必須拒絕理賠 ＿＿＿ 15 ＿＿＿ 留住客戶。你可以拒調低價，甚至賣出更多商品或提供更多服務給客戶。當用戶可能生氣、失望或感到不便時，就馬上要進行溝通。

11. 題句：這些訴求包括換貨、退貨、物品功能 ＿＿＿ 11 ＿＿＿
　　選項：(A) is correct 現在式　(B) to be correct 正確的　(C) is corrected 被　(D) be corrected

解析
⑴答題關鍵在「這些訴求包括換貨、退貨、物品功能 ＿＿＿ 11 ＿＿＿ ，」。
⑵只有選 (D) 項的「be corrected」放入空格，才符合「用 be correct 二字代替 should be correct」的文法規定，亦即 should be 的 should 可省略。

12. 題句：一些對調低價的要求必須 ＿＿＿ 12 ＿＿＿
　　選項：(A) retailed 零售　(B) denied 否認、拒絕　(C) appreciated 賞識　(D) elaborated 精巧的

解析
⑴答題關鍵在「不過，一些對調價的要求必須 ＿＿＿ 12 ＿＿＿ ，且必須……」。
⑵只有(B)選項的「拒絕」放入空格，才是符合題意的正確選項。

13. 題句：當用戶 ＿＿＿ 13 ＿＿＿，或者賣主已合理或合法盡到該負的責任時，發出拒調低價通知是必要的。
　　選項：(A) at fault 有過失　(B) on call 在外應診　(C) in tears 哭泣　(D) off guard 無防備

解析
⑴答題關鍵在「當用戶 ＿＿＿ 13 ＿＿＿，或者賣主已合理或合法盡到該負的責任時，」
⑵只有選(A)項的「有過失」放入空格，才是符合題意的正確選項。

14. 題句：這個通知需要你的高度溝通技巧 ＿＿＿ 14 ＿＿＿ 這是受方的壞消息。
　　選項：(A) till 一直到　(B) unless 除非　(C) because 因為　(D) therefore 因此

解析
⑴答題關鍵在「這個通知需要你的高度溝通技巧 ＿＿＿ 14 ＿＿＿ 這是受方的壞消息」。
⑵只有選(C)項的「因為」放入空格，才符合題意，且「前後兩子句需有連接詞」的文法規定。

15. 題句：你必須拒絕理賠 _____15_____ 留住客戶。

選項：(A) by and large 總的來說　(B) over and over 重複　(C) at the same time 同時　(D) for the same reason 同一理由

解析

⑴答題關鍵在「你必須拒絕理賠 _____15_____ 留住客戶」。

⑵只有選(C)項的「同時」放入空格，才是符合題意的正確選項。

第 16 至 20 題為題組

People may express their feelings differently on different occasions. Cultures sometimes vary greatly in this regard. A group of researchers in Japan, _____16_____ , studied the facial reactions of students to a horror film. When the Japanese students watched the film _____17_____ the teacher present, their faces showed only the slightest hints of reaction. But when they thought they were alone (though they _____18_____ by a secret camera), their faces twisted into vivid mixes of anguished distress, fear, and disgust.

The study also shows that there are several unspoken rules about how feelings should be _____19_____ shown on different occasions. One of the most common rules is minimizing the show of emotion. This is the Japanese norm for feelings of distress _____20_____ someone in authority, which explains why the students masked their upset with a poker face in the experiment.

人們在不同的場合可能會表達不同的感受。不同的文化在這部分會有很大的差異。以日本的一組研究人員 _____16_____ ，觀察學生看恐怖電影時的臉上表情。_____17_____ 在場的教師看電影時，他們的表情只顯出輕微的反應。但當他們認為他們是單獨看電影時，（他們正 _____18_____ 被一架祕密照像機錄影著），他們的表情卻是滿臉扭曲、痛苦、懼怕、與厭惡。

研究也顯示有關感覺部分的不成文規定在不同的場合應 _____19_____ 表示出來。最通常的規定是減低情感的表達。這是有當權人物 _____20_____ 時的日本規範，這解釋那些學生為什麼在實驗過程中要做到毫無表情。

16. 題句：以日本的一組研究人員 _____16_____ ……

選項：(A) as usual 一如往常　(B) in some cases 某些情況　(C) to be frank 坦白說　(D) for example 為例、舉例來說

解析

⑴答題關鍵在「以日本的一組研究人員 _____16_____ ，」。

⑵只有(D)選項的「為例、舉例來說」放入空格，才是符合題意的正確選項。

17. 題句：_____17_____ 在場的教師看電影時……。

選項：(A) of 的　(B) as 如　(C) from 從　(D) with 與

解析

⑴答題關鍵在「_____17_____ 在場的教師看電影時」。

(2)只有選(D)項的「與」放入空格，才是符合題意的正確選項。

18. 題句：（他們正 ＿＿＿18＿＿＿ 被一架祕密照像機錄影著），
　　選項：(A) were being taped 被動語態過去進行式　(B) had taped 過去完成式　(C) are taping 現在進行式　(D) have been taped 被動語態

解析

(1)答題關鍵在「＿＿＿18＿＿＿ 在場的教師看電影時」。

(2)只有選(A)項的「were being taped」放入空格，才是符合文法規定的正確選項。

19. 題句：研究也顯示有關感覺部分的不成文規定在不同的場合應該 ＿＿＿19＿＿＿ 表達出來。
　　選項：(A) rarely 稀有的　(B) similarly 同樣的　(C) properly 適當地　(D) critically 批判地

解析

(1)答題關鍵在「在不同的場合應該 ＿＿＿19＿＿＿ 表達出來」。

(2)只有(C)選項的「適當地」放入空格，才是符合題意的正確選項。

20. 題句：這是有當權人物 ＿＿＿20＿＿＿ 時的日本規範
　　選項：(A) with the help of 有了～幫助　(B) in the presence of 出席、在場　(C) on top of 除～之外　(D) in place of 站～立場

解析

(1)答題關鍵在「這是有當權人物 ＿＿＿20＿＿＿ 時的日本規範」。

(2)只有(B)選項的「出席、在場」放入空格，才是符合「in the present of」的片語說法。才是符合題意的正確選項。

三、文意選填（10分）

說明：第21題至第30題，每題1個空格。請依文意在文章後所提供的(A)到(L)選項中分別選出最適當者，並將其英文字母代號畫記在答案卡之「選擇題答案區」。各題答對得1分，未作答、答錯、或畫記多於1個選項者，該題以零分計算。

第 21 至 30 題為題組

The history of the written word goes back 6,000 years. Words express feelings, open doors into the ＿＿＿21＿＿＿ , create pictures of worlds never seen, and allow adventures never dared. Therefore, the original ＿＿＿22＿＿＿ of words, such as storytellers, poets, and singers, were respected in all cultures in the past.

But now the romance is ＿＿＿23＿＿＿ Imagination is being surpassed by the instant picture. In a triumphant march, movies, TV, videos, and DVDs are ＿＿＿24＿＿＿ storytellers and books. A visual culture is taking over the world—at the ＿＿＿25＿＿＿ of the written word. Our literacy, and with it our verbal and communication skills, are in ＿＿＿26＿＿＿ decline.

The only category of novel that is _____27_____ ground in our increasingly visual world is the graphic novel. A growing number of adults and young people worldwide are reading graphic novels, and educators are beginning to realize the power of this _____28_____ The graphic novel looks like a comic book, but it is longer, more sophisticated, and may come in black and white or multiple _____29_____ and appear in many sizes. In fact, some of the most interesting, daring, and most heartbreaking art being created right now is being published in graphic novels. Graphic novels _____30_____ the opportunity to examine the increasingly visual world of communications today while exploring serious social and literary topics. The graphic novel can be used to develop a sense of visual literacy, in much the same way that students are introduced to art appreciation.

在 6,000 年前就有文字記載的歷史。文字表達情感，打開 _____21_____ 大門，創作出從未見過的畫面及從未有過的冒險之旅。因此，文字的原先 _____22_____ ，像是講故事的人、詩人與歌手，過去在所有不同文化裡都受到尊重。

但是現在傳奇故事 _____23_____ 。立即影像優於想像力。在勝利的行軍、電影、電視、錄影帶和 DVD _____24_____ 了講故事者和書籍。視覺文化以書面為 _____25_____ 通行全世界。我們的識字、口說和溝通技能，都在 _____26_____ 衰退。

在不斷成長之視覺世界裡，唯一 _____27_____ 的是寫實小說。全球很多的大人小孩還在閱讀寫實小說，教育工作者開始意識到這種 _____28_____ 的能力。寫實小說看起來像一本連環漫畫，但是更長，更複雜，有黑白或多種 _____29_____ ，尺寸大小也有很多種。事實上，當今一些最有趣的、最大膽及最令人心碎的藝術創作，是以寫實小說的方式出版。寫實小說在探索嚴重的社會與文學議題之同時，也 _____30_____ 機會來檢視這個視覺世界。寫實小說能用來發展一種視覺文學意識，就像教育學生養成有欣賞藝術的能力是一樣的。

(A) expense 費用　(B) fading 褪色　(C) colors 色彩　(D) research 研究
(E) replacing 取代　(F) offer 提供　(G) users 使用者　(H) rapid 快速
(I) gaining 獲得　(J) medium 媒介　(K) circular 循環　(L) unknown 未知

21. 題句：文字表達情感，打開 _____21_____ 大門，
解析
(1)答題關鍵在「打開 _____21_____ 大門，」。
(2)只有(L) 選項的「未知」放入空格，才是符合題意的正確選項。

22. 題句：文字的原先 _____22_____ ，像是講故事的人、詩人與歌手
解析
(1)答題關鍵在「文字的原先 _____22_____ ，」。
(2)只有(G) 選項的「使用者」放入空格，才是符合題意的正確選項。

23. 題句：但是現在傳奇故事 ＿＿＿＿23＿＿＿＿

解析

(1)答題關鍵在「但是現在傳奇故事 ＿＿＿＿23＿＿＿＿ 」。

(2)只有(B)選項的「褪色」放入空格，才是符合題意的正確選項。

24. 題句：在勝利的行軍、電影、電視、錄影帶和 DVD ＿＿＿＿24＿＿＿＿ 了講故事者和書籍。

解析

(1)答題關鍵在「錄影帶和 DVD ＿＿＿＿24＿＿＿＿ 了講故事者和書籍」。

(2)只有(E)選項的「取代」放入空格，才是符合題意的正確選項。

25. 題句：視覺文化以書面為 ＿＿＿＿25＿＿＿＿ 通行全世界

解析

(1)答題關鍵在「視覺文化以書面為 ＿＿＿＿25＿＿＿＿ 通行全世界」。

(2)只有(A)選項的「代價、費用」放入空格，才是符合題意的正確選項。

(3)at the expense of 中譯為「以～為代價」。

26. 題句：我們的識字、口說和溝通技能，都在 ＿＿＿＿26＿＿＿＿ 衰退。

解析

(1)答題關鍵在「我們的識字、口說和溝通技能，都在 ＿＿＿＿26＿＿＿＿ 衰退。」。

(2)只有(H)選項的「快速」放入空格，才是符合題意的正確選項。

27. 題句：在不斷成長之視覺世界裡，唯一 ＿＿＿＿27＿＿＿＿ 的是寫實小說

解析

(1)答題關鍵在「唯一 ＿＿＿＿27＿＿＿＿ 的是寫實小說」。

(2)只有(I)選項的「尚有進展」放入空格，才是符合題意的正確選項。

28. 題句：教育工作者開始意識到這種 ＿＿＿＿28＿＿＿＿ 的能力

解析

(1)答題關鍵在「教育工作者開始意識到這種 ＿＿＿＿28＿＿＿＿ 的能力」。

(2)只有(J)選項的「媒介、媒體」放入空格，才是符合題意的正確選項。

29. 題句：但是更長，更複雜，有黑白或多種 ＿＿＿＿29＿＿＿＿

解析

(1)答題關鍵在「有黑白或多種 ＿＿＿＿29＿＿＿＿ 」。

(2)只有(C)選項的「顏色」放入空格，才是符合題意的正確選項。

30. 題句：在探索嚴重的社會與文學議題之同時，也 _____30_____ 機會來檢視這個視覺世界

解析

(1)答題關鍵在「也 _____30_____ 機會來檢視這個視覺世界」。

(2)只有(F)選項的「提供」放入空格，才是符合題意的正確選項。

四、篇章結構（10分）

> 說明：第 31 題至第 35 題，每題 1 個空格。請依文意在文章後所提供的(A)到(F)選項中分別選出最適當者，填入空格中，使篇章結構清晰有條理，並將其英文字母代號標示在答案卡之「選擇題答案區」。每題答對得 2 分，未作答、答錯、或畫記多於 1 個選項者，該題以零分計算。

第 31 至 35 題為題組

The effect of bullying can be serious and even lead to tragedy. Unfortunately, it is still a mostly unresearched area. _____31_____ That year two shotgun-wielding students, both of whom had been identified as gifted and who had been bullied for years, killed 13 people, wounded 24 and then committed suicide. A year later an analysis by the US government found that bullying played a major role in more than two-thirds of the campus violence. _____32_____ Numerous dictators and invaders throughout history have tried to justify their bullying behavior by claiming that they themselves were bullied. _____33_____ Although it is no justification for bullying, many of the worst humans in history have indeed been bullies and victims of bullying.

霸凌的後果可能很嚴重甚至產生悲劇。不幸的是，這部分一直都沒被研究過。_____31_____ 那年兩個揮舞獵槍的學生，都被證實天賦資質不錯，多年來受到霸凌，殺死 13 人，射傷的有 24 人而最後自殺身亡。一年後，一份政府的分析指出，霸凌案件占校園暴力的三分之二以上。_____32_____ 歷史上有許多獨裁與侵略者說，他們本身也是受霸凌者，想藉此把他們的霸凌行為正當化。_____33_____ 雖然霸凌是不對的，在歷史上還是有很多的倒楣的受到霸凌成為受害人。

Since bullying is mostly ignored, it may provide an important clue in crowd behavior and passer-by behavior. _____34_____ Many of them have suggested bullying as one of the reasons of this decline in emotional sensitivity and acceptance of violence as normal. When someone is bullied, it is not only the bully and the victim who are becoming less sensitive to violence. _____35_____ In this sense, bullying affects not only the bullied but his friends and classmates and the whole society.

由於多數的霸凌案件被忽視，它也許可以在群眾或路人行為裡提供一份重要的線索。_____34_____ 他們之中有許多人暗示霸凌是情感低潮時所以認為接受霸凌是正常的。一個人受到霸凌時，不只是霸凌者及受害者都較無理性。_____35_____ 這樣的話，受影響的不只是受害者，也包括他的同學、友人及整個社會。

(A) Hitler, for example, is claimed to have been a victim of bullying in his childhood.

以希特勒為例，聲稱在他孩提時代受到霸凌。

(B) Campus bullying is becoming a serious problem in some high schools in big cities.

大城市的一些高中的校園霸凌已變成是嚴重的問題。

(C) The friends and classmates of the bully and the victim may accept the violence as normal.

霸凌加害與受害雙方同學或友人，有可能視霸凌暴力為正常行為。

(D) Research indicates that bullying may form a chain reaction and the victim often becomes the bully.

學術研究指出霸凌可能形成連鎖反應，而受害者最後常會變成加害者。

(E) Psychologists have been puzzled by the inactivity of crowds and bystanders in urban centers when crimes occur in crowded places.

群眾與路人對當街霸凌事件的袖手旁觀使心理學家很迷惑。

(F) The link between bullying and school violence has attracted increasing attention since the 1999 tragedy at a Colorado high school.

自從科羅拉多高中在 1999 年發生霸凌悲劇後，霸凌與學校暴力的連結已引起更多注意。

31. 題句：不幸的是，這部分一直都沒被研究過。 ＿＿＿31＿＿＿ 那年兩個揮舞獵槍的學生，都被證實天賦資質不錯……。

解析

依題意只有 (F) 選項的「自從科羅拉多高中在 1999 年發生霸凌悲劇後，霸凌與學校暴力的連結已引起更多注意」才是連接空格前後兩句的正確選項。

32. 題句：霸凌案件占校園暴力的三分之二以上。 ＿＿＿32＿＿＿ 歷史上有許多獨裁與侵略者說，他們本身也是受霸凌者

解析

依題意只有 (D) 選項的「學術研究指出霸凌可能形成連鎖反應，而受害者最後常會變成加害者。」才是連接空格前後兩句的正確選項。

33. 題句：想藉此把他們的霸凌行為正當化。 ＿＿＿33＿＿＿ 雖然霸凌是不對的，……

解析

依題意只有 (A) 選項的「以希特勒為例，聲稱在他孩提時代受到霸凌。」才是連接空格前後兩句的正確選項。

34. 題句：它也許可以在群眾或路人行為裡提供一份重要的線索。 ＿＿＿34＿＿＿ 他們之中有許多人暗示霸凌是情感低潮時……。

解析

依題意只有 (E) 選項的「群眾與路人對當街霸凌事件的袖手旁觀使心理學家很迷惑。」才是連接空格前後兩句的正確選項。

35. 題句：不只是霸凌者及受害者都較無理性。　　35　　這樣的話，受影響的不只是受害者……

解析

依題意只有 (C) 選項的「霸凌加害與受害雙方同學或友人，有可能視霸凌暴力為正常行為。」才是連接空格前後兩句的正確選項。

五、閱讀測驗（32分）

說明：第 36 題至第 51 題，每題請分別根據各篇文章的文意選出最適當的 1 個選項，畫記在答案卡之「選擇題答案區」。各題答對得 2 分，未作答、答錯、或畫記多於 1 個選項者，該題以零分計算。

第 36 至 39 題為題組

Since the times of the Greeks and Romans, truffles have been used in Europe as delicacies and even as medicines. They are among the most expensive of the world's natural foods, often commanding as much as US$250 to US$450 per pound. Truffles are actually mushrooms, but unusual ones. They live in close association with the roots of specific trees and their fruiting bodies grow underground. This is why they are difficult to find.

從希臘和羅馬時代起，松露巧克力糖在歐洲經已被作為美食甚至可作藥。它們在天然食物裡，要價高達每英磅 250 美元到 450 美元的昂貴食物。松露實際上是蘑菇，但非一般蘑菇。它們棲息在某些特定樹根，而它們的多果之身是長在土壤下，這是他們難被找到的原因。

Truffles are harvested in Europe with the aid of female pigs or truffle dogs, which are able to detect the strong smell of mature truffles underneath the surface of the ground. Female pigs are especially sensitive to the odor of the truffles because it is similar to the smell given off by male pigs. The use of pigs is risky, though, because of their natural tendency to eat any remotely edible thing. : For this reason, dogs have been trained to dig into the ground wherever they find this odor, and they willingly exchange their truffle for a piece of bread and a pat on the head. Some truffle merchants dig for their prizes themselves when they see truffle flies hovering around the base of a tree. Once a site has been discovered, truffles can be collected in subsequent years.

在歐洲，松露巧克力樹是用母豬和松露狗來幫助收成，狗能在土壤下聞到濃味的成熟松露。母豬對松露的氣味特別敏感，因為那氣味很類似公豬氣味。使用豬隻是有風險的，因為牠們的自然習性會吃掉深入土壤的食物。因此，狗已經被訓練在他們找到這種氣味的地方往下深挖，並且牠們很樂意用松露與主人換一片麵包或被主人拍拍頭部。松露商人看到蒼蠅在大樹根部盤旋時，也會自己動手挖掘。一旦好的場子被發現，在隨後幾年都有松露可收成。

To enjoy the wonderful flavor of what has been described as an earthly jewel, you must eat fresh, uncooked specimens shortly after they have been harvested. The strength of their flavor decreases rapidly with time, and much of it is lost before some truffles reach the market. To preserve them, gourmet experts suggest putting them in closed glass jars in a refrigerator. Another recommendation is to store them whole in bland oil.

為了享有被譽為塵世珠寶的好口味，你必須收成後不要煮，趁新鮮吃。它的美味很快會越來越淡，而在運送到市場前，大部分松露會變得沒有味道。為了收藏它們，美食專家建議用玻璃罐子裝好，放在冰箱保存。另一個建議是浸泡在溫和食物油裡。

36. Why do some people prefer using dogs than pigs in search of truffles?

　　為尋找松露，為什麼有些人喜歡用狗而不用豬？

　　(A) Dogs have stronger paws to dig.

　　　　狗有更強壯的爪子挖。

　　(B) Dogs usually won't eat the truffles found.

　　　　狗通常不會吃找到的松露。

　　(C) Dogs have a better sense of smell than pigs.

　　　　狗有比豬更好的嗅覺。

　　(D) Dogs are less likely to get excited than pigs.

　　　　狗不會像豬激動。

解析

從答題關鍵的「使用豬隻是有風險的，因為牠們的自然習性會吃掉深入土壤的食物。」可看出，只有(B)選項的「狗通常不會吃找到的松露」才是符合題意的正確選項。

37. What is the best way to enjoy truffles as a delicacy?

　　最好的食用松露的方法是什麼？

　　(A) Eating them cooked with pork.

　　　　用豬肉一起煮來吃。

　　(B) Eating them uncooked with bland oil.

　　　　與柔性油生吃。

　　(C) Eating them fresh right after being collected.

　　　　採收後立即趁鮮吃。

　　(D) Eating them after being refrigerated.

　　　　冷藏之後才吃。

解析

從答題關鍵的「你必須收成後不要煮，趁新鮮吃。」可看出，只有(C)選項的「採收後立即趁鮮吃。」才是符合題意的正確選項。

38. Which of the following statements is true?

　　下列陳述中哪項為真？

　　(A) Truffles are roots of some old trees.

　　　　松露是一些古樹的根。

(B) Truffles can be found only by dogs and pigs.

松露只能透過狗和豬發現。

(C) Truffles send out a strong odor when they mature.

當他們成熟時，松露發出一種味濃的氣味。

(D) Truffles cannot be collected at the same place repeatedly.

松露在同地不能反覆收成。

解析

根據文章內容，只有 (C) 選項的「當他們成熟時，松露發出一種味濃的氣味」 才是符合題意的正確選項。

39. Which of the following can be inferred from the passage?

下列哪一項可從文章推斷出？

(A) Truffles sold in glass jars are tasteless.

用玻璃杯罐子出售的松露是無味的。

(B) Truffles taste like fruit when eaten fresh.

松露新鮮吃時味道像水果。

(C) Truffles are only used for cooking nowadays.

松露目前只用於烹飪。

(D) Truffles are expensive because they are difficult to find.

松露是昂貴的，因為他們難被找到。

解析

從答題關鍵的「它們棲息在某些特定樹根，而它們的多果之身是長在土壤下，這是他們難被找到的原因。」可看出，只有 (D) 選項的「松露是昂貴的，因為他們難被找到。」才是符合題意的正確選項。

第 40 至 43 題為題組

In an ideal world, people would not test medicines on animals. Such experiments are stressful and sometimes painful for animals, and expensive and time-consuming for people. Yet animal experimentation is still needed to help bridge vast gaps in medical knowledge. That is why there are some 50 to 100 million animals used in research around the world each year.

在一個理想的世界，人們將不再用動物測試藥性。這樣的實驗是緊張的，有時候使動物很痛苦，對人而言算是昂貴與費時。然而動物實驗仍然有需要，幫助減少醫學差距。那就是為什麼全球每年要花大約 5 千萬到 1 億隻動物作實驗的原因。

Europe, on the whole, has the world's most restrictive laws on animal experiments. Even so, its scientists use some 12 million animals a year, most of them mice and rats, for medical research. Official statistics show that just 1.1 million animals are used in research in America each year. But that is misleading. The American authorities do not think mice and rats are worth counting and, as these are the most common laboratory animals, the true figure is much higher.

Japan and China have even less comprehensive data than America.

　　歐洲，總的來說，有全世界最嚴格的動物實驗限制。即使如此，他們的科學家一年使用大約 1200 萬隻動物，大多數是作醫學研究的老鼠。官方統計數據顯示光是美國一年就要用掉 110 萬隻動物做研究。但這是誤導的美國當局認為老鼠不值得一隻一隻數清楚，因為老鼠只是最普通的實驗室動物，真實的數字高很多。與美國相比較，日本和中國的數據沒有那麼廣泛。

　　Now Europe is reforming the rules governing animal experiments by restricting the number of animals used in labs. Alternatives to animal testing, such as using human tissue or computer models, are now strongly recommended.

　　In addition, sharing all research results freely should help to reduce the number of animals for scientific use. At present, scientists often share only the results of successful experiments. If their findings do not fit the hypothesis being tested, the work never sees the light of day. This practice means wasting time, money, and animals' lives in endlessly repeating the failed experiments.

　　現下歐洲透過限制在實驗室的動物使用量訂下改革測試動物的選擇，例如使用人類組織或電腦模組，且已大力的被推薦使用。另外，自由分享所有研究結果應有助減少供科學用途的動物數量。目前，科學家經常只分享成功的實驗案例。如果他們的結論不適於測試的假設，就不算成功。這樣無止境的失敗經驗，是在浪費時間、金錢與動物的生命。

　　Animal experimentation has taught humanity a great deal and saved countless lives. It needs to continue, even if that means animals sometimes suffer. Europe's new measures should eventually both reduce the number of animals used in experiments and improve the way in which scientific research is conducted.

　　動物實驗有助教導人性並且拯救無數生命，即使這些動物有時候會受罪，而實驗必須持續下去歐洲的新措施最終會減少實驗動物的數量，也會改進科學研究的執行方式。

40. What is the main idea of this passage?

　　這篇文章的大意是什麼？

(A) The success of animal experiments should be ensured.

　　動物實驗的成功應被確保。

(B) Ban on the use of animals in the lab should be enforced.

　　禁止實驗動物的使用應該加強。

(C) Greater efforts need to be taken to reduce the number of lab animals.

　　要有更大的努力來降低實驗動物的數量。

(D) Scientists should be required to share their research results with each other.

　　應該要求科學家彼此分享研究結果。

解析

根據文章內容，只有 (C) 選項的「要有更大的努力來降低實驗動物的數量。」才是本文的大意。

41. Which of the following statements is true about animals used in the lab?

下列有關實驗動物之使用，哪項為真？

(A) America uses only about 1.1 million lab animals per year.

美國每年大約使用 110 萬隻實驗動物。

(B) Europe does not use mice and rats as lab animals at all.

歐洲根本不使用老鼠作為實驗動物。

(C) Britain does not use as many lab animals as China does.

英國使用的實驗室動物比中國少。

(D) Japan has limited data on the number of lab animals used each year.

日本已經限制每年使用的實驗室動物的數量。

解析

從答題關鍵的「官方統計數據顯示光是美國一年就要用掉 110 萬隻動物做研究」可看出，只有 (A) 選項的「美國每年大約使用 110 萬隻實驗動物」才是符合題意的正確選項。

42. Which of the following is mentioned as an alternative to replace animal experiments?

下列的哪一項在文章中被提及用來做動物實驗的替代選項？

(A) Statistical studies.

統計研究。

(B) Computer models.

電腦模組。

(C) DNA planted in animals.

動物的 DNA。

(D) Tissue from dead animals.

死去動物的組織。

解析

從答題關鍵的「例如使用人類組織或電腦模組，且已大力的被推薦使用。」可看出，只有 (B) 選項的「電腦模組」才是符合題意的正確選項。

43. What usually happens to unsuccessful animal experiments?

不成功的動物實驗通常會怎樣？

(A) They are not revealed to the public.

失敗結果沒對外公開。

(B) They are made into teaching materials.

失敗結果被編成教材。

(C) They are collected for future publication.

失敗結果被彙集成冊。

(D) They are not removed from the research topic list.

失敗結果未從研究清單中移除。

解析

從答題關鍵的「如果他們的結論不適於測試的假設，就不算成功」可看出，只有 (A) 選項的「失敗結果沒對外公開。」才是符合題意的正確選項。

第 44 至 47 題為題組

Spider webs are one of the most fascinating examples of animal architecture. The most beautiful and structurally ordered are the orb webs. The main function of the web is to intercept and hold flying prey, such as flies, bees and other insects, long enough for the spider to catch them.

In order to do so, the threads of the web have to withstand the impact forces from large and heavy prey as well as environmental forces from wind and rain for at least a day in most cases.

蜘蛛網是動物建築的最迷人的例子之一。最美麗和結構最井然有序的是球狀網。蛛網的主要功能是攔截並且捉住飛舞的獵物，像是蒼蠅，蜜蜂和其他昆蟲，並有足夠的時間讓蜘蛛抓住牠的獵物。為了這麼做，蛛絲必須禁得起大型或過重獵物所帶來的衝擊，以及能對抗自然風雨的力量。多數情況下，蛛絲的強度至少要能維持一天以上。

The orb web is found to have two main characteristics. The first is its geometry, which consists of an outer frame and a central part from which threads radiate outward. Enclosed in the frame are capture spirals winding round and round from the web center out to the frame The whole web is in tension and held in place by anchor threads, which connect the frame to the surrounding vegetation or objects. The second and perhaps most important characteristic is the material with which it is built. Spider silk is a kind of natural composite that gives this lightweight fiber a tensile strength comparable to that of steel, while at the same time making it very elastic.

球狀網被認為有兩個主要特徵。首先，是它的幾何圖形，這包括一個外框和中心結構，網絲由此以幅射狀向外織出。網框內部是具捕捉功能的螺旋網絲，由內向外層層擴充。整個蛛蜘網處於繃緊狀，並有錨絲固定住，這條錨絲將蜘蛛網連結起在植物或其他物體上。第 2 個特色，或許是最重要的特色是造網的材料。蜘蛛絲是一種自然合成物，使這種極輕纖維比同樣纖細的鋼鐵更具抗張力強度，同時它非常有彈性。

Two types of silk threads are used in the web. One is highly elastic and can stretch to almost twice its original length before breaking and, for most types of spiders, is covered in glue. This type is used in the capture spiral for catching and holding prey. The other is stiffer and stronger, and is used for the radius, frames and anchor threads, which allows the web to withstand prey impact and to keep its structural strength through a wide range of environmental conditions.

蜘蛛網有兩種網絲。一種是非常有彈性，並能伸展到原有尺寸的兩倍長才會折斷，多數類型的蜘蛛，有隱藏的黏貼劑。這種黏劑被用在誘捕螺旋網，並可抓住獵物。另一種網絲更硬更有韌性，用在幅射狀蛛網、網框與錨絲，這個錨絲更能耐受獵物衝擊且於大部分的週遭環境下還能保持它的蜘蛛網結構。

44. What is this passage mainly about?

本文主要大意是什麼？

(A) The food network in nature.

自然的食品網路。

(B) The construction of orb webs.

球狀網的建造。

(C) The network of geometrical studies.

幾何研究的網路。

(D) The environmental challenges for spider webs.

蜘蛛網的環境挑戰。

解析
根據文章內容，只有(B)選項的「球狀網的建造。」才是符合題意的正確選項。

45. What does the word "so" in the first paragraph refer to?

本文第一個段「so」是指何意？

(A) To catch and keep small creatures.

捕獲並留住小生物。

(B) To find a good material for the web.

找到做網的好材料。

(C) To observe the behavior patterns of spiders.

觀察蜘蛛的行為模式。

(D) To present a fantastic architecture by animals.

透過動物提出一座美妙的建築。

解析
根據第一段文章內容，只有(A)選項的「捕獲並留住小生物」才是符合題意的正確選項。

46. Which part of the web is used for supporting the web itself?

網中的哪個部分用於支撐整個蛛網？

(A) The center of the web.

網的中心部分。

(B) The glue on the lines.

　　線上的膠水。

(C) The anchor threads.

　　錨絲。

(D) The capture spiral.

　　誘捕螺旋網。

解析

從答題關鍵的「並有錨絲固定住，這條錨絲將蜘蛛網連結起在植物或其他物體上。」可看出，只有 (C) 選項的「錨絲」才是符合題意的正確選項。

47. According to the passage, which statement is true about the silk threads?

　　根據本文，關於絲線哪個陳述是眞實的？

(A) They are all sticky and extendable.

　　它們都有黏性也可延伸。

(B) They are usually strong enough to last for a day.

　　它們通常的韌性足以持續一天。

(C) They remove harmful chemicals from insects.

　　它們從會去除昆蟲的化學物質。

(D) They are made of rare plants in the environment.

　　它們由週邊的稀有植物做成。

解析

從答題關鍵的「並有錨絲固定住，這條錨絲將蜘蛛網連結起在植物或其他物體上。」可看出，只有 (B) 選項的「它們通常的韌性足以持續一天」才是符合題意的正確選項。

第 48 至 51 題為題組

　　Doctor of Philosophy, usually abbreviated as PhD or Ph.D., is an advanced academic degree awarded by universities. The first Doctor of Philosophy degree was awarded in Paris in 1150, but the degree did not acquire its modern status until the early 19th century. The doctorate of philosophy as it exists today originated at Humboldt University. The German practice was later adopted by American and Canadian universities, eventually becoming common in large parts of the world in the 20th century.

　　哲學博士，通常簡寫爲博士或者哲學博士，是大學所授予的進階學位。第一個博士學位是 1150 年在巴黎授予，但是直到第十九世紀初葉它才獲得它現有的社會地位。當今的博士學位源自漢伯特大學。美國和加拿大的大學後來採用了德國的慣例，到了二十世紀這個慣例在全世界變得更普及。

　　For most of history, even a bachelor's degree at a university was the privilege of a rich few, and many academic staff did not hold doctorates. But as higher education expanded after the Second World War, the number of PhDs increased accordingly. American universities geared up first: By 1970, America was graduating half of the world's PhDs in science and technology. Since then, America's annual output of PhDs has doubled, to 64,000. Other countries are catching up. PhD production has sped up most dramatically in Mexico, Portugal, Italy, and Slovakia. Even Japan, where the number of young people is shrinking, has churned out about 46% more PhDs.

大多數的歷史記載，即使大學的學士學位，也是富者少有的特權，而很多學術工作人員根本不具博士學位。但是當高等教育在第二次世界大戰之後擴展，博士的數量也隨著增加。美國大學首先起步，到 1970 年，美國在科學與技術方面的博士占全世界的一半。從那以後，美國的博士人數每年以倍數成長到 64,000 人。其他國家正在趕上。在墨西哥，葡萄牙，義大利和斯洛伐克等國家，博士的數量快速且戲劇性的成長。即使日本，年輕人的數量正在減縮，已經大量產生多出大約 46% 的博士。

Researchers now warn that the supply of PhDs has far outstripped demand. America produced more than 100,000 doctoral degrees between 2005 and 2009, while there were just 16,000 new professorships. In research, the story is similar. Even graduates who find work outside universities may not fare all that well. Statistics show that five years after receiving their degrees, more than 60% of PhDs in Slovakia and more than 45% in Belgium, the Czech Republic, Germany, and Spain are still on temporary contracts. About one-third of Austria's PhD graduates take jobs unrelated to their degrees.

研究人員警告博士的供應已經遠超過需求。美國在 2005 和 2009 之間創造超過 100,000 個博士學位，而僅有 16,000 個新的教授職務。研究過程發現，情況差不多。即使研究生在校外找工作可能沒進展得很順利。統計資料顯示，獲得學位的 5 年後，在斯洛伐克超過 60% 的博士、在比利時超過 45% 的博士。捷克共和國，德國和西班牙仍然適用暫時的合約。大約 3 分之 1 的奧地利的博士畢業生擔任與他們的學位無關的工作。

Today, top universities around the world are still picking bright students and grooming them as potential PhDs. After all, it isn't in their interests to turn the smart students away: The more bright students stay at universities, the better it is for academics. But considering the oversupply of PhDs, some people have already begun to wonder whether doing a PhD is a good choice for an individual.

今天，全世界的大學仍然挑選聰明的學生並且培養 他們為潛在的博士。終究 他們不會拒絕聰明的學生：大學收的聰明學生越多，對學校越好。但是考慮到博士的供應過多，已經有人開始想知道，當個博士是否為個人的好選擇。

48. In which country did the modern practice of granting doctoral degrees start?

　　批准博士學位的現代慣例始於哪個國家？

　(A) France. 法蘭西。　　(B) Germany. 德國。　　(C) Canada. 加拿大。　　(D) The U.S. 美國

解析

從答題關鍵的「美國和加拿大的大學後來採用了德國的慣例，」可看出，只有 (B) 選項的「德國」才是符合題意的正確選項。

49. Which of the following words is closest in meaning to "churned out" in the second paragraph?

　　下列哪一個意思最接近第二章節裡所提的「churned out」？

　　(A) Failed 失敗　(B) Warned 警告　(C) Demanded 要求　(D) produce 生產

解析

churned out 中譯為「大量生產」只有(D)選項的「生產」才是與其意思最接進的選項。

50. Which of the following may be inferred from the third paragraph?

　　第 3 段內容可推斷出下列哪一項？

　　(A) PhD graduates in Austria are not encouraged to work outside university.

　　　　在奧地利的博士畢業生沒被鼓勵在大學外邊工作。

　　(B) Most German PhDs work at permanent jobs immediately after graduation.

　　　　大多數德國博士在畢業之後立即找到固定工作。

　　(C) It is much easier for American PhD holders to find a teaching position than a research job.

　　　　與一個研究工作相比較，美國博士持有者要找教學工作容易得多。

　　(D) It is more difficult for PhDs to get a permanent job five years after graduation in Slovakia than in Spain.

　　　　在斯洛伐克畢業 5 年後的博士，要找固定工作比在西班牙難。

解析

根據第 3 段文章內容，只有 (D) 選項的「畢業 5 年後的博士，要在斯洛伐克找固定工作會比在西班牙難。」才是符合題意的正確選項。

51. Which of the following best describes the author's attitude　toward the increase of PhDs in recent years?

　　有關博士人數近年來不斷增加一事，下列哪一項最能描述作者的態度？

　　(A) Concerned. 關心　(B) Supportive.　(C) Indifferent. 漠視　(D) Optimistic. 樂觀

解析

根據文章內容，只有(A)選項的「關心」才是最能描述作者態度的正確選項。

第貳部分：非選擇題（28分）

一、中譯英（8分）

説明：1.請將以下中文句子譯成正確、通順、達意的英文，並將答案寫在「答案卷」上。

　　　　2.請依序作答，並標明題號。每題 4 分，共 8 分。

1. 日本的核電廠爆炸已經引起全球對核子能源安全的疑慮。

解析

先將題句內相關字詞寫出中譯：

日本的核電廠爆炸 The nuclear explosion in Japan

已經引起 has caused

全球 world-wide / global worry

對核能安全 to the safety of nuclear energy.

整句英譯

The nuclear explosion in Japan has caused world-wide doubt to the safety of nuclear energy.

2. 科學家正尋求安全、乾淨又不昂貴的綠色能源，以滿足我們對電的需求。

解析

科學家 Scientists 正在尋求 are seeking

安全、乾淨又不昂貴的 the safe, clean and inexpensive 電力

綠色能源 green energy 以滿足～的需求 to meet

我們對電的需求 our needs to electric power

整句英譯

Scientists are seeking a safe, clean and inexpensive green energy to meet our needs for electric power.

二、英文作文（20分）

> 說明：1.依提示在「答案卷」上寫一篇英文作文。
> 　　　2.文長至少 120 個單詞（words）。

提示：你認為畢業典禮應該是個溫馨感人、活潑熱鬧、或是嚴肅傷感的場景？請寫一篇
　　　英文作文說明你對畢業典禮的看法，第一段寫出畢業典禮對你而言意義是什麼，
　　　第二段說明要如何安排或進行活動才能呈現出這個意義。

解析

(1)先將題句內相關字詞寫出中譯：

畢業典禮 The graduation ceremony　　應該是 be supposed to be

溫馨感人 warm and touching　　　　　活潑熱鬧 active and joyful

嚴肅傷感的 serious and sentimental　　情景 scene

你對畢業典禮的看法 your prospect to the graduation ceremony

第一段：畢業典禮對你的意義為何？

　　To me, the graduation ceremony is not only the ending of one of my life phases but also the beginning of another phase. It means a lot to me because I become more mature in both phsically and mentally. It's also the time for me to make one step forward to be able to make better decisions, to be more humble in interactive while dealing with others.

（對我來說畢業典禮不只是我人生階段的結束，同時也是另一階段的開始。畢業典禮對我的意義重大，因爲我在身、心兩方面都變得更成熟了。這也是我要再往前誇出一大步的時刻，遇到事情就能夠做出更好的決定，待人處事間也能夠更爲謙虛成熟。）

第二段：説明要如何安排或進行活動，才能呈現這個意義

　　I intend to continue my school to the university. My father keep reminding me of studying while I can, he said our family doesn't need my financial aid, and all my parents want me to do is study hard, concentrating on school studying is my first priority I can also take a part-time job in one condition: I am okay with my school grading and be able to afford to work part-time physically.

　　（我有意繼續我的學業去念大學，家父不斷提醒我，趁能夠念書時要多念書。父親説，家裡不用我賺錢貼補家用。我的父母親要我做的事就是用功讀書，念書才是我的本份。他們又説，只有在一種條件之下我才可以打工，那就是：「在校的學科成績都過關，而且體力上也可以撐得過去」。）

學測（學科能力測驗）

（97～100年學測）

97 年學測（學科能力測驗）

一、詞彙（15%）

說明：第 1 至 15 題，每題選出最適當的一個選項，標示在答案卡之「選擇題答案區」。每題答對得 1 分，答錯不倒扣。

1. Amy did not ＿＿＿＿＿＿ changes in the course schedule and therefore missed the class.
   艾咪沒 ＿＿＿＿＿＿ 在課程表方面的變化因此曠課。
   (A) arrest 逮捕　(B) alarm 警報　(C) notice 注意到　(D) delay 延遲

   解析
   (1)答題關鍵在「艾咪沒 ＿＿＿＿＿＿ 在課程表方面的變化」。
   (2)只有(C) 選項的「注意到」放入空格，才是符合整句題意的正確選項。

2. It is not easy for old people to ＿＿＿＿＿＿ their backs, so they need help when their backs itch.
   老年人 ＿＿＿＿＿＿ 他們的背有困難，因此當背癢時他們需要幫助。
   (A) label 標籤　(B) scratch 搔癢　(C) lighten 減輕　(D) squeeze 壓縮

   解析
   (1)答題關鍵在「老年人 ＿＿＿＿＿＿ 他們的背有困難」。
   (2)只有(B) 選項的「搔癢」放入空格，才是符合整句題意的正確選項。

3. Mary is suffering from a stomachache and needs to eat food which is easy to ＿＿＿＿＿＿.
   瑪莉遭受胃痛之苦並且需要吃容易 ＿＿＿＿＿＿ 食品。
   (A) launch 啟動　(B) invade 侵入　(C) adopt 採用　(D) digest 消化

   解析
   (1)答題關鍵在「需要吃容易 ＿＿＿＿＿＿ 食品。」
   (2)只有(D) 選項的「消化」放入空格，才是符合整句題意的正確選項。

4. Since our classroom is not air-conditioned, we have to ＿＿＿＿＿＿ the heat during the hot summer days.
   由於我們的教室沒裝空調，我們必須 ＿＿＿＿＿＿ 炎夏的熱氣。
   (A) consume 消費　(B) tolerate 忍受　(C) recover 恢復　(D) promote 推廣

解析

(1)答題關鍵在「我們必須 ＿＿＿＿＿＿＿＿ 炎夏的熱氣。」

(2)只有(B)選項的「忍受」放入空格，才是符合整句題意的正確選項。

5. Sue is so ＿＿＿＿＿＿＿＿ that she always breaks something when she is shopping at a store.

蘇是如此 ＿＿＿＿＿＿＿＿ 當她在一家商店採買時，她總會弄壞一些東西。

(A) religious 宗教的　(B) visual 視覺的　(C) clumsy 笨拙的　(D) intimate 親密

解析

(1)答題關鍵在「蘇是如此 ＿＿＿＿＿＿＿＿ ……她總會弄壞一些東西。」

(2)只有(C)選項的「笨拙」放入空格，才是符合整句題意的正確選項。

6. Ann enjoyed going to the flower market. She believed that the ＿＿＿＿＿＿＿＿ of flowers refreshed her mind.

安喜歡去花市。她相信花的 ＿＿＿＿＿＿＿＿ 使她的心情愉快。

(A) instance 實例　(B) dominance 支配　(C) appliance 器具　(D) fragrance 芳香

解析

(1)答題關鍵在「她相信花的 ＿＿＿＿＿＿＿＿ 使她的心情愉快」。

(2)只有(D)選項的「芳香」放入空格，才是符合整句題意的正確選項。

7. The profits of Prince Charles's organic farm go to ＿＿＿＿＿＿＿＿ to help the poor and the sick.

查理斯王子的有機農場利潤捐給 ＿＿＿＿＿＿＿＿ 幫助貧病者。

(A) charities 慈善機構　(B) bulletins 公報　(C) harvests 農作收成　(D) rebels 叛亂者

解析

(1)答題關鍵在「有機農場利潤捐給 ＿＿＿＿＿＿＿＿ 幫助貧病者」。

(2)只有(A)選項的「慈善機構」放入空格，才是符合整句題意的正確選項。

8. Jack was given the rare ＿＿＿＿＿＿＿＿ of using the president's office, which made others quite jealous.

傑克被給予難得的 ＿＿＿＿＿＿＿＿ 使用總統府，使其它人十分妒忌。

(A) mischief 惡作劇　(B) privilege 特權　(C) involvement 介入　(D) occupation 職業

解析

(1)答題關鍵在「傑克被給予難得的 ＿＿＿＿＿＿＿＿ 使用總統府」。

(2)只有(B)選項的「特權」放入空格，才是符合整句題意的正確選項。

9. This new computer is obviously ＿＿＿＿＿＿＿＿ to the old one because it has many new functions.

這台新款電腦比舊款電腦 ＿＿＿＿＿＿＿＿ 因為它有很多新功能。

(A) technical 技術　(B) suitable 合適　(C) superior 較高的　(D) typical 典型

解析

⑴答題關鍵在「新款電腦比舊款電腦 _____ 」。

⑵只有(C)選項的「superior」放入空格，才是符合整句題意的正確選項。

⑶片語 superior to 中譯爲「比～優、好、年長」之意。

10. Simon loves his work. To him, work always comes first, and family and friends are _____.

賽門熱愛他的工作。對他來說，工作總是優先而家庭和朋友是 _____ 。

(A) secondary 第二　(B) temporary 暫時的　(C) sociable 愛交際的　(D) capable 有能力

解析

⑴答題關鍵在「工作總是優先而家庭和朋友是 _____ 」。

⑵只有(A)選項的「第二」放入空格，才是符合整句題意的正確選項。

11. Although your plans look good, you have to be _____ and consider what you can actually do.

雖然你的計畫看起來好，但是你必須 _____ 並考慮你實際上能做多少。

(A) dramatic 戲劇化　(B) realistic 務實地　(C) stressful 緊張的　(D) manageable 可管理的

解析

⑴答題關鍵在「但是你必須 _____ 並考慮你實際上能做多少。」

⑵只有(B)選項的「務實地」放入空格，才是符合整句題意的正確選項。

12. Built under the sea in 1994, the _____ between England and France connects the UK more closely with mainland Europe.

1994年在海底建造，在英國和法國之間的 _____ 使英國更靠近歐洲大陸。

(A) waterfall 瀑布　(B) temple 寺廟　(C) tunnel 隧道　(D) channel 海峽

解析

⑴答題關鍵在「在英國和法國之間的 _____ 使英國更靠近歐洲大陸。」

⑵只有(C)選項的「隧道」放入空格，才是符合整句題意的正確選項。

13. This tour package is very appealing, and that one looks _____ attractive. I don't know which one to choose.

這個旅遊套餐很有魅力，而那個看起來 _____ 有吸引力。我不知要選哪一個。

(A) equally 同樣地　(B) annually 每年　(C) merely 僅僅　(D) gratefully 充滿感激

解析

⑴答題關鍵在「而那個看起來 _____ 有吸引力。」

(2)只有(A)選項的「同樣地」放入空格，才是符合整句題意的正確選項。

14. Hsu Fang-yi, a young Taiwanese dancer, recently ＿＿＿＿＿ at Lincoln Center in New York and won a great deal of praise.

徐芳宜，一位年輕的台灣舞蹈家，最近在紐約的林肯中心 ＿＿＿＿＿ 且贏得很多讚揚。

(A) performed 表演　(B) pretended 假裝　(C) postponed 延期　(D) persuaded 說服

解析

(1)答題關鍵在「最近在紐約的林肯中心 ＿＿＿＿＿ 且贏得很多讚揚」。

(2)只有(A)選項的「表演」放入空格，才是符合整句題意的正確選項。

15. The police searched the house of the suspect ＿＿＿＿＿ They almost turned the whole house upside down.

警察 ＿＿＿＿＿ 搜查嫌犯的房子。他們幾乎把整個房子裡裡外外都搜遍了。

(A) relatively 相對地　(B) thoroughly 徹底地　(C) casually 隨意的　(D) permanently 永久地

解析

(1)答題關鍵在「警察 ＿＿＿＿＿ 搜查嫌犯的房子」。

(2)只有(B)選項的「徹底地」放入空格，才是符合整句題意的正確選項。

二、綜合測驗（15%）

說明：第 16 至 30 題，每題一個空格，請依文意選出最適當的一個選項，標示在答案卡之「選擇題答案區」。每題答對得 1 分，答錯不倒扣。

　　What is so special about green tea? The Chinese and Indians＿＿＿16＿＿＿ it for at least 4,000 years to treat everything from headache to depression. Researchers at Purdue University recently concluded that a compound in green tea ＿＿＿17＿＿＿ the growth of cancer cells. Green tea is also helpful ＿＿＿18＿＿＿ nfection and damaged immune function. The secret power of green tea is its richness in a powerful anti-oxidant.

　　為什麼綠茶如此特別？中國人與印第安人至少已經 ＿＿＿16＿＿＿ 4,000 年的綠茶來治病，從頭痛到精神沮喪都會有幫助。珀杜大學的研究人員最近斷定，在綠茶裡的一種化合物會 ＿＿＿17＿＿＿ 癌細胞的成長。綠茶也 ＿＿＿18＿＿＿ 對感染或受損的免疫功能有幫助。綠茶的祕密的是，它是很強效的抗氧化劑。

　　Green tea and black tea come from the same plant. Their ＿＿＿19＿＿＿ is in the processing. Green tea is dried but not fermented, and this shorter processing gives it a lighter flavor than black tea. It also helps retain the tea's beneficial chemicals. That is ＿＿＿20＿＿＿ green tea is so good for health. The only reported negative effect of drinking green tea is a possible allergic reaction and insomnia due to the caffeine it contains.

　　綠茶和紅茶來自相同的植物。他們的 ＿＿＿19＿＿＿ 在於處理過程。綠茶是乾燥且烘焙、不發酵，而在更短的處理過程中，它的味道比紅茶淡。它也有助於保留茶的有

益化學物質。那是 _____20_____ 綠茶是如此有益健康的原因。喝綠茶的唯一的負面報告是，它本身的咖啡因，會有過敏反應與失眠的可能性。

16. 題句：The Chinese and Indians _____16_____ it for at least 4,000 years to treat ...
中國人與印第安人至少已經 _____16_____ 4,000 年的綠茶來治病……

　　選項：(A) would use 使用　(B) are using　(C) had used　(D) have been using

解析
(1)答題關鍵在，「已經 _____16_____ 4,000 年的綠茶來治病……」。
(2)只有選(D)項的「have been using」放入空格，才符合現在完成進行式的文法規定。

17. 題句：在綠茶裡的一種化合物會 _____17_____ 癌細胞的成長。
　　選項：(A) looks after 照料　(B) slows down 減慢　(C) takes over 接手　(D) turns out 變成

解析
(1)答題關鍵在「在綠茶裡的一種化合物會 _____17_____ 癌細胞的成長」。
(2)只有(B)選項的「減慢」放入空格，才是符合題意的正確選項。

18. 題句：Green tea is also helpful _____18_____ infection and damaged immune function.
　　選項：(A) for 為　(B) from 從　(C) at 在　(D) inside 裡邊

解析
(1)答題關鍵在「Green tea is also helpful _____18_____ infection and damaged immune function」。
(2)只有選(A)項的「for」放入空格，才是符合題意的正確選項。

19. 題句：他們的 _____19_____ 在於處理過程。
　　選項：(A) weight 重量　(B) purpose 目的　(C) difference 不同之處　(D) structure 結構

解析
(1)答題關鍵在「他們的 _____19_____ 在於處理過程」。
(2)只有(C)選項的「不同之處」放入空格，才是符合題意的正確選項。

20. 題句：That is _____20_____ green tea is so good for health.
　　(A) whether 是否　(B) whenever 何時　(C) what 什麼　(D) why 為什麼

解析
(1)答題關鍵在 「That is _____20_____ green tea is so good for health」。
(2)只有(D)選項的「why」放入空格，才符合「That is way」的正確選項。

　　A wise woman traveling in the mountains found a precious stone. The next day she met another traveler who was hungry. The wise woman generously opened her bag to _____21_____ her food with the traveler. When the hungry traveler saw the precious stone, he asked her to give it to him. The woman did _____22_____ without hesitation. The traveler left, rejoicing.

　　一名聰明婦女在山中旅行時撿到一塊寶石。第二天她遇見一名飢餓的旅遊者。聰明的婦女慷慨地打開她的包包與旅遊者 _____21_____ 她的食品。當飢餓的旅遊者看見寶石時，要求她把寶石送給他。該婦女毫不猶豫地 _____22_____ 。旅遊者高興地離開。

If he sold the stone, he thought, he _____23_____ enough money for the rest of his life. But in a few days he came back to find the woman. When he found her, he said, "I know how valuable this stone is, but I'm giving it back to you, _____24_____ that you can give me something even more precious. You gave me the stone without asking for anything _____25_____ .Please teach me what you have in your heart that makes you so generous."

　　如果他出售這塊寶石，他這一輩子都會 _____23_____ 足夠的錢。但是在幾天之後他回來找到了那婦女。，他說，「我知道這塊石頭多麼有價值，但是我要把它還給你，_____24_____ 你能給我更寶貴的東西。當初你給我石頭時並沒要求任何 _____25_____ 。請教教我，你的內心有些什麼會讓妳那麼慷慨」。

21. 題句：打開她的包包與旅遊者 _____21_____ 她的食品
　　選項：(A) give給　(B) bring攜帶　(C) share分享　(D) earn賺取
    解析
　(1)答題關鍵在「與旅遊者 _____21_____ 她的食品」。
　(2)只有(D)選項的「分享」放入空格，才是符合題意的正確選項。

22. 題句：該婦女毫不猶豫地 _____22_____ 。
　　選項：(A) so 因此　(B) such 如此　(C) as 當　(D) thus 因此
    解析
　(1)答題關鍵在「該婦女毫不猶豫地 _____22_____ 」。
　(2)只有(A)選項的「so」放入空格，才是符合題意的正確選項。

23. 題句：如果他出售這塊寶石，他這一輩子都會 _____23_____ 足夠的錢。
　　選項：(A) had 過去式的有　(B) had had 過完式的有　(C) would have 現在式的有
　　　　　(D) would have had 假設語氣的過去事實
    解析
　(1)答題關鍵在「他這一輩子都會 _____23_____ 足夠的錢」。
　(2)只有(C)選項的「would have」放入空格，才是符合題意的正確選項。

24. 題句：_____24_____ that you can give me something even more precious.
　　　(A) hope 希望　(B) hoping 動名詞　(C) hoped 過去式　(D) to hope 不定詞

解析
(1)答題關鍵在「_____24_____ that you can give me something...」。
(2)只有(B)選項的「Hoping」放入空格，才符合「動名詞當主詞」的文法規定。

25. 題句：當初你給我石頭時並沒要求任何_____25_____

　　　選項：(A) on leave 請假　(B) by surprise 驚喜　(C) off record 非正式的　(D) in return 回報

解析
(1)答題關鍵在「當初你給我石頭時並沒要求任何_____25_____」。
(2)只有(D)選項的「回報」放入空格，才是符合題意的正確選項。

　　Prague, the capital of the Czech Republic, is a very beautiful city. Situated on both banks of the winding River Vltava, Prague is like one big open-air museum. _____26_____ some six hundred years of architecture nearly untouched by natural disaster or war, the city retains much of its medieval appearance. _____27_____ you go, there are buildings in Romanic, Baroque, and Rococo styles that were popular hundreds of years ago. All of them successfully _____28_____ the destruction of postwar redevelopment and remained unchanged. While the Iron Curtain was still in place under the communist government, Prague was _____29_____ visited by foreigners. Since the 1990s, _____30_____ all that has changed. Prague is now one of the most popular tourist attractions in Europe.

　　布拉格，捷克共和國的首都，是一座非常美麗的城市。位於蜿蜒沃他瓦河的兩岸，布拉格看起來象一座大型的戶外博物館。一些_____26_____600年歷史的古建築，沒有遭受天災或戰爭的破壞。城市盡量保留它的中世紀風貌。_____27_____你走到那裡，都會看到數百年前流行的羅馬式、巴洛克與洛克克式等建築。所有這些都幸運地_____28_____戰火的破壞，保留原樣不變。

　　在以前的鐵幕共產時代，_____29_____外國人造訪布拉格。然而，從20世紀90年代_____30_____，所有的都改變了。布拉格現在是歐洲最受歡迎的旅遊勝地之一。

26. 題句：_____26_____ some six hundred years of architecture
　　選項：(A) For 為　(B) With 有　(C) Upon 由於　(D) Along 沿著

解析
(1)答題關鍵在「some six hundred years...」。
(2)只有(B)選項的「with 有」放入空格，才符合 with 的正確用法。

27. 題句：_____27_____ you go, there are buildings in Romanic...
　　選項：(A) Since 自從　(B) Before 之前　(C) Whatever 不論什麼　(D) Wherever 不論何處

解析

(1)關鍵字在「you go」。

(2)只有選(D)項的「wherever」連成 wherever you go「不論你走到何處」才是正確答案。

28. 題句：All of them successfully_____28_____ the destruction of postwar
選項：(A) escaped 逃過、避過　(B) featured 有特色　(C) defended 防衛　(D) inspired 受啓發

解析

(1)答題關鍵在「destruction of postwar...」。

(2)只有(A)選項的「逃過、避過」放入空格，才是符合整句題意的正確選項。

29. 題句：Prague was _____29_____ visited by foreigners.
選項：　(A) ever 以前　(B) seldom 很少　(C) nearly 近於　(D) wholly 全部

解析

(1)答題關鍵在「visited by foreigners」。

(2)只有(B)選項的「seldom」放入空格，才是符合整句題意的正確選項。

30. 題句：Since the 1990s, _____30_____ all that has changed.
選項：(A) afterwards 之後　(B) therefore 所以　(C) however 然而　(D) furthermore 而且

解析

(1)答題關鍵在「空格左右兩邊的兩句」。

(2)只有(C)選項的「however」放入空格，才符合「however 當連接詞的用法」的文法規定。

三、文意選填（10%）

說明：第 31 至 40 題，每題一個空格，請依文意在文章後所提供的(A) 到 (J) 選項中分別選出最適當者，並將其英文字母代號標示在答案卡之「選擇題答案區」。每題答對得 1 分，答錯不倒扣。

One day, a guru foresaw in a vision what he would be in his next life. Then he called his favorite disciple and asked him, "What would you do to thank me for all you have received from me?" The disciple said he would do whatever his guru asked him to do. Having received this _____31_____, the guru said, "Then this is what I'd like you to do for me. I've just _____32_____ that I'll die very soon and I'm going to be reborn as a pig. Do you see that sow eating garbage there in the yard? I'm going to be the fourth piglet of its next litter. You'll _____33_____ me by a mark on my brow. After that sow gives birth, find the fourth piglet with a mark on its brow and, with one _____34_____ of your knife, slaughter it. I'll be _____35_____ from a pig's life. Will you do this for me?"

The disciple felt sad to hear this, but he agreed to do as he was told. Soon after their

_____36_____ , the guru died and the sow did have a litter of four little pigs. Then the disciple _____37_____ his knife and picked out the little pig with a mark on its brow. When he was about to cut its throat, the little pig suddenly _____38_____ , "Stop!" Before the disciple could recover from the _____39_____ of hearing the little pig speak in a human voice, it continued, "Don't kill me. I want to live on as a pig. When I asked you to kill me, I didn't know what a pig's life would be _____40_____ . It's great! Just let me go".

　　有一天，一名印度教導師看到了他未來生命裡的樣子。然後他打電話給他最喜愛的弟子並且問他，「你要怎麼謝我你從我這裡所學到的全部？」弟子說他將會做到導師要他做的任何事情。得到這個 _____31_____ 後，導師繼續說：「以下就是我要你為我做的事：我剛剛才 _____32_____ 我很快就會死，然後投胎為豬。你有看到那頭母豬在院子裡吃垃圾嗎？我將會是他的下一窩仔豬裡的第4頭小豬。你會看到我眉上的標記 _____33_____ 我。在母豬分娩之後，找到那頭眉上有記號的仔豬，用你的刀子_____34_____ 殺了牠。這樣我就可以 _____35_____ 繼續當做豬。你會幫我這個忙嗎？」

　　聽到這麼說這名弟子很悲哀，但是他同意導師的要求去做。就在他們 _____36_____ 之後，導師死了，而母豬確實生出一窩有4隻的仔豬。然後弟子 _____37_____ 他的刀，挑出那隻眉上有標記的小豬。當他正要割斷小豬的咽喉時，小豬突然 _____38_____ ，「停止！」在弟子還沒有能從小豬講人話的_____39_____ 中恢復過來之前，牠繼續說，「不要殺死我。我還是想要繼續當作豬活下去。先前當我要求你殺死我時，我並不知道豬的生活是 _____40_____ 樣子。太棒了！就讓我去吧。」

(A) shock 驚嚇　　(B) conversation 談話　　(C) like 像什麼　　(D) promise 承諾

(E) released 豁免　　(F) screamed 大聲尖叫　　(G) learned 獲知　　(H) recognize 認出

(I) stroke 劃一下　　(J) sharpened 磨利

31. 題句：得到這個 _____31_____ 後，導師繼續說……

解析
(1)答題關鍵在 「得到這個 _____31_____ 後」。
(2)只有(D) 選項的「承諾」放入空格，才是符合題意的正確選項。

32. 題句：我剛才 _____32_____ 我很快就會死，

解析
(1)答題關鍵在「剛才 _____32_____ 我很快就會死，」。
(2)只有(F) 選項的「獲知」放入空格，才是符合題意的正確選項。
(3)I have learned … 中譯為「我剛才獲知……」之意。

33. 題句：你會看到我眉上的標記 _____33_____ 我。

解析

(1) 答題關鍵在「你會看到我眉上的標記 _____33_____ 我。」。

(2) 只有(H)選項的「認出」放入空格，才是符合題意的正確選項。

34. 題句：用你的刀子 _____34_____ 殺了牠。

解析

(1)答題關鍵在「用你的刀子 _____34_____ 殺了牠。」。

(2)只有(D)選項的「劃一下」放入空格，才是符合題意的正確選項。

35. 題句：這樣我就可以 _____35_____ 繼續當做豬

解析

(1)答題關鍵在「我就可以 _____35_____ 繼續當做豬」。

(2)只有(E)選項的「豁免」放入空格，才是符合題意的正確選項。

36. 題句：就在他們 _____36_____ 之後，導師死了

解析

(1)答題關鍵在「就在他們 _____36_____ 之後，導師死了」。

(2)只有(B)選項的「對話」放入空格，才是符合題意的正確選項。

37. 題句：然後弟子 _____37_____ 他的刀……

解析

(1)答題關鍵在「然後弟子 _____37_____ 他的刀……」。

(2)只有(J)選項的「磨利」放入空格，才是符合題意的正確選項。

38. 題句：小豬突然 _____38_____ ，「停止！」

解析

(1)答題關鍵在「停止」。

(2)只有(F)選項的「大聲尖叫」放入空格，才是符合題意的正確選項。

39. 題句：還沒有能從小豬講人話的 _____39_____ 中恢復過來之前

解析

(1)答題關鍵在「還沒有能從小豬講人話的 _____39_____ 中恢復過來之前」。

(2)只有(A)選項的「驚嚇」放入空格，才是符合題意的正確選項。

40. 題句：先前當我要求你殺死我時，我並不知道豬的一生是＿＿＿＿40＿＿＿＿樣子

解析

⑴答題關鍵在「我並不知道豬的一生是＿＿＿＿40＿＿＿＿樣子」。

⑵只有 (D) 選項的「like」放入空格，才是符合題意的正確選項。

⑶what a pig's life would be like. 中譯為豬的一生是什麼樣子
　　　　　　　　　　　　　　＝豬隻過什麼樣的生活

四、閱讀測驗（32%）

> 說明：第 41 至 56 題，每題請分別根據各篇文章之文意選出最適當的一個選項，標示在
> 答案卡之「選擇題答案區」。每題答對得 2 分，答錯不倒扣。

41-44 為題組

Howler monkeys are named for the long loud cries, or howls, that they make every day. They are the loudest land animal and their howls can be heard three miles away through dense forests. Male howler monkeys use their loud voices to fight for food, mates, or territory. Everyone starts and ends the day by howling to check out where their nearest competitors are.

吼猴是因有又長又大的吼叫聲而得名，他們每天都會吼叫。他們是陸上叫聲最大的動物，而牠們的吼叫聲在濃密森林三哩外的地方都聽得到。公吼猴利用牠們的吼聲來搶食物、交配或爭地盤。每隻吼猴在清晨與黃昏都會用吼叫聲來查出最接近的競爭者在哪裡。

Interestingly, when there are few howler monkeys in an area, the howling routine takes on a different pattern. In Belize, where howler monkeys were newly reintroduced into a wildlife sanctuary, the howler monkeys were heard only a few times a week rather than every day.

Apparently, with plenty of space and no other howler monkeys around, there was no need to check on the whereabouts of their competitors.

有趣的是，一個地區如果吼猴不多時，吼叫的模式會不一樣。在貝里斯，在那裡吼猴是最近才被引進到某一個野生動物禁獵區，這些吼猴一周才吼叫幾次而不是每天吼叫。

顯然，在很大的空間且附近沒有其他吼猴出現，沒有必要檢查他們的競爭者在哪裡。

At the sanctuary, keepers now use recorded howler sounds from a distance so that the monkeys feel the need to make the territorial calls as they would do in the wild. In the future when the population grows, there will be no need for the recording because the howler monkeys will have more reason to check in with the neighbors to define their own territories.

在禁獵區，動物管理人使用預錄的吼猴聲，拿到遠處播放，使園區裡的這些猴子感到，還是有必要像在荒野一樣的吼叫。將來，區內的吼猴數量增加時，就不會再用預錄的聲音，到時眾多的吼猴有更多的理由去清查競爭者與地盤。

41. Why do howler monkeys howl?

吼猴為什麼吼叫？

(A) To claim their territory.

聲稱他們的地盤。

(B) To check how popular they are.

查看他們有多麼受歡迎。

(C) To tell others they are going to leave.

告訴它猴他們將要離開。

(D) To show friendliness to their neighbors.

向鄰居表示友好。

解析

從答題關鍵的「公吼猴利用牠們的吼聲來搶食物、交配或爭地盤」可看出，只有 (A) 選項的「聲稱他們的地盤」才是符合題意的正確選項。

42. Why did the howler monkeys in Belize howl less often?

吼猴為什麼在貝里斯吼叫的次數少？

(A) They lived too close to each other.

他們住得太接近。

(B) There was enough food for all of them.

他們有足夠的食物。

(C) There were no other competitors around.

在周遭沒有其他競爭者。

(D) They were not used to the weather there.

他們不習慣當地天氣。

解析

從答題關鍵的「在很大的空間且附近沒有其他吼猴出現，沒有必要檢查他們的競爭者在哪裡。」可看出，只有 (C) 選項的「在周遭沒有其他競爭者。」才是符合題意的正確選項。

43. Why do the keepers at the sanctuary use recorded howls?

在園區的看護人為什麼用預錄吼猴聲？

(A) To prevent the howler monkeys from getting homesick.

不讓吼猴有思家之苦。

(B) To help howler monkeys maintain their howling ability.

為了幫助吼猴保持吼叫的能力。

(C) To trick the monkeys into the belief that there is plenty of space around.

誘騙猴子周遭土地空間很大。

(D) To teach the monkeys how to make the loudest cries to scare people away.

教猴子怎樣叫出最大聲來嚇人。

解析

從答題關鍵的「使園區裡的這些猴子感到，還是有必要像在荒野一樣的吼叫。」可看出，只有(B)選項的「為了幫助吼猴保持吼叫的能力。」才是符合題意的正確選項。

44. According to the passage, which of the following is true about howler monkeys?

根據本文，如下內容中哪項關於吼猴說法才是屬實？

(A) They howl most often at noon.

他們最常在中午吼叫。

(B) They originally came from Belize.

他們最初來自貝里斯。

(C) People can hear their howls three miles away.

人們在 3 英里外就能聽到吼猴叫聲。

(D) Female monkeys howl to protect their babies.

母猴吼叫來保護嬰兒。

解析

從答題關鍵的「牠們的吼叫聲在濃密森林三哩外的地方都聽得到。」可看出，只有 (C) 選項的「人們在 3 英里外就能聽到吼猴叫聲。」才是正確選項。

45-48為題組

After the creation of the Glacier National Park in Montana, the growing number of park visitors increased the need for roads. Eventually, the demand for a road across the mountains led to the building of the Going-to-the-Sun Road. The construction of the Going-to-the-Sun Road was a huge task. After 11 years of work, the final section of the road was completed in 1932. The road is considered an engineering feat. Even today, visitors to the park marvel at how such a road could have been built. It is one of the most scenic roads in North America.

The construction of the road has changed the way visitors experience the Glacier National Park. Visitors now can drive over sections of the park that previously took days of horseback riding to see. Just across the border, in Canada, is the Waterton Lakes National Park. In 1931, members of the Rotary Clubs of Alberta and Montana suggested joining the two parks as a symbol of peace and friendship between the two countries. In 1932, the United States and Canadian governments renamed the parks the Waterton-Glacier International Peace Park, the world's first. More recently, the parks have received several international honors. They were named as a World Heritage Site in 1995. This international recognition highlights the importance of this area, not just to the United States and Canada, but to the entire world.

在蒙大拿有了冰河國家公園之後，日益增多的公園訪客數量使當地道路需求增加。最後，會需要一條穿過山脈的道路，導致「通向太陽之路」的興建。通向太陽之

路是一項巨大工程。施工 11 年之後，道路的末段部分在 1932 年完工。這條道路被認爲爲一項英勇工程。即使今天，去公園訪客對還感到驚訝，這樣的道路是怎麼建造起來的。這是在北美洲風景最美的道路之一。

　　道路的建設已經改變參觀者觀賞冰河國家公園的方式。參觀者現在已能開車越過以前要騎馬好幾天才看得到的公園景色。只需穿過邊境，在加拿大這一邊是沃特頓湖國家公園。在 1931 年，亞伯特和蒙大拿的扶輪社會員建議，結合這兩個國家公園，作爲在兩個國家之間的一個和平和友誼的象徵。到了 1932 年，美國和加拿大政府給公園重新命名沃特頓冰河國際和平公園，世界的第一個這一類公園。近年來，公園已經獲得幾種國際榮譽，在 1995 年被列爲世界文化遺產。這個國際榮譽強調的是這個地區的重要性，不屬美國和加拿大，而是屬於全世界。

45. What made it necessary to build a road through the Glacier National Park?

爲什麼要穿過冰河國家公園建造道路？

(A) There were too many parks in Montana.

在蒙大拿有太多公園。

(B) The park was not sunny enough for visitors.

公園對參觀者來說不夠晴朗。

(C) The existing mountain roads were destroyed.

現有的山區道路被破壞。

(D) More visitors were interested in going to the park.

更多的參觀者有興趣去公園。

解析

根據文章內容，只有(D)選項的「更多的參觀者有興趣去公園。」才是符合題意的正確選項。

46. How has the Going-to-the-Sun Road influenced the way people experience the Glacier National Park?

「通向太陽之路」怎樣影響人們觀賞冰河國家公園的方式？

(A) The scenery along the road is too beautiful for visitors to drive carefully.

沿著道路的風景太美麗，參觀者無法小心駕駛。

(B) It has become a marvelous experience for people to ride horses on this road.

人們在這條道路上騎馬賞景已成爲一種奇妙的經驗。

(C) The road has allowed people to see more of the park in a shorter period of time.

道路的便捷使人們在更短的時間期看到更多的公園美景。

(D) The transportation on the road was so difficult that few people could really enjoy the trip.

在道路上的運輸很困難以致很少人能眞正享受旅行的樂趣。

從答題關鍵的「參觀者現在已能開車越過以前要騎馬好幾天才看得到的公園景色。」可看出，只有 (C) 選項的「道路的便捷使人們在更短的時間期看到更多的公園美景。」才是符合題意的正確選項。

47. What does "an engineering feat" mean?

是指何意？

(A) A big success in construction.

建築史上的大成功。

(B) A magical building machine.

一台有魔法的造路機。

(C) A great disaster for the travelers.

對旅遊者的大災難。

(D) An enjoyable process for engineers.

給工程師的愉快過程。

根據文章內容，只有 (A) 選項的「建築史上的大成功。」才是符合題意的正確選項。

48. What is special about the Waterton-Glacier International Peace Park?

沃特頓冰河國際和平公園有何特別？

(A) It is where the glacier runs to the lake.

冰河在此流向湖泊。

(B) It is the first park funded by the whole world.

這是被全世界提供資金的第一個公園。

(C) It is a special park built to protect wild animals.

它是一個特別的公園建造來保護野生動物。

(D) It is composed of two parks located in two countries.

它由兩個國家的兩個公園組成。

從答題關鍵的「到了 1932 年，美國和加拿大政府給公園重新命名沃特頓冰河國際和平公園，世界的第一個這一類公園。」可看出，只有 (D) 選項的「它由兩個國家的兩個公園組成。」才是符合題意的正確選項。

49-52 為題組

　　Ice sculpting is a difficult process. First, ice must be carefully selected so that it is suitable for sculpting. Its ideal material is pure, clean water with high clarity. It should also have the minimum amount of air bubbles. Perfectly clear ice blocks weighing 140 kg and measuring 100 cm × 50 cm × 25 cm are available from the Clinebell Company in Colorado. Much larger clear blocks are produced in Europe and Canada or harvested from a frozen river in Sweden. These large ice blocks are used for large ice sculpting events and for building ice hotels.

冰雕是一個艱難的過程。首先，必須仔細挑選適於雕刻的冰塊。它的理想材料不要有雜質、乾淨透明的水。它也應該有最小數量的氣泡。完全的冰塊重 140 公斤，尺寸約 100 公分 × 50 公分 × 25 公分，這些都來自科羅拉多的 Clinebell 公司。超大且透明的冰塊產自歐洲與加拿大或來自瑞典的結冰河川。這些超大冰塊用於大規模的冰雕場合或用來建設冰凍旅館。

Another difficulty in the process of ice sculpting is time control. The temperature of the environment affects how quickly the piece must be completed to avoid the effects of melting. If the sculpting does not take place in a cold environment, then the sculptor must work quickly to finish his piece. The tools used for sculpting also affect when the task can be accomplished. Some sculptures can be completed in as little as ten minutes if power tools are used. Ice sculptors also use razor-sharp chisels that are specifically designed for cutting ice. The best ice chisels are made in Japan, a country that, along with China, has a long tradition of magnificent ice sculptures.

另一個冰雕過程中的困難是時間的控制。環境的溫度影響冰雕必須在多少時間內完成，以避免融化掉。如果雕刻不在低溫的環境裡進行，那麼雕刻師必須快速完成他的作品。用於雕刻的工具也會影工作進度。如果使用電動工具，有些雕刻品可能在10分鐘內就可完成。冰雕師也會用像剃刀那樣鋒利的鑿刀，用來切割特定花樣。最好的冰雕鑿刀產自日本，跟中國一樣，都有冰雕悠久傳統。

Ice sculptures are used as decorations in some cuisines, especially in Asia. When holding a dinner party, some large restaurants or hotels will use an ice sculpture to decorate the table. For example, in a wedding banquet it is common to see a pair of ice-sculpted swans that represent the union of the new couple.

冰雕作品多半用做爲菜餚的裝飾品，特別是亞洲。當舉行晚宴時，一些大的餐廳或者飯店將使用冰雕品來裝飾桌子。例如，在婚宴場合用一對冰雕天鵝是很普遍的，牠們代表新婚夫婦的結合。

49. What kind of ice is ideal for sculpting?

哪種冰做冰雕最理想？

(A) Ice from ice hotels.

來自冰飯店的冰。

(B) Ice from clean water.

來自淨水的冰。

(C) Ice with lots of bubbles in it.

裡頭有很多水泡的冰。

(D) Ice weighing over 100 kilograms.

重量超過 100 公斤的冰。

解析

從答題關鍵的「它的理想材料不要有雜質、乾淨透明的水。」可看出，只有 (B) 選項的「來自淨水的冰」才是符合題意的正確選項。

50. Why is ice sculpting difficult?

冰雕為什麼很難？

(A) It is hard to control the size and shape of the ice.

不容易控制冰的大小與形狀。

(B) The right theme for ice sculpting is not easy to find.

不容易找到冰雕的的正確主題。

(C) The appropriate tools are only available in some countries.

只有某些國家才有合適的工具。

(D) It is not easy to find the right kind of ice and work environment.

不容易找到合適的冰塊與工作環境。

解析

根據文章內容，只有 (D) 選項的「不容易找到合適的冰塊與工作環境。」才是符合題意的正確選項。

51. What is paragraph 3 mainly about?

第 3 段落的大意為何？

(A) The uses of ice sculptures.

冰雕品的用途。

(B) The places where ice is sculpted.

冰塊被雕刻的地方。

(C) The quality of ice sculptures.

冰雕的品質。

(D) The origin of ice sculpting parties.

冰雕聚會的起源。

解析

根據文章第3段內容來看，只有(A)選項的「冰雕品的用途。」才是符合題意的正確選項。

52. Which of the following statements is true about the process of sculpting ice?

有關冰雕過程，下列陳述哪項為真？

(A) It takes more time to carve with razor-sharp chisels.

用剃刀式鑿刀雕刻須花更多的時間。

(B) It can be finished in 10 minutes if the right tools are used.

如果使用合適的工具，可能在 10 分鐘內完成冰雕。

(C) Larger blocks of ice from Sweden are easier to handle for sculptors.

來自瑞典的大型冰塊使雕刻師更容易於處理。

(D) The carver must work fast in a cold environment to avoid catching cold.

雕刻師在冰冷的環境裡工作動作要快以免感冒。

解析

從答題關鍵的「如果使用電動工具，有些雕刻品可能在10分鐘內就可完成。」可看出，只有(B)選項的「如果使用合適的工具，可能在10分鐘內完成冰雕。」才是符合題意的正確選項。

53-56 為題組

beforehand that the pain won't be so bad, you might not suffer as much. According to a recent study, the part of your brain that reacts to severe pain is largely the same part that reacts to expectation of pain. Researchers in this study worked with 10 volunteers, ages 24 to 46. Each volunteer wore a device that gave out 20-second-long pulses of heat to the right leg. There were three levels of heat, producing mild, moderate, or strong pain. During training, the volunteers would first hear a tone, followed by a period of silence, and then feel a heat pulse. They then learned to associate the length of the silent pause with the intensity of the upcoming heat pulse. The longer the pause, the stronger the heat pulse would be, causing more severe pain.

如果你的手指破觸到熱爐，那會很痛。不過，如果你事先說服你自己，疼痛不會那麼糟，你可能就不會那麼痛苦。根據一項最近的研究，你大腦內反應劇痛的部分，與想像會很痛的部分基本上兩者是相同的部分。研究人員與 10 位志願者合作，年齡 24 到 46 歲。每位志願者穿一套能夠傳遞 20 秒長振動熱度到右腿的裝置，有三種等級的熱，會產生溫和、適度、或強烈的疼痛。這期間志願者會先聽到一個音調，隨後會寂靜一段時間，然後感到熱振動。他們然後要學習處理靜止的長度，與即將到來的熱脈衝的強度。 靜止時間越長，熱脈衝越強，疼痛越劇烈。

A day or two later, the real experiment began. The researchers found that the parts of the brain involved in learning, memory, emotion, and touch became more active as the volunteers expected higher levels of pain. These were mainly the same areas that became active when participants actually felt pain. Interestingly, when the volunteers expected only mild or moderate pain but experienced severe pain, they reported feeling 28 percent less pain than when they expected severe pain and actually got it. The new study emphasizes that pain has both physical and psychological elements. Understanding how pain works in the mind and brain could eventually give doctors tools for helping people cope with painful medical treatments.

一兩天後，真正的實驗開始。那些研究人員發現，當那些志願者想像會更痛時，他們大腦內負責學習、記憶、情感與觸覺的部分，活動變得更積極。 這與參加者實際感到痛苦時的腦部反應是同一部分。有趣的是，當那些志願者只期待溫和或適度痛苦時，卻也會感到劇痛。當他們期待劇痛也實際感到劇痛時，他們的報告卻顯示有百分之28的較少疼痛。新研究強調痛苦有身體和心理兩要素。了解疼痛怎樣在精神上與大腦裡運作，在將來會讓醫師做些有助人們處理疼痛醫療之事。

53. What is the main idea of the passage?

本文的大意是什麼？

(A) We should learn to be sensitive to pain.

我們應該學習對痛苦敏感些。

(B) Our feeling of pain is decided by our environment.

我們對痛苦的感覺由週遭環境決定。

(C) How people feel pain remains unknown to scientists.

人們怎樣感到疼痛在科學上還是未知。

(D) Our reaction to pain is closely related to our expectation of pain.

我們對疼痛的反應與我們對疼痛預期密切相關。

解析

根據文章內容，只有 (D) 選項的「我們對疼痛的反應與我們對疼痛預期密切相關。」才是本文大意。

54. Which of the following is true about the pulses of heat in the study?

如下內容中的哪些在研究過程中關於熱脈衝是真實的？

(A) Each heat pulse lasted for 20 seconds.

每一熱脈衝持續20秒。

(B) The pulses were given to the arms of the volunteers.

脈衝被傳到那些志願者的手臂。

(C) Different devices gave out different levels of heat pulses.

不同的設備發出熱漲落的不同的水準。

(D) There were two levels of heat intensity given to the volunteers.

有給那些志願者的熱強度的兩步。

解析

從答題關鍵的「每位志願者穿一套能夠傳遞 20 秒長振動熱度到右腿的裝置」可看出，只有 (A) 選項的「每一熱脈衝持續 20 秒。」才是符合題意的正確選項。

55. How did the volunteers learn to expect different levels of heat?

那些志願者怎樣學習期待不同等級的熱度？

(A) From the loudness of the tone they heard.

從他們聽到音調的音量。

(B) From the instruction given to them by the researchers.

從研究人員給他們的指示。

(C) From the color of a light flashing on the device they wore.

從他們所穿裝置上閃燈的顏色。

(D) From the length of the pause between a tone and the heat pulse.

從音調和熱脈衝之間的中止長度。

解析

從答題關鍵的「他們然後要學習處理靜止的長度，與即將到來的熱脈衝的強度。」可看出，只有
(D) 選項的「從音調和熱脈衝之間的中止長度。」才是符合題意的正確選項。

56. According to the passage, what may be the author's advice to a doctor before a surgery?

根據本文，在手術作者對醫生的建議可能是什麼？

(A) To provide the patient with more pain killers.

為病患提供更多的止痛藥。

(B) To talk to the patient and ease his/her worries.

和病患交談以緩和他 / 她的耽心。

(C) To give the patient strong heat pulses beforehand.

事先給病患強壯的熱脈衝

(D) To emphasize the possible severe pain to the patient.

對病患強調可能的劇痛。

解析

從答題關鍵的「了解疼痛怎樣在精神上與大腦裡運作，在將來會讓醫師做些有助人們處理疼痛醫
療之事。」可看出，只有 (B) 選項的「和病患交談以緩和他 / 她的耽心。」才是符合題意的正確
選項。

第貳部分：非選擇題

一、翻譯題（8%）

說明：1. 請將以下兩句中文譯成正確而通順達意的英文，並將答案寫在「答案卷」上。
　　　2. 請依序作答，並標明題號。每題 4 分，共 8 分。

1. 聽音樂是一個你可以終生享受的嗜好。

解析

本題的重要字彙如下：

聽音樂 Listening to the music　是一個 is a / an　你可以 you may / can　終身享用的 enjoy the
lifetime　嗜好 a hobby

整句英譯

Listening to the music is a hobby that you may enjoy the livetime.

2. 但能彈奏樂器可以為你帶來更多的喜悦。

解析

本題的重要字彙如下：

但 but 能彈奏樂器 to be able to play musical instruments 可以 may / can 為你帶來 bring you 更多的喜悦 more joy

整句英譯

But it will bring you more joy if you are able to play musical instruments.

二、英文作文（20%）

說明：1. 依提示在「答案卷」上寫一篇英文作文。

　　　2. 文長 120 個單詞（words）左右。

提示：你（英文名字必須假設為 George 或 Mary）向朋友（英文名字必須假設為 Adam 或 Eve）借了一件相當珍貴的物品，但不慎遺失，一時又買不到替代品。請寫一封信，第一段說明物品遺失的經過，第二段則表達歉意並提出可能的解決方案。

請注意：為避免評分困擾，請使用上述提示的 George 或 Mary 在信末署名，<u>不得使用自己真實的中文或英文姓名</u>。

解析

(1) 先將題句內相關字詞寫出中譯：

借 borrow　　　　相當 pretty　　　　珍貴的 precious　　　物品 article　　但是 but

不慎遺失 lost it carelessly / by accident　　一時 in the meantime　　買不到 not able to buy

替代品 substitution / replacement　　表達歉意 to express one's apology　　提出 offer

可能的解決方案 possible solution

第一段：說明物品遺失的經過

　Dear Adam:

　I am terribly sorry that I have lost the camera that I borrowed from you last week. It was last weekend when my wife and I went to Taipei 101 for our wedding anniversary. we took quite a few pictures there, especially the largest damper in the world on the 88th floor. But when I wanted to take more pictures after we came down the ground floor, I suddenly realized that my camera has gone. And my wife said that she didn't see me carrying the camera ever since I came out the men's room on the 89th floor. I dashed back to the toilet, and even checked with the Lost & Found Desk. It wasn't my day, the camera has gone for sure.

　（親愛的亞當：）

　很抱歉我把上個禮拜向你借的照相機弄丟了。上一個週末我和我太太慶結婚週年去了台北 101 大樓，我們在那裡拍了很多照片，特別是 88 樓的全世界最大的阻尼。

但是當我們回到一樓想要再拍幾張照片時，我突然發現照相機不見了。我太太說我從 89 樓的男廁出來後就沒有看到我揹照相機。我趕快衝回廁所，甚至於也問了失物招領處的人，照相機確定被人檢走了。

I've checked with the camera shop, wish to buy you a new one but the clerk said the factory has stopped producing the model of your camera. In the meantime there is no way of getting the same model camera in Taiwan. Adam my friend, can I buy you the same brand but different model camera instead ? Hope to hear from you soon.

　　Your friend,

　　George

　　我去了相機店，想要買一台新的相機還你，但店員說工廠已停產你那一款相機了。而一時之間在台灣又買不到同款相機。亞當我的好友，我可否買一台同廠牌但不同款式的相機還給你呢？請儘快回覆。

　　你的好友　喬治　上

98 年學測（學科能力測驗）

第壹部分：選擇題（72分）

一、詞彙（15分）

説明：第 1 至 15 題，每題選出最適當的一個選項，標示在答案卡之「選擇題答案區」。每題答對得 1 分，答錯不倒扣。

1. Steve's description of the place was so ＿＿＿＿＿＿ that I could almost picture it in my mind.

   史蒂夫對該地方的描述相當 ＿＿＿＿＿＿ 我幾乎可以在我腦海中想像得到。

   (A) bitter 苦味　(B) vivid 生動　(C) sensitive 敏感　(D) courageous 英勇的

   解析

   (1)答題關鍵在題目空格左、右方的「描述相當」與「我幾乎可以」。

   (2)四個選項中，只有選(B)項的「生動」，才可有意義連成「描述相當生動我幾乎可以……」。

2. When people feel uncomfortable or nervous, they may ＿＿＿＿＿＿ their arms across their chests as if to protect themselves.

   當人們感到不舒服或緊張時，他們可能會在胸前 ＿＿＿＿＿＿ 雙臂好像來保護自己

   (A) toss 拋出　(B) fold 摺疊　(C) veil 戴面紗　(D) yield 出產

   解析

   (1)答題關鍵在題目空格右方的「在胸前」與「雙臂」。

   (2)四個選項中，只有選(B)項的「摺疊」，才可有意義連成「在胸前摺疊雙臂」。

3. The doors of these department stores slide open ＿＿＿＿＿＿ when you approach them. You don't have to open them yourself.

   當你踏觸到時百貨公司的門都是打開 ＿＿＿＿＿＿ 。你不必自己打開。

   (A) necessarily 必須地　(B) diligently 勤勉地　(C) automatically 自動地　(D) intentionally 有意地

   解析

   (1)答題關鍵在題目空格左方的「打開」。

   (2)四個選項中，只有選(C)項的「自動地」，才可有意義連成「那些門會自動打開」（自動打開的英文說法是「打開自動 open automatically」與中文順序想反）。

4. Nicole is a _____ language learner. Within a short period of time, she has developed a good command of Chinese and Japanese.

妮可是一個 _____ 的語言學習者。短期間內她就能流利地說華語和日語。

(A) convenient 方便　(B) popular 流行　(C) regular 規律的　(D) brilliant 優秀的

解析

(1)答題關鍵在題目空格右方的「語言學習者」。

(2)四個選項中，只有選(D)項的「優秀的」，才可有意義連成「是一個優秀的語言學習者」。

5. With rising oil prices, there is an increasing _____ for people to ride bicycles to work.

隨著油價的上升，騎腳踏車上班的人有增加的 _____ 。

(A) permit 允許　(B) instrument 工具　(C) appearance 出現　(D) tendency 趨勢

解析

(1)答題關鍵在題目空格左方的「增加的」。

(2)四個選項中，只有選(D)項的「趨勢」，才可有意義連成「……增加的趨勢」。

6. This information came from a very _____ source, so you don't have to worry about being cheated.

這消息來自 _____ 來源，你不用擔心被騙。

(A) reliable 可靠的　(B) flexible 有彈性的　(C) clumsy 笨拙的　(D) brutal 殘酷的

解析

(1)答題關鍵在題目空格左、右方的「來自」與「來源」。

(2)四個選項中，只有選(A)項的「可靠的」，才可有意義連成「來自可靠的來源」。

7. We hope that there will be no war in the world and that all people live in peace and _____ with each other.

希望世界上沒有戰爭而人們有和平的生活並且互相 _____ 相處。

(A) complaint 抱怨　(B) harmony 和諧　(C) mission 任務　(D) texture 結構

解析

(1)答題關鍵在題目空格左、右方的「互相」與「相處」。

(2)四個選項中，只有選(B)項的「和諧地」，才可有意義連成「互相和諧相處」。

8. To have a full discussion of the issue, the committee spent a whole hour _____ their ideas at the meeting.

為了對該議題有全面的討論，委員會花了整整一小時 _____ 他們的想法。

(A) depositing 寄存　(B) exchanging 交換　(C) governing 管理　(D) interrupting 干擾

解析

(1)答題關鍵在題目空格右方的「他們的想法」。

(2)四個選項中，只有選(B)項的「交換」，才可有意義連成「交換他們的想法」。

9. While adapting to western ways of living, many Asian immigrants in the US still try hard to
_____ their own cultures and traditions.

在適應西式生活的同時，很多移美的亞洲人仍努力地 _____ 他們自己的文化與傳統。

(A) volunteer 志願者　(B) scatter 分散　(C) preserve 保留　(D) motivate 有動機

解析

(1)答題關鍵在題目空格左、右方的「努力地」與「他們自己的」。

(2)四個選項中，只有選(C)項的「保留」，才可有意義連成「努力地保留他們自己的文化與傳統」。

10. With the worsening of global economic conditions, it seems wiser and more _____ to keep cash in the bank rather than to invest in the stock market.

有了全球經濟的惡化，在銀行存款比投資股票應該是比較 _____ 。

(A) sensible 明智的　(B) portable 手提的　(C) explicit 清楚地　(D) anxious 焦慮地

解析

(1)答題關鍵在題目空格左、右方的「比較」與「在銀行存款」 _____ 。

(2)四個選項中，只有選(A)項的「明智的」，才可有意義連成「在銀行存款……是比較明智的」。

11. Under the _____ of newly elected president Barack Obama, the US is expected to turn a new page in politics and economy.

在新當選的歐巴馬總統 _____ 之下，人們期待美國在政經方面會有新的做法。

(A) adoption 採用　(B) fragrance 香味　(C) identity 身分　(D) leadership 領導

解析

(1)答題關鍵在題目空格左、右方的「歐巴馬總統」與「之下」。

(2)四個選項中，只有選(D)項的「領導」，才可有意義連成「在歐巴馬總統領導之下……」。

12. Rapid advancement in motor engineering makes it _____ possible to build a flying car in the near future.

機動工程的快速進步 _____ 可能在不久將來就可以建造飛行車輛。

(A) individually 個別的　(B) narrowly 狹窄的　(C) punctually 準時地　(D) technically 技術上來說

解析

(1)答題關鍵在題目空格右方的「可能」。

(2)四個選項中，只有選 (D) 項的「技術上來說」，才可有意義連成「技術上來說有可能在不久的將來……」。

13. When you take photos, you can move around to shoot the target object from different _____ .

拍照時你可從不同的 _____ 拍攝影像。

(A) moods 心情　(B) trends 趨勢　(C) angles 角度　(D) inputs 輸入

解析

(1)答題關鍵在題目空格左方的「不同的」與「拍攝影像」。

(2)四個選項中，只有選 (C) 項的「角度」，才可有意義連成「從不同的角度拍攝影像」。

14. Students were asked to _____ or rewrite their compositions based on the teacher's comments.

學生被要求 _____ 或依老師的意見重寫作文。

(A) revise 修改　(B) resign 辭職　(C) refresh 使清新　(D) remind 提醒

解析

(1)答題關鍵在題目空格左、右方的「被要求」與「或依老師的意見」。

(2)四個選項中，只有選 (A) 項的「修改（作文）」，才可有意義連成「被要求修改或依老師的意見重寫作文」。

15. Besides lung cancer, another _____ of smoking is wrinkles, a premature sign of aging.

除了肺癌外，另一個吸菸的 _____ 是有皺紋，提前老化的現象。

(A) blessing 祝福　(B) campaign 活動　(C) consequence 後果　(D) breakthrough 突破

解析

(1)答題關鍵在題目空格左、右方的「另一個」與「吸菸的」。

(2)四個選項中，只有選 (C) 項的「後果」，才可有意義連成「另一個吸菸的後果是有皺紋」。

二、綜合測驗（15分）

說明：第 16 至 30 題，每題一個空格，請依文意選出最適當的一個選項，標示在答案卡之「選擇題答案區」。每題答對得 1 分，答錯不倒扣。

　　Art Fry was a researcher in the 3M Company. He was bothered by a small irritation every Sunday as he sang in the church choir. That is, after he _____16_____ his pages in the hymn book with small bits of paper, the small pieces would invariably fall out all over the floor. One day, an idea _____17_____ Art Fry. He remembered a kind of glue developed by a colleague that everyone thought _____18_____ a failure because it did not stick very well. He then coated the glue on a paper sample and found that it was not only a good bookmark, but it was great for writing notes. It would stay in place _____19_____ you wanted it to. Then you could remove it

_____20_____ damage. The resulting product was called the Post-it, one of 3M's most successful office products.

　　阿特・福萊是 3 M 公司的研究員。他每個星期日在教堂唱詩班唱歌時，都會有點困擾。 那就是， 在他用小紙片在唱詩書內 _____16_____ 頁數後，小紙片總是掉落滿地。有一天，阿特 _____17_____ 一個辦法。他記得一位同事開發的一種膠水，每人都認爲那 _____18_____ 一次敗筆，因爲它黏不牢。他之後將紙板樣品塗上膠並且發現它不但是一個好書簽，而且作筆記也很好用。它會黏在 _____19_____ 你想黏的地方，也可以把它拿下來 _____20_____ 損壞。這種有效的產品被叫作「方便貼」，是 3 M 最暢銷的辦公用品之一。

16. 題句：after he _____16_____ his pages in the hymn book with small bits of paper,
　　　　　在他用小紙片在唱詩書內 _____16_____ 頁數後，小紙片總是掉落滿地。
　　選項：(A) marked 做標記　(B) tore 撕毀　(C) served 保留　(D) took 攜帶

解析
依題意只有選(A)項的「做標記」（把某頁做標記之意）才是正確選項。

17. 題句：One day, an idea _____17_____ Art Fry.
　　　　　有一天，阿特 _____17_____ 。
　　選項：(A) threw at 投擲　(B) occurred to 有……想法　(C) looked down upon 看不起　(D) came up with 想出辦法

解析
(1)依題意只有選(B)項的「occurred to」才是正確選項。
(2)occurred to 爲「想起」之意。當及物動詞用時，其後受詞是「某人」。如 A good idea occurred to me.
(3)(D) 選項的 come up with 是陷阱選項，它與 occurred to 兩片語的差別是，前一片語之前，要有「人」的主詞，後一片語的人稱主詞，是放片語後當受詞。如： He came up with a good idea. 與 A good idea occurred to me.

**18. 題句：that everyone thought _____18_____ a failure because it did not stick very well.
　　　　　每個人都認爲那 _____18_____ 一次敗筆，因爲它黏不牢。
　　選項：(A) is 是　(B) was （過去式）　(C) will be （未來式）　(D) has been （現在完成式）

解析
(1)答題關鍵在連接詞 because 的前後兩個子句。 從屬子句已有 did not 二字。
(2)因此四選項中要選(B)項過去式動詞的 was，才是符合文法的正確選項。

**19. 題句：It would stay in place _____19_____ you wanted it to.

它會黏在 _____19_____ 你想黏的地方。

選項：(A) despite that 不管…… (B) rather than 而不是 (C) as long as 只要 (D) no matter what 不論什麼

解析

(1)空格左右方是兩個子句，需要連接詞放入空格。

(2)依題意只有選 (C) 項的從屬片語連接詞的「as long as只要」，才能有意義連成「只要你要它留（黏）在哪裡它就黏在哪裡」，才是正確選項。

20. 題句：Then you could remove it _____20_____ damage.

也可以把它拿下來 _____20_____ 損壞。

選項：(A) into 到……裡 (B) out of 自……離開 (C) within…… 之內 (D) without 不會、沒有

解析

依題意只有選(D)項的「不會、沒有」才是正確選項。

The pineapple, long a symbol of Hawaii, was not a native plant. _____21_____ , pineapples did not appear there until 1813. The pineapple was _____22_____ found in Paraguay and in the southern part of Brazil. Natives planted the fruit across South and Central America and in the Caribbean region, _____23_____ Christopher Columbus first found it. Columbus brought it, along with many other new things, back to Europe with him. From there, the tasty fruit _____24_____ throughout other parts of civilization. It was carried on sailing ships around the world because it was found to help prevent scurvy, a disease that often _____25_____ sailors on long voyages. It was at the end of one of these long voyages that the pineapple came to Hawaii to stay.

鳳梨，長久以來一直是夏威夷的象徵，但它不是本地植物。 _____21_____ 鳳梨直到1813年才出現在那裡。鳳梨 _____22_____ 巴拉圭與巴西南方。當地人在美國中、南部及加勒比海地區栽種鳳梨， _____23_____ 哥倫布首先發現了鳳梨。哥倫布帶了鳳梨與其他新奇的東西回歐洲。此後，這個可口的水果 _____24_____ 整個文明國度。載送鳳梨的船運一直不停因為鳳梨被發現可以預防壞血病，那是一種經常使長程航行船員 _____25_____ 疾病。這些長程航行最後把鳳梨運到夏威夷。

21. 題句：The pineapple... was not a native plant. _____21_____ , pineapples did not appear there until 1813.

它不是本地植物。 _____21_____ 鳳梨直到1813年才出現在那裡。

選項：(A) For example 舉例 (B) In fact 事實上 (C) As a result 結果 (D) Little by little 漸漸地

解析

依題意只有選(B)項的「事實上」才是正確選項。

22. 題句：The pineapple was _____22_____ found in Paraguay and in the southern part of Brazil.

鳳梨 _____22_____ 巴拉圭與巴西南方。

選項：(A) nearly 幾乎 (B) recently 最近地 (C) originally 原先、源自 (D) shortly 短時間

解析

依題意只有選(C)項的「原先、源自」才是正確選項。

**23. 題句：Natives planted the fruit across South and Central America and in the Caribbean region, _____23_____ Christopher Columbus first found it.

當地人在美國中、南部及加勒比海地區栽種鳳梨，_____23_____ 哥倫布首先發現了鳳梨。

選項：(A) that 那個 (B) what 什麼 (C) which 哪一 (D) where 何處

解析

(1)答題關鍵在空格左邊的前述詞也是地方副詞的 region 一字，其後接關係副詞 where。

(2)四個選項中，只有選(D)項、同時也是表示地方的關係副詞，才是符合文法的正確選項。

**24. 題句：From there, the tasty fruit _____24_____ throughout other parts of civilization.

此後，這個可口的水果 _____24_____ 整個文明國度。

選項：(A) spread 散布、普及 (B) to spread （不定詞） (C) should spread 應該散布

(D) will spread （未來式）

解析

依本題句是在敘述一件事實，所以選(A)項現在式動詞的「spread」才是正確選項。

25. 題句：it was found to help prevent scurvy, a disease that often _____25_____ sailors on long voyages.

鳳梨被發現可以預防壞血病，那是一種經常使長程航行船員 _____25_____ 疾病。

選項：(A) bothered 受困擾 (B) contacted 接觸 (C) suffered 受苦 (D) wounded 受傷

解析

依題意只有選(A)項的「受困擾」才是正確選項。

The Paralympics are Olympic-style games for athletes with a disability. They were organized for the first time in Rome in 1960. In Toronto in 1976, the idea of putting together different disability groups _____26_____ sports competitions was born. Today, the Paralympics are sports events for athletes from six different disability groups. They emphasize the participants' athletic achievements _____27_____ their physical disability. The games have grown in size gradually. The number of athletes _____28_____ in the Summer Paralympic Games has increased from 400 athletes from 23 countries in 1960 to 3,806 athletes from 136 countries in 2004.

The Paralympic Games have always been held in the same year as the Olympic Games. Since the Seoul 1988 Paralympic Games and the Albertville 1992 Winter Paralympic Games, they have also _____29_____ in the same city as the Olympics. On June 19, 2001, an agreement was signed between the International Olympic Committee and the International Paralympics Committee to keep this _____30_____ in the future. From the 2012 bid onwards, the city chosen to host the Olympic Games will also host the Paralympics.

　　殘障奧運會是殘障人士的奧運形式的競賽。這種比賽在 1960 年於羅馬第一次舉辦。1976 年在多倫多，_____26_____ 不同的殘障團體參加比賽的想法落實了。今天，殘奧會是由六種不同的殘障團體組成的比賽。他們強調參加者的運動成就，_____27_____ 他們的身體殘障。比賽規模逐漸擴大。_____28_____ 夏季殘奧會從 1960年的 23 個國家 400 名運動員增加到 2004 年的 136 個國家 3,806 名。

　　殘奧會都會與一般奧運會同年舉行。自 1988 年的首爾殘奧會與 1992 年的阿爾貝維爾的冬季殘奧會以來，1992 年冬季殘奧會，他們就改在與奧運會相同的城市_____29_____。到了 2001 年 6 月 19 日，一項由國際奧運會與國際殘奧會委員們簽署一項同意書，以後要繼續的舉辦這類 _____30_____。且自 2012 年以後被選為主辦奧運會的城市，也要同時舉辦殘奧會。

**26. 題句：the idea of putting together different disability groups _____26_____ sports competitions was born.

　　　　_____26_____ 不同的殘障團體參加比賽的想法落實了。

選項：(A) for 為了　(B) with 與　(C) as 當　(D) on 在……上

解析

依題意只有選(A)項的「for」（為了讓不同……參加之意）才是正確選項。

27. 題句：They emphasize the participants' athletic achievements _____27_____ their physical disability.

　　　　他們強調參加者的運動成就，_____27_____ 他們的身體殘障。

選項：(A) in terms of 就……而論　(B) instead of 取代、而不是　(C) at the risk of 冒……險　(D) at the cost of 以……為代價

解析

依題意只有選(B)項的「取代、而不是」才是正確選項。

**28. 題句：The number of athletes _____28_____ in the Summer Paralympic Games has increased....

選項：(A) participate 參加　(B) participated（過去式）　(C) participating（動名詞）　(D) to participate（不定詞）

解析

(1)依題意只有選(C)項的「participating」才是正確選項。

(2)參加者從1960年的多少人到2004年的多少人，已不是單純的過去式用法，因此，在緊接athletes（運動員）字後就用分詞片語「athletes participating in the Summer Paralympic...」來修飾athletes，所以(C)項的 participating 才是正確選項。

29. 題句：they have also _____29_____ in the same city as the Olympics 1992
　　　　1992年冬季殘奧會，他們就改在與奧運會相同的城市 _____29_____ 。
　　選項：(A) taken turns 輪流　(B) taken place 舉行　(C) taken off 脫下　(D) taken over 接管

解析

依題意只有選(B)項「舉行」才是正確選項。

30. 題句：International Olympic Committee and the International Paralympics Committee to keep this _____30_____ in the future.
　　　　將來，國際奧委會與國際輪椅奧運會都會保持這類的 _____30_____ 。
　　選項：(A) piece 一片　(B) deadline 最後期限　(C) date 日期　(D) practice 練習、訓練

解析

依題意只有選 (D) 項的「練習、訓練」才是正確選項。

三、文意選填（10分）

說明：第 31 至 40 題，每題一個空格，請依文意在文章後所提供的(A)到(J)選項中分別選出最適當者，並將其英文字母代號標示在答案卡之「選擇題答案區」。每題答對得 1 分，答錯不倒扣。

　　Familiar fables can be narrated differently or extended in interesting and humorous ways. The end of the famous fable of "The Tortoise and the Hare" is well known to all: the tortoise wins the race against the hare. The moral lesson is that slow and steady wins the race. We all have grown up with this popular version, but the _____31_____ fable can be extended with different twists. At the request of the hare, a second race is _____32_____ and this time, the hare runs without taking a rest and wins. The moral lesson is that _____33_____ and consistent will always beat slow and steady. Then it is the tortoise that _____34_____ the hare to a third race along a different route in which there is a river just before the final destination. This time, the tortoise wins the race because the hare cannot swim. The moral lesson is "First _____35_____ your strengths, and then change the playing field to suit them."

　　But the story continues. Both _____36_____ know their own drawbacks and limitations very well; therefore, they jointly decide to have one last race-not to decide who the winner or loser is, but just for their own pleasure and satisfaction. The two _____37_____ as a team. Firstly, the hare carries the tortoise on its back to the river. Then, the tortoise carries the hare and swims to the _____38_____ bank of the river. Lastly, the hare carries the tortoise again on its back. Thus they reach the _____39_____ line together. Overall, many moral lessons from the last match are highlighted. The most obvious one is the importance of _____40_____ . Another moral which also means a great deal is "competition against situations rather than against rivals."

　　熟悉的寓言可以有不同的詮釋，或者在有趣和幽默的模式裡誇張一些。著名寓言

「龜兔賽跑」的結局眾所皆知：烏龜贏得比賽。寓意所說的是，緩慢但穩定者贏！我們都是在這種版本的環境中長大。但是 ____31____ 寓言也會有不同的詮釋。應兔子的要求，第二場比賽 ____32____ ，這次，兔子沒有休息所以跑贏。寓意則是指 ____33____ 和一致性贏過緩慢與穩定。然後是烏龜 ____34____ 兔子要跑第三次比賽，但是路線不同，且在抵達終點前會有一條小河。這次，烏龜贏得比賽，因為兔子不能游泳。這則的寓意是「首先要 ____35____ 你的力量，然後改變運動場適應它」。

　　但是故事繼續著。兩個 ____36____ 都非常了解自己的缺點和限制；因此，他們共同決定有最後一場比賽不是用來決定誰勝誰敗，只要比賽快樂和滿意就好。這兩個 ____37____ 成為一個團隊。首先，兔子把烏龜背到河邊，然後，烏龜背著兔子游到 ____38____ 岸。最後，兔子再次背著烏龜。因此他們一同到達 ____39____ 線。總的來說，來自最後比賽的很多寓意被強調出來。最明顯的一種是 ____40____ 的重要性。另一種意義重大的寓意是，「為所處環境競爭而不是為對手競爭」。

(A) arranged 安排的　(B) challenges 挑戰　(C) competitors 競爭者
(D) cooperate 合作　(E) fast 快　(F) finishing 完成、終點　(G) identify 確認
(H) opposite 相反地　(I) same 相同　(J) teamwork 團隊

31. 題句：We all have grown up with this popular version, but the ____31____ fable can be extended with different twists.

　　　　但是 ____31____ 寓言也會有不同的詮釋。

解析

依題意只有選(I)項的「相同的」才是正確選項。

32. 題句：a second race is ____32____ and this time, the hare runs without taking a rest and wins.

　　　　應兔子的要求，第二場比賽 ____32____ 。

解析

依題意只有選(A)項的「被安排了」才是正確選項。

33. 題句：The moral lesson is that ____33____ and consistent will always beat slow and steady.

　　　　寓意則是指 ____33____ 和一致性贏過緩慢與穩定。

解析

依題意只有選(E)項的「快」才是正確選項。

34. 題句：Then it is the tortoise that _____34_____ the hare to a third race.
　　　　然後是烏龜 _____34_____ 兔子要跑第三次比賽。

解析

依題意只有選(B)項的「挑戰」才是正確選項。

35. 題句：Then it is the tortoise that _____34_____ the hare to a third race along a different route.
　　　　首先要 _____35_____ 你的力量，然後改變運動場適應它。

解析

依題意只有選(G)項的「確認」才是正確選項。

36. 題句：Both _____36_____ know their own drawbacks and limitations very well;
　　　　兩個 _____36_____ 都非常了解自己的缺點和限制。

解析

依題意只有選(C)項的「競爭者」才是正確選項。

37. 題句：The two _____37_____ as a team.
　　　　這兩個 _____37_____ 成為一個團隊。

解析

依題意只有選(D)項的「合作」才是正確選項。

38. 題句：The tortoise carries the hare and swims to the _____38_____ bank of the river.
　　　　然後，烏龜背著兔子游到 _____38_____ 岸。

解析

依題意只有選(H)項的「相反的」（即對岸之意）才是正確選項。

39. 題句：Thus they reach the _____39_____ line together.
　　　　因此他們一同到達 _____39_____ 線。

解析

依題意只有選(F)項的「完成」（終點線之意）才是正確選項。

40. 題句：The most obvious one is the importance of _____40_____.
　　　　最明顯的一種是 _____40_____ 的重要性。

解析

依題意只有選 (J) 項的「團隊配合」才是正確選項。

四、閱讀測驗（32分）

說明：第41至56題，每題請分別根據各篇文章之文意選出最適當的一個選項，標示在答案卡之「選擇題答案區」。每題答對得2分，答錯不倒扣。

41-44 為題組

To Whom It May Concern:

　　Your address was forwarded to us by Why Bother Magazine. All of us here think The International Institute of Not Doing Much is the best organization in the world. You know how to avoid unnecessary activities!

　　We closely followed the advice in your article. First, we replaced all our telephones with carrier pigeons. Simply removing the jingle of telephones and replacing them with the pleasant sounds of birds has had a remarkable effect on everyone. Besides, birds are cheaper than telephone service. After all, we are a business. We have to think of the bottom line. As a side benefit, the birds also fertilize the lawn outside the new employee sauna.

　　Next, we sold the computers off to Stab, Grab, Grit, and Nasty, a firm of lawyers nearby. Our electricity bill went way down. Big savings! The boss is impressed. We have completely embraced paper technology. Now that we all use pencils, doodling is on the increase, and the quality of pencilwomanship is impressive, as you can tell from my handwriting in this letter. By the way, if you can, please send this letter back to us. We can erase and reuse it. Just tie it to **Maggie**'s leg and she'll know where to take it.

　　Now it's very calm and quiet here. You can notice the difference. No more loud chatter on the telephones! All we hear is the scratching of pencil on paper, the sound of pigeons, and the delivery of inter-office correspondence by paper airplane.

　　Wonderful! I've always wanted to work for an insurance company ever since I was a little girl. Now it's perfect.

　　Sincerely yours,

　　Eleanor Lightly

　　Spokeswoman and Company Hair Stylist

　　ABC Activity Insurance: Insure against overdoing it

敬啓者（敬啓有關的人）

　　Why Brother 雜誌將您的演講內容給了我們，我們認為，「不必多做國際機構」是世界上最好的組織。你們知道如何避免不必要的活動。

　　我們採用你們文章裡的建言。首先，我們用信鴿替代我們的全部電話。僅僅用鳥聲替代電話鈴聲就大大地影響了每一個人。而且，鳥比電話服務便宜。終究，我們是在商言商。我們必須考慮到底線作為附加價值，鳥也會在新蓋的員工三溫暖館外的草坪上施點肥。

　　下一步，我們把電腦賣給 Stab、Grab、Grit 及 Nasty，這是附近的一家律師事務所。我們的電費馬上少很多。省太多了！這使老闆大為滿意。我們完全擁護書面科技。既然我們都使用鉛筆，亂畫情形不斷增加，並且手寫的品質也進步了。從本函我

的手寫筆跡你應該看得出來。還有，如果可行的話，請把這這張信紙寄還給我們。我們能擦掉筆跡重新使用。請把紙綁在瑪姬（鴿子名）的腳上，牠就知道要送去哪裡。

　　這裡現在非常寧靜。你會感覺到與先前有所差別。不再有大聲喋喋不休的講電話聲，我們聽到的只有鉛筆在紙上的摩擦聲、鴿子聲，以及紙摺飛機在各部門之間飛來飛去的聲音。太棒了，從小我就一直想要在保險公司上班。現在那太好了。

　　誠懇的，

　　伊蓮娜賴利

　　女發言人兼公司髮型師

　　ABC 活動保險：保障不必過勞

41. Which of the following best describes the life the author is leading?

下列哪一項最能描述作者導引的生活？

(A) A simple, slow-paced life.

單純，放慢腳步的生活。

(B) A life of hard work and security.

努力工作且有保障的生活。

(C) A religious, peasant-like life.

有宗教信仰，像農民一樣的生活。

(D) A life away from paper and pencils.

不用紙筆的生活。

解析

從答題關鍵的「All of us here think The International Institute of Not Doing Much is the best organization in the world. You know how to avoid unnecessary activities!」可看出，(A) 項的「A simple, slow-paced life.」才是正確選項。

42. Where is Eleanor's letter sent to?

伊蓮娜的信會寄去哪裡？

(A) Why Bother Magazine.

「不做太多」雜誌社。

(B) ABC Activity Insurance Company.

ABC 活動保險公司。

(C) Stab, Grab, Grit, and Nasty Law Firm.

Stab, Grab, Grit, and Nasty 律師事務所。

(D) The International Institute of Not Doing Much.

「不做太多」的國際機構。

> 解析

從答題關鍵的「The International Institute of Not Doing Much is the best organization in the world. You know how to avoid unnecessary activities!」可看出，(D) 項的「The International Institute of Not Doing Much.」才是正確選項。

43. Which of the following is practiced in the author's company?

下列哪一項在作者的公司實踐過？

(A) Replacing the manual work system with modern technology.

用現代技術替換手工做法。

(B) Turning off lights in the daytime to save electricity.

在白天關燈以省電。

(C) Recycling paper resources whenever possible.

隨時回收紙資源。

(D) Buying birds and pets as company for the staff.

買鳥和寵物與員工作伴。

> 解析

從答題關鍵的「By the way, if you can, please send this letter back to us. We can erase and reuse it.」可看出，(C) 項的「Recycling paper resources whenever possible.」才是正確選項。

44. What is true about **Maggie**?

關於瑪姬哪項為真？

(A) She works as a manager in the author's company.

她在作者的公司當經理。

(B) She sometimes helps fertilize the lawn outside the sauna.

她有時會在三溫暖間外面草坪施肥。

(C) She often helps with inter-office correspondence using e-mail.

她經常用電子郵件幫助傳遞部門之間的郵件。

(D) Her handwriting has improved a lot after entering the company.

進入公司後她的字寫得更好看。

> 解析

從答題關鍵的「Just tie it to Maggie's leg and she'll know where to take it.」可看出，(B) 項的「She sometimes helps fertilize the lawn outside the sauna.」才是正確選項。

45-48 為題組

The Galapagos Islands are the Pacific island paradise where Darwin's theory of evolution was born. They are places filled with giant tree lizards, sandy beaches, and tropical plants. Now they will be famous for one more thing: the world's first green airport.

This group of islands off the coast of Ecuador has recently contracted Argentine Corporacion America to manage the redevelopment of the airport on the island of Baltra. It is estimated that US$20 million is needed to complete **the project** by 2009. The new development has several important features: use of wind and solar energy, passive heating and cooling systems, as well as concrete runways in place of asphalt, which has a greater carbon footprint during its production cycle. This new development couldn't be coming at a better time for the Galápagos, which were added to an environmental "danger list" in 2007.

Pacific islands like the Galápagos, Easter Island, and Tahiti, have economies that are driven almost completely by tourism. However, some people think these are "unsustainable models of development." The number of visitors to the Galápagos rose more than 250% from 1990 to 2006, while the number of commercial flights to the area rose 193% from 2001 to 2006. These increases put great stress on the islands' resources and environment. Air travel is especially criticized for exhausting natural resources and causing environmental damage. Thus, efforts are being made to reduce the environmental impact of the tourism industry. The greening of airports is just one of these attempts.

加拉帕戈斯島是達爾文想出進化論的太平洋島國。在那裡充滿大型樹蜥蜴、沙灘和熱帶植物。他們將會因擁有世界第一個綠色機場而聞名。

這個在厄瓜多外海的群島最近與阿根廷公司簽約，以經營 Baltra 島的機場重新開發事宜。估計將需要 2,000 萬美元而會在 2009 年完工。新開發案有幾個重要的特色：使用風力與太陽能源、被動式冷暖系統，以及使用堅固的混凝土而不是瀝青，瀝青在生產期間所造成的碳跡較大。新開發案對加拉帕戈斯來說正是時候，該市在 2007 年被列入「環保危險名單」。

像加拉帕戈斯島、復活節島和大溪地等的太平洋群島，幾乎都是倚賴觀光事業。不過，有些人認為這些開發無法持續發展。在 1990～2006 年期間，到加拉帕戈斯的觀光客人數增加了 250%，而商業航班數量從 2001 年到 2006 年成長了 193%。這些發展給該島的資源和環境上，造成極大壓力。航空旅行因耗盡自然資源、造成環境污染，更是受到批評。因此，各部門都努力地降低旅遊業的環境影響。飛機場的綠化就是多種努力的一部分。

45. What is this article mainly about?

本文的主題是什麼？

(A) The problems of Darwin's theory.

達爾文理論的問題。

(B) The background of building a green airport.

建造綠色飛機場的背景。

(C) The history of the Galapagos Islands.

加拉帕戈斯島的歷史。

(D) The ease of transportation to the Pacific islands.

到太平洋群島的交通很方便。

解析

從整篇文章內容來看，是在說明該地要建綠色機場的始末，因此 (B) 項的「The background of building a green airport.」才是正確選項。

46. Where will the world's first green airport be built?

世界的第一個綠色機場將會建在哪裡？

(A) In Tahiti. 在大溪地。　　(B) In Argentina. 在阿根廷。

(C) In Baltra. 在 Baltra。　　(D) In the United States. 在美國。

解析

從答題關鍵的「has recently contracted Argentine Corporacion America to manage the redevelopment of the airport on the island of Baltra」可看出，(C) 項的「In Baltra.」才是正確選項。

47. What is true about the Galapagos Islands?

關於加拉帕戈斯島哪項為真？

(A) They are located near Ecuador in the Pacific Ocean.

他們位在太平洋的厄瓜多附近。

(B) They have had a great increase in population since 2001.

從 2001 年起他們人口增加很多。

(C) They will invest US$20 million to promote their tourism.

他們將投資 2,000 萬美元推廣觀光。

(D) They have become one of the most dangerous places in the world.

他們已成為在世界上最危險的地方之一。

解析

從答題關鍵的「This group of islands off the coast of Ecuador」可看出，(A) 項的「They are located near Ecuador in the Pacific Ocean.」才是正確選項。

48. What does the project in the second paragraph refer to?

第二段文章內容與什麼有關？

(A) The plan to build a green airport.

計畫建造綠色機場。

(B) The research on the production of solar energy.

創造太陽能的的研究。

(C) The task of calculating a carbon footprint.

　　計算碳足跡的任務。

(D) The study on the exhaustion of natural resources.

　　在自然資源的竭盡上的研究。

解析

從整段文章內容來看，只提到建綠色機場之事，並無提到三選項的內容，因此 (A) 項的「The plan to build a green airport」才是正確選項。

49-52 為題組

According to popular folklore, many animals are smarter than they appear. Dogs bark before earthquakes; cattle predict rainfall by sitting on the ground. But cattle may have another hidden talent in telling which way is north.

Small animals such as mole rats living underground are known for the use of magnetism to navigate. Dr. Begall and her colleagues wanted to know whether larger mammals also have the ability to perceive magnetic fields. They investigated this possibility by studying images of thousands of cattle captured on Google Earth, a website that stitches together satellite photographs to produce an image of the Earth's surface.

Grazing animals are known to orient themselves in a way that minimizes wind chill from the north and maximizes the warmth of the sun when they are cold. The researchers therefore had to study a lot of cows grazing in lots of different places at different times of day, in order to average out these factors and see whether cattle could act like compass needles.

The researchers concluded that cattle do generally orient themselves in a north-south direction. This north-south preference has also been noted in flies, termites and honeybees. But unfortunately, even the high resolution of Google Earth is not powerful enough to tell which end of the cow is its head, and which its tail. The researchers were therefore unable to answer their research questions of whether cattle prefer to look north or south, and whether that differs in the northern and southern hemispheres.

根據廣為流傳的民間傳說，很多動物比他們的外表看起來更聰明。狗會在地震發生前狂吠；牛會坐在地上來預測下雨。但是牛可能還有另一種隱藏的能力，牠會辨識北方。

小動物像是生活在地下的錢鼠，知道利用磁場認方向。Begall 與她的同事一直想知道大型哺乳動物是否有能力去感覺磁場。他們透過在「Google Earth」上捕捉的數千頭牛隻的圖像調查這種可能性，它是一個連結衛星照片的網站，可顯示地球表面的圖像。

草食動物被認為會調整自己的方向，把北方來的冷風減到最低，在天冷時，也會把太陽的熱能保持久一些。因此研究人員必須在每天的不同時間與地點觀察牛隻吃草的情形，以便平均出這些因素，也要看看牛隻會否像羅盤指針一樣的辨識方向。

研究人員的結論是，牛隻通常會站於南北向的方位。這種南北向的現象也會發生在蒼蠅，白蟻和蜜蜂等身上。但是令人遺憾，即使 GoogleEarth 的高解析度也無法分

辨牛隻的哪一端是頭，哪一端是尾巴。研究人員因此無法回答他們的研究問題，牛隻喜歡朝北還是朝南？另外，在北半球與南半球會不會不同？。

49. What is the article mainly about?

本文大意爲何？

(A) The usefulness of Google Earth.

Google Earth的實用。

(B) Whether cattle are superior to other animals.

是否牛隻優於其他動物。

(C) Animals' sensitivity to natural disasters.

動物對自然災害的敏感性。

(D) Whether cattle behave like compass needles.

是否牛隻行爲像羅盤磁針。

解析

從整段文章談的都是牛隻與方向的問題，沒有提到其他三選項的內容，所以，(D) 項的「Whether cattle behave like compass needles.」才是正確選項。

50. Which of the following factors might affect Dr. Begall's research result?

下列哪一項可能影響 Begall 博士的研究結果？

(A) Rainfall 降雨。　(B) Earthquakes 地震。　(C) Location 位置。　(D) Cost 費用。

解析

從答題關鍵的「cattle do generally orient themselves in a north-south direction.」可看出，(C) 項的「Location」才是正確選項。

51. What is the major finding of Dr. Begall's study?

博士的主要發現是什麼？

(A) Cattle point north-south.

牛隻朝向北方南方。

(B) Magnetism can't be studied scientifically.

無法用科學研究磁性。

(C) Animals prefer to look south.

動物喜歡向南方看。

(D) Google Earth is a reliable research tool.

Google Earth是一件可靠的研究工具。

解析

從答題關鍵的「The researchers concluded that cattle do generally orient hemselves in a north-south direction. This north-south preference has also been noted in flies, termites and honeybees. But unfortunately, even the high resolution of Google Earth is not powerful enough to tell which end of the cow is its head, and which its tail.」可看出，(A) 項的「Cattle point north-south.」才是正確選項。

52. Why couldn't the researchers get the answer to their research questions?

研究人員爲什麼不能得到他們研究問題的答案？

(A) Many cattle in their study were sitting on the ground.

他們研究的很多牛隻坐在地上。

(B) The cattle constantly change directions to avoid wind chill.

牛隻經常改變方向以避免寒風。

(C) There is magnetic difference between the two hemispheres.

在兩個半球之間有磁性的差異。

(D) They couldn't tell a cow's head from its tail in the satellite pictures.

衛星畫面裡看不出牛的頭或尾巴。

解析

從答題關鍵的「even the high resolution of Google Earth is not powerful enough to tell which end of the cow is its head, and which its tail. The researchers were therefore unable to answer their research questions of whether cattle prefer to look north or south,」可看出，(D) 項的「They couldn't tell a cow's head from its tail in the satellite pictures.」才是正確選項。

53-56 爲題組

Children normally have a distrust of new foods. But it's the parents' job to serve a variety of foods and expose their children to healthy dieting habits.

Some simple strategies can help even the pickiest eater learn to like a more varied diet. First of all, you don't have to send children out of the kitchen. With hot stoves, boiling water and sharp knives at hand, it is understandable that parents don't want children in the kitchen when they're making dinner. But studies suggest that involving children in meal preparation is an important first step in getting them to try new foods. In one study, nearly 600 children from kindergarten to sixth grade took part in a nutrition curriculum intended to get them to eat more vegetables and whole grains. The researchers found that children who had cooked their own foods were more likely to eat those foods in the cafeteria than children who had not. Kids don't usually like radishes, but if kids cut them up and put them in the salad, they will love the dish.

Another strategy is not to diet in front of your children. Kids are tuned into their parents' eating preferences and are far more likely to try foods if they see their mother or father eating them. Given this powerful effect, parents who are trying to lose weight should be careful of how their dieting habits can influence a child's perceptions about food and healthful eating. In one study of 5-year-old girls about dieting, one child noted that dieting involved drinking chocolate milkshakes, because her mother was using Slim-Fast drinks. Another child said dieting meant "you fix food but you don't eat it." By exposing young children to **erratic** dieting habits, parents may be putting them at risk for eating disorders.

孩子通常不相信新食品。提供不同食品且引導孩子吃健康食品的習慣，是父母親的工作。

一些簡單的策略能幫助或甚至是最愛挑食者，去學習喜歡不同的飲食。首先，你不必將孩子趕出廚房。有了熱爐、沸水和鋒利的刀在手上，可以理解雙親準備晚餐時，不要孩子跑來廚房。但是研究報告建議，讓孩子參與準備餐食是要他們嘗試新食品的重要的第一步。在一項研究，將近六百個孩子，從幼稚園到六年級生都有，參加目的要孩子多吃蔬菜與穀類營養課程。研究人員發現曾經自己烹飪的小孩，比不曾自己烹飪的小孩，比較會吃自助餐廳的食物。孩子通常不喜歡小蘿蔔，但如果孩子自己切蘿蔔，並放進沙拉，他們就會喜歡吃。

另一個策略就是，在你的孩子面前不要節食。如果孩子看見父母親吃某些食物，就更會想吃那些食物。有了這種強力效應，想減重的父母應該注意他們的忌食習慣會如何地影響孩子的想法。有關五歲女孩的節食研究裡，一個孩子注意到節食竟然可以吃熱巧克力奶昔，因為她母親使用「快瘦」飲料。另一個孩子說，節食的意思是「你準備食物，但你不吃它」。讓孩子養成怪異的節食習慣，父母可能已使小孩處於飲食失調的風險。

53. What is the main purpose of this article?

　　本文的主要用意是什麼？

　(A) To explain what causes children's eating disorder.

　　　解釋引起孩子亂吃的原因。

　(B) To teach children about the meal preparation process.

　　　教孩子餐食準備的過程。

　(C) To advocate the importance of vegetables and whole grains.

　　　提倡菜蔬和全穀類的重要性。

　(D) To inform parents how they can help their children like varied foods.

　　　告知父母他們怎樣幫助孩子喜歡不同的食物。

解析

從整篇文章的內容，談的都是父母親教孩子們不要挑挑食、親子共同準備晚餐等事情，可看出，(D) 項的「To inform parents how they can help their children like varied foods.」才是正確選項。

54. Which of the following groups will eat more balanced meals?

　　下列哪一項比較會吃均衡的飲食？

　(A) The children who help cook food.

　　　幫助烹飪的那些孩子。

　(B) The children whose parents are on a diet.

有父母在節食的那些孩子。

(C) The children who do not love radishes.

不愛小蘿蔔的那些孩子。

(D) The children whose parents work in a cafeteria.

父母在自助餐廳工作的那些孩子。

解析

從答題關鍵的「The researchers found that children who had cooked their own foods were more likely to eat those foods in the cafeteria than children who had not. Kids don't usually like radishes, but if kids cut them up and put them in the salad, they will love the dish.」可看出，(A) 項的「The children who help cook food.」才是正確選項。

55. What does erratic in the last sentence imply?

最後一句的「erratic」是指何意？

(A) Obvious. 明顯。　(B) Healthful. 有益於健康。　(C) Dishonest. 不誠實。

(D) Inappropriate. 不適當。

解析

erratic 為古怪的、怪癖的之意，只有 (D) 項的「Inappropriate.」才是最接近選項。

56. Which of the following is true about Slim-Fast?

有關「快瘦」下列哪一項為真？

(A) It is children's favorite food.

它是孩子最喜愛的食品。

(B) It looks like a chocolate milkshake.

它看起來像巧克力奶昔。

(C) It contains a variety of vegetables.

它含有多種菜蔬。

(D) It is intended for slim, fast people.

有意給快瘦的人。

解析

從答題關鍵的「one child noted that dieting involved drinking chocolate milkshakes, because her mother was using Slim-Fast drinks.」可看出，(B) 項的「It looks like a chocolate milkshake」才是正確選項。（選項 (D) 怎不能選？）

第貳部分：非選擇題（28分）

一、翻譯題（8分）

> 說明：1. 請將以下兩題中文譯成正確而通順達意的英文，並將答案寫在「答案卷」上。
> 　　　2. 請依序作答，並標明題號，每題僅能譯成一個英文句子。每題4分，共8分。

1. 大部分學生不習慣自己解決問題，他們總是期待老師提供標準答案。

解析

先將題句內相關字詞寫出中譯：

大部分學生 most students　不習慣 are not used to　自己解決問題 to solve their own problems 他們總是期待 they are expecting　老師提供標準答案 standard answer /solution from their teachers.

整句英譯

Most students are not used to solve their own problems, they are always expecting standard answers / solutions from their teachers.

2. 除了用功讀書獲取知識外，學生也應該培養獨立思考的能力。

解析

先將題句內相關字詞寫出中譯：

除了……外 besides　用功讀書 study hard　獲取知識 to get the knowledge　學生也應該 students should　培養 cultivate　獨立思考的能力 their thinking ability independently

整句英譯

Besides studying hard to get the knowledge, students should also cultivate their thinking ability independently.

二、英文作文（20分）

> 說明：1. 依提示在「答案卷」上寫一篇英文作文。
> 　　　2. 文長120個單詞（words）左右。

提示：請根據右方圖片的場景，描述整個事件發生的前因後果。文章請分兩段，第一段說明<u>之前</u>發生了什麼事情，並根據圖片內容描述<u>現在</u>的狀況；第二段請合理說明<u>接下來</u>可能會發生什麼事，或者<u>未來</u>該做些什麼。

解析

(1)這種看圖說故事的作文很容易發揮，它並沒有固定的格式要求考生怎麼寫，只要寫出來的文章，不離圖意太遠、加上語句通順、文語法不要錯，都可得高分。

(2)該圖看出來是一個簡陋房屋倒塌的圖片，內有一位背籮筐、戴斗笠的農人回到災難現場。只要圖上有的通通把它寫下來，最後再把所有的單句串聯起來就可以了。

相關字詞：從圖片推斷 an inference from the picture　倒塌的農舍或穀倉 collapsed farm house / barn　一位背籮筐戴斗笠農民 a farmer wearing a straw hat, and back-packed with a large basket　回到受災現場 returned to the site

To infer from what we see in the picture, it looks very much like a collapsed farm house stroke by the earthquack. You see the gravel all over, and you car hardly see what was in it before the house collapsed. There is no way of knowing whether the farmer has any family, or, perhaps he is alone.

Feeling sympathy for the farmer is one thing, to help him apply for aid from goverrment or private charity institute is another. The farmer should go directly to the town office seeking for any legal relief fund by the local government, there are so many different kinds of law concerning something so called "disaster relief fund", further more, there will be someone at the town offices to assist any illiterate citizen in filling up all kinds of forms.

相關字詞：從圖片推斷 an inference from the picture　倒塌的農舍或穀倉 collapsed farm house / barn　一位背籮筐戴斗笠農民 a farmer wearing a straw hat, and back-packed with a large basket　回到受災現場 returned to the site

99 年學測（學科能力測驗）

第壹部分：選擇題（72分）

一、詞彙（15分）

1. Mr. Lin is a very _____ writer; he publishes at least five novels every year.

   林先生是一位非常 _____ 作家，他每年最少出版五本小說。

   (A) moderate 適度的　(B) temporary 臨時的　(C) productive 多產的　(D) reluctant 勉強的

   解析
   (1)解題關鍵字在題目空格左、右方的「非常的」與「作家」二字。
   (2)四個答項中，只有選 (C) 項的「多產的」，才可有意義地連成「非常多產的作家」，也才符合後句的「每年出版五本小說」。

2. Using a heating pad or taking warm baths can sometimes help to _____ pain in the lower back.

   利用電熱板或洗溫水澡，有助於 _____ 下背部的疼痛。

   (A) polish 打蠟　(B) relieve 減輕　(C) switch 開關　(D) maintain 保持

   解析
   (1)解題關鍵字在題目空格左、右方的「有助於」與「疼痛」二字。
   (2)四個答項中，只有選 (B) 項的「減輕」，才可有意義地連成「有助於減輕疼痛」（下背部的疼痛）。

3. Peter stayed up late last night, so he drank a lot of coffee this morning to keep himself _____ in class.

   彼德昨晚晚睡，所以他今早喝很多咖啡，可在課堂上使他保持 _____ 。

   (A) acceptable 可接受　(B) amazed 驚奇的　(C) accurate 準確　(D) awake 清醒

   解析
   (1)答題關鍵在題目空格左方的「使他保持」。
   (2)四個選項中，只有選 (D) 項的「清醒」，才可有意義地連成「在課堂上使他保持清醒」。

4. Due to _____ , prices for daily necessities have gone up and we have to pay more for the same items now.

由於 _____ ，民生必須品的物價上升，而同樣的東西現在要付更多錢。

(A) inflation 通貨膨漲　(B) solution 解決辦法　(C) objection 反對　(D) condition 條件

解析

(1)答題關鍵在題目空格左、右方的「由於」與「民生必須品的物價上升」。

(2)四個選項中，只有選 (A) 項的「通貨膨漲」，才可有意義地連成「由於通貨膨漲，民生必須品的物價上升」。

5. The government is doing its best to _____ the cultures of the tribal people for fear that they may soon die out.

政府正盡力在 _____ 原住民文化以防其消失。

(A) preserve 保護　(B) frustrate 挫敗　(C) hesitate 猶豫　(D) overthrow 推翻

解析

(1)答題關鍵在題目空格右方的「原住民文化以防其消失」。

(2)四個選項中，只有選(A)項的「保護」，才可有意義地連成「保護原住民文化以防其消失」。

6. I could not _____ the sweet smell from the bakery, so I walked in and bought a fresh loaf of bread.

我無法 _____ 麵包店傳出的香味，所以我進去買了一條麵包。

(A) insist 堅持　(B) resist 抗拒　(C) obtain 獲得　(D) contain 包含

解析

(1)答題關鍵在題目空格左、右方的「無法」與「傳出的香味」。

(2)四個選項中，只有選(B)項的「抗拒」，才可有意義地連成「無法抗拒麵包店傳出的香味」。

7. Steve has several meetings to attend every day; therefore, he has to work on a very _____ schedule.

史帝芬每天要參加好幾個會議，所以他要有一個非常 _____ 工作表。

(A) dense 稠密的　(B) various 不同的　(C) tight 緊密的　(D) current 當前的

解析

(1)答題關鍵在題目空格左、右方的「一個非常」與「工作表」。

(2)四個選項中，只有選 (C) 項的「緊密的」，才可有意義地連成「他要有一個非常緊密的工作表」，也才能對應句前的「每天要參加好幾個會議」。

8. Michael Phelps, an American swimmer, broke seven world records and won eight gold medals in men's swimming _____ in the 2008 Olympics.

麥可，一位美國游泳選手，在 2008 奧運男子游泳 _____ 中，打破七次世界記錄並獲八面金牌。

(A) drills鑽孔　(B) techniques技術　(C) routines例行事務　(D) contests比賽

解析

(1)答題關鍵在題目空格左方的「男子游泳」。

(2)四個選項中，只有選 (D) 項的「比賽」，才可有意義地連成「在2008奧運男子遊泳比賽中，打破……」。

9. Those college students work at the orphanage on a _____ basis, helping the children with their studies without receiving any pay.

那些大學生以 _____ 方式，在孤兒院免費協助院童作功課。

(A) voluntary 志願的　(B) competitive 競爭的　(C) sorrowful 悲傷的　(D) realistic 現實的

解析

(1)答題關鍵在題目空格左方的「以」與「方式」。

(2)四個選項中，只有選 (A) 項的「志願的」，才可有意義地連成「以志願的方式，在孤兒院……」。

10. Studies show that asking children to do house _____ such as taking out the trash or doing the dishes, helps them grow into responsible adults.

研究調查顯示出，要求小孩做 _____ 像是倒垃圾或洗碗盤，有助於幫他們長大後更有責任感。

(A) missions 任務　(B) chores 家裡雜事　(C) approaches 接近　(D) incidents 事件

解析

(1)答題關鍵在題目空格左、右方的「做」與「像是」。

(2)四個選項中，只有選 (B) 項的「家裡雜事」，才可有意義地連成「要求小孩做雜事，像是倒垃圾……」。

11. John has been scolded by his boss for over ten minutes now. _____ she is not happy about his being late again.

約翰被老闆罵了十多分鐘。_____ 她是不高興他再次遲到。

(A) Expressively 表現地　(B) Apparently 顯然地　(C) Immediately 立即　(D) Originally 起初

解析

(1)答題關鍵在題目空格左、右方的「被老闆罵了十多分鐘」與「她是不高興……」。

(2)四個選項中，只有選 (B) 項的「顯然地」，才可有意義地連成「被老闆罵了 10 多分鐘。顯然地她是不高興……」。

12. Since the orange trees suffered _____ damage from a storm in the summer, the farmers are expecting a sharp decline in harvests this winter.

由於柳橙樹在夏天遭到暴風雨的 _____ 傷害，樹農們預期今年冬天的收成量

會劇減。

(A) potential 潛力　(B) relative 親戚　(C) severe 嚴重的　(D) mutual 互相

解析

(1)答題關鍵在題目空格右方的「傷害」。

(2)四個選項中，只有選(C)項的「嚴重的」，才可有意義地連成「遭到暴風雨的嚴重傷害」。

13. Typhoon Morakot claimed more than six hundred lives in early August of 2009, making it the most serious natural _____ in Taiwan in recent decades.

2009 年 8 月初的莫拉克颱風奪去 600 條人命，造成臺灣近十年來最嚴重的天然 _____ 。

(A) disaster 災難　(B) barrier 障礙　(C) anxiety 焦慮　(D) collapse 倒塌

解析

(1)答題關鍵在題目空格左方的「天然」。

(2)四個選項中，只有選(A)項的「災難」，才可有意義地連成「造成臺灣近十年來最嚴重的天然災難」。

14. Robert was the only _____ to the car accident. The police had to count on him to find out exactly how the accident happened.

羅伯是車禍的唯一 _____ 。警方指望他協助查出車禍是怎麼發生的。

(A) dealer 業者　(B) guide 導遊　(C) witness 目擊者　(D) client 客戶

解析

(1)答題關鍵在題目空格左、右方的「唯一」與「車禍」。

(2)四個選項中，只有選(C)項的「目擊者」，才可有意義地連成「車禍的唯一目擊者」。

15. Badly injured in the car accident, Jason could _____ move his legs and was sent to the hospital right away.

在車禍中嚴重受傷，傑森_____移動雙腿並立即送醫。

(A) accordingly 依照　(B) undoubtedly 肯定地　(C) handily 熟練地　(D) scarcely 幾乎不

解析

(1)答題關鍵在題目空格左方的「could」與「move his legs」。

(2)四個選項中，只有選(D)項的「幾乎不」，才可有意義地連成「傑森幾乎不能移動雙腿」。

(3)本題考副詞 hardly, scarcely 用法。could hardly, could scarcely 的中譯都是「幾乎不」之意。

二、綜合測驗（15分）

Anita was shopping with her mother and enjoying it. Interestingly, both of them _____16_____ buying the same pair of jeans.

According to a recent marketing study, young adults influence 88% of household clothing purchases. More often than not, those in their early twenties are the more _____17_____ consumers. There isn't a brand or a trend that these young people are not aware of. That is why mothers who want to keep abreast of trends usually _____18_____ the experts－their daughters. This tells the retailers of the world that if you want to get into a mother's _____19_____ , you've got to win her daughter over first.

With a DJ playing various kinds of music rather than just rap, and a mix of clothing labels designed more for taste and fashion than for a precise age, department stores have managed to appeal to successful middle-aged women _____20_____ losing their younger customers. They have created a shopping environment where the needs of both mother and daughter are satisfied.

阿妮塔很高興地與她的母親上街購物。有趣的是，她們母女兩個 _____16_____ 都買了相同的牛仔褲。

根據新近的市場研究，年輕人影響了家人 88% 的衣物購買意願。通常，那些二十出頭的人是 _____17_____ 消費者。沒有一個品牌或者流行趨勢是這些年輕人不知道的。那就是為什麼想跟上趨勢的母親通常會 _____18_____ 專家──她們的女兒。這告訴世界上的零售商先要贏得女兒的認同才有辦法要母親 _____19_____ 。

一個 DJ 播放各種各樣的音樂而不是僅僅只有繞舌歌，不同的混合衣物商標是為品味與風尚而非為某一固定年齡層。百貨商店已經設法訴求於成功的中年婦女而 _____20_____ 失去他們家中的更年輕顧客。他們創造母親和女兒的需要且滿意的購物環境。

16. 題句：Interestingly, both of them _____16_____ buying the same pair of jeans.

　　　有趣的是，她們母女兩個 _____16_____ 都買了相同的牛仔褲。

　　(A) gave up 放棄　(B) ended up 到最後　(C) took to 開始從事　(D) used to 過去的習慣

解析

依題意只有選(B)項的「到最後」才是正確選項。

**17. 題句：those in their early twenties are the more _____17_____ consumers.

選項：(A) informed 消息靈通的　(B) informative 情報的　(C) informal 非正式的　(D) informational 新聞的

解析

⑴答題關鍵在空格左方的「more」，其後一定要放形容詞。

⑵依題意只有選(A)項的「消息靈通的」才是正確選項。

⑶(B)項的 informative 隨也有「見聞廣博」之意，但本篇短文是敘述購物，及對商品的流行、價位等，因此(A)項的「informed消息靈通的」才是正確選項。

18. 題句：That is why mothers who want to keep abreast of trends usually _____18_____ the experts－their daughters.

那就是為什麼想跟上趨勢的母親通常會 _____18_____ 專家——她們的女兒

選項：(A) deal with 交易　(B) head for 前往　(C) turn to 轉向　(D) look into 查資料

解析

依題意只有選(C)項的「轉向」（轉而向專家求助之意）才是正確選項。

19. 題句：This tells the retailers of the world that if you want to get into a mother's _____19_____ ,

這告訴世界上的零售商先要贏得女兒的認同才有辦法要母親 _____19_____ 。

選項：(A) textbook 教科書　(B) notebook 錢包、筆記本　(C) workbook 練習簿
(D) pocketbook 錢包

解析

依題意只有選(D)項的「錢包」才是正確選項。Get into a mother's pocketbook 為「讓母親掏錢」之意。

**20. 題句：department stores have managed to appeal to successful middle-aged women _____20_____ losing their younger customers.

百貨商店已經設法訴求於成功的中年婦女而 _____20_____ 失去他們家中的更年輕顧客。

選項：(A) in 之內　(B) while 當　(C) after 之後　(D) without 無、不、沒有

解析

對照空格前後兩句的題意，只有選(D)項的「without」才是正確選項。

Onions can be divided into two categories: fresh onions and storage onions. Fresh onions are available _____21_____ yellow, red and white throughout their season, March through August. They can be _____22_____ by their thin, light-colored skin. Because they have a higher water content, they are typically sweeter and milder tasting than storage onions. This higher water content also makes _____23_____ easier for them to bruise. With its delicate taste, the fresh onion is an ideal choice for salads and other lightly-cooked dishes. Storage onions, on the other hand, are available August through April. _____24_____ fresh onions, they have multiple layers of thick, dark, papery skin. They also have an _____25_____ flavor and a higher percentage of solids. For these reasons, storage onions are the best choice for spicy dishes that require longer cooking times or more flavor.

　　洋蔥可以分成兩大類：新鮮洋蔥和儲存洋蔥。在 3 月到 8 月的洋蔥季節裡，它們的顏色 _____21_____ 黃色、紅色和白色都有。從洋蔥的淺色薄皮可 _____22_____ 它的好壞。它們比儲存洋蔥有較高的含水率，通常嘗起來甜一些也溫和一些。本身較高的含水率也使 _____23_____ 較易碰傷。由於它的美味的口味，新鮮的洋蔥是沙拉和其他輕煮食物理想的選擇。儲存洋蔥，另一方面，洋蔥可用期從 8 月到 4 月。_____24_____ 新鮮洋蔥，有多層深色像紙的外皮，同時也有 _____25_____ 的味道和實心部分較多。由於這些原因，儲存洋蔥是需要長時間烹煮之辛辣菜餚的最佳選擇。

**21. 題句：Fresh onions are available _____21_____ yellow, red and white

　　選項：(A) from 從……　(B) for 為……　(C) in　(D) of

解析

依題意只有選(C)項的「in」才是正確選項。顏色之前的介係詞要用「in」。

22. 題句：They can be _____22_____ by their thin, light-colored skin.
　　　　從洋蔥的淺色薄皮可 _____22_____ 它的好壞。

　　選項：(A) grown 成長　(B) tasted 嘗味道　(C) identified 識別、判斷　(D) emphasized 強調

解析

依題意只有選(C)項的「識別、判斷」才是正確選項。

**23. 題句：This higher water content also makes _____23_____ easier for them to bruise.
　　　　本身較高的含水量也使 _____23_____ 較易碰傷。

　　選項：(A) such 如此　(B) much 多　(C) that 那個　(D) it 它

解析

依題意只有選(D)項的「it」才可有意義連成「makes it easier（使它更容易）」才是正確選項。

**24. 題句：_____24_____ fresh onions, they have multiple layers of thick, dark, papery skin.
　　　　_____24_____ 新鮮洋蔥，有多層深色像紙的外皮。

　　選項：(A) Unlike 不像　(B) Through 經由　(C) Besides 在旁　(D) Despite 儘管

解析

依題意只有選(A)項的「Unlike不像」才可有意義連成「不像新鮮洋蔥……」，才是正確選項。

25. 題句：They also have an _____25_____ flavor and a higher percentage of solids.
　　　　同時也有 _____25_____ 的味道和實心部分較多。

　　選項：(A) anxious 焦慮的　(B) intense 強烈的　(C) organic 有機的　(D) effective 有效率的

依題意只有選(B)項的「強烈的」才是正確選項。

Many people like to drink bottled water because they feel that tap water may not be safe, but is bottled water really any better?

Bottled water is mostly sold in plastic bottles and that's why it is potentially health ____26____ . Processing the plastic can lead to the release of harmful chemical substances into the water contained in the bottles. The chemicals can be absorbed into the body and ____27____ physical discomfort, such as stomach cramps and diarrhea.

Health risks can also result from inappropriate storage of bottled water. Bacteria can multiply if the water is kept on the shelves for too long or if it is exposed to heat or direct sunlight. ____28____ the information on storage and shipment is not always readily available to consumers, bottled water may not be a better alternative to tap water.

Besides these ____29____ issues, bottled water has other disadvantages. It contributes to global warming. An estimated 2.5 million tons of carbon dioxide were generated in 2006 by the production of plastic for bottled water. In addition, bottled water produces an incredible amount of solid ____30____ . According to one research, 90% of the bottles used are not recycled and lie for ages in landfills.

很多人喜歡喝瓶裝水因為他們覺得自來水可能不安全，但是瓶裝水真的更好嗎？

瓶裝水多數裝在塑膠瓶出售，那也就是它有潛在健康 ____26____ 的原因。處理塑膠瓶會釋出有害的化學物質到瓶裝水。這些化學物質會被人體吸收並 ____27____ 身體的不舒服，像是胃痙攣和腹瀉。

瓶裝水的不適當貯存也能引起健康風險。如果那些水被存放太久或者暴露高溫或受陽光直接照射，細菌都會倍數增加。 ____28____ 消費者無法隨時得知關於貯存和運送瓶裝水的資訊，瓶裝水可能不是自來水以外的更好選擇。

除這些 ____29____ 問題以外，瓶裝水有其他不利條件。它促使地球暖化。2006年在生產裝水的塑膠瓶時，估計產生約 250 萬公噸的二氧化碳。另外，瓶裝水產生極多的固體 ____30____ 。根據一份研究，用過的瓶子有 90% 沒被回收處理，而是多年放在垃圾場裡。

26. 題句：Bottled water is mostly sold in plastic bottles and that's why it is potentially health ____26____ .
那也就是它有潛在健康 ____26____ 的原因。
選項：(A) frightening 害怕　(B) threatening 威脅　(C) appealing 上訴　(D) promoting 推廣

解析
依題意只有選(B)項的「威脅」才是正確選項。

**27. 題句：The chemicals can be absorbed into the body and ____27____ physical discomfort,

這些化學物質會被人體吸收並 _____27_____ 身體的不舒服。

選項：(A) cause 導致　(B) causing（現在分詞）　(C) caused（過去式）　(D) to cause（不定詞）

解析

依題意只有選(A)項的「導致」才是正確選項。

**28. 題句： _____28_____ the information on storage and shipment is not always readily available to consumers,

_____28_____ 消費者無法隨時得知關於貯存和運送瓶裝水的資訊。

選項：(A) Although 雖然　(B) Despite 不管　(C) Since 由於　(D) So 如此的

解析

依題意只有選(C)項的「由於」才能連成「由於消費者無法……」是正確選項。

29. 題句：Besides these _____29_____ issues, bottled water has other disadvantages.

除這些 _____29_____ 問題以外，瓶裝水有其他不利條件。

選項：(A) display 展示　(B) production 生產　(C) shipment 裝運　(D) safety 安全

解析

依題意只有選(D)項的「安全」才是正確選項。

30. 題句：bottled water produces an incredible amount of solid _____30_____ .

瓶裝水產生極多的固體 _____30_____ 。

選項：(A) waste 浪費　(B) resource 資源　(C) ground 地面　(D) profit 獲利

解析

依題意只有選(A)項的「浪費」才是正確選項。

三、文意選填（10分）

> 說明：第 31 至 40 題，每題一個空格，請依文意在文章後所提供的 (A) 到 (J) 選項中分別選出最適當者，並將其英文字母代號標示在答案卡之「選擇題答案區」。每題答對得 1 分，答錯不倒扣。

　　Football is more than a sport; it is also an invaluable _____31_____ . In teaching young players to cooperate with their fellows on the practice _____32_____ , the game shows them the necessity of teamwork in society. It prepares them to be _____33_____ citizens and persons.

　　Wherever football is played, the players learn the rough-and-tumble lesson that only through the _____34_____ of each member can the team win. It is a lesson they must always _____35_____ on the field. Off the field, they continue to keep it in mind. In society, the former player does not look upon himself as a lone wolf who has the right to remain _____36_____ from the society and go his own way. He understands his place in the team; he knows he is a member of society and must _____37_____ himself as such. He realizes that only by cooperating can he do his _____ 38 _____ in making society what it should be. The man who has played football knows that teamwork is _____ 39 _____ in modern living. He is also aware that every citizen must do his part if the nation is to _____ 40 _____ . So he has little difficulty in adjusting himself to his role in family life and in the business world, and to his duties as a citizen.

　　足球是不僅是一種運動；它同時也是一名無價的 _____ 31 _____ 。在練習 _____ 32 _____ 它教年輕運動員與隊員合作，比賽也讓球員看到群體裡團隊合作的必要性。它使球員要成為 _____ 33 _____ 的公民和為人預作準備。無論在哪裡比賽，隊員們學習只有透過每球員間的 _____ 34 _____ ，在混戰中球隊才能獲勝。這是他們在球場上必須 _____ 35 _____ 的教訓。即使離開球場他們也都記住這個法則。在社會裡，老一輩的運動員不把自己看作是有權與社會 _____ 36 _____ 的孤獨份子。他在團隊裡能了解自己的立場，他知道他是社會的成員並且必須 _____ 37 _____ 良好。他意識到只有合作才能使他 _____ 38 _____ 而使社會祥和。踢足球的人都知道團隊合作在現代生活裡是 _____ 39 _____ 。他也意識到要使國家 _____ 40 _____ ，每位公民必須盡他的職責。因此他幾乎沒有困難地，可以在家庭與商場去適應他的角色，成為一個好國民。

　　(A) cooperation 合作　(B) prosper 繁榮　(C) teacher 教師　(D) behave 行為
　　(E) isolated 隔離　(F) essential 必要的　(G) better 更好的　(H) share 分享
　　(I) field 場地　(J) remember 記住

31. 題句：它同時也是一名無價的 _____ 31 _____ 。
解析
依題意只有選(C)項的「教師」才是正確選項。

32. 題句：在練習 _____ 32 _____ 它教年輕運動員與隊員合作。
解析
依題意只有選(I)項的「場地」才是正確選項。

33. 題句：它使球員要成為 _____ 33 _____ 的公民和為人預作準備。
解析
依題意只有選(G)項的「更好的」才是正確選項。

34. 題句：隊員們學習只有透過每球員間的 _____ 34 _____ ，在混戰中球隊才能獲勝。
解析
依題意只有選(A)項的「合作」才是正確選項。

35. 題句：這是他們在球場上必須 _____ 35 _____ 的教訓。
解析
依題意只有選(J)項的「記住」才是正確選項。

36. 題句：老一輩的運動員不把自己看作是有權與社會 ＿＿＿＿36＿＿＿＿ 的孤獨份子。
解析
依題意只有選 (E) 項的「隔離」才是正確選項。

37. 題句：他知道他是社會的成員並且必須 ＿＿＿＿37＿＿＿＿ 良好。
解析
依題意只有選 (D) 項的「行為」才是正確選項。

38. 題句：他意識到只有合作才能使他 ＿＿＿＿38＿＿＿＿ 而使社會祥和。
解析
依題意只有選 (H) 項的「分享」才是正確選項。

39. 題句：踢足球的人都知道團隊合作在現代生活裡是 ＿＿＿＿39＿＿＿＿ 。
解析
依題意只有選 (F) 項的「必要的」才是正確選項。

40. 題句：他也意識到要使國家 ＿＿＿＿40＿＿＿＿ ，每位公民必須盡他的職責。
解析
依題意只有選 (B) 項的「繁榮」才是正確選項。

四、閱讀測驗（32分）

說明：第 41 至 56 題，每題請分別根據各篇文章之文意選出最適當的一個選項，標示在答案卡之「選擇題答案區」。每題答對得 2 分，答錯不倒扣。

　　On the island of New Zealand, there is a grasshopper-like species of insect that is found nowhere else on earth. New Zealanders have given it the nickname *weta*, which is a native Maori word meaning "god of bad looks." It's easy to see why anyone would call this insect a bad-looking bug. Most people feel disgusted at the sight of these bulky, slow-moving creatures.

　　Wetas are nocturnal creatures; they come out of their caves and holes only after dark. A giant weta can grow to over three inches long and weigh as much as 1.5 ounces. Giant wetas can hop up to two feet at a time. Some of them live in trees, and others live in caves. They are very long-lived for insects, and some adult wetas can live as long as two years. Just like their cousins grasshoppers and crickets, wetas are able to "sing" by rubbing their leg parts together, or against their lower bodies.

　　Most people probably don't feel sympathy for these endangered creatures, but they do need protecting. The slow and clumsy wetas have been around on the island since the times of the dinosaurs, and have evolved and survived in an environment where they had no enemies until rats came to the island with European immigrants. Since rats love to hunt and eat wetas, the rat population on the island has grown into a real problem for many of the native species that are unaccustomed to **its** presence, and poses a serious threat to the native weta population.

　　在紐西蘭島上，有種長得像蚱蜢一樣、但在其他地方看不到的昆蟲。紐西蘭人給它取個綽號叫「唯它」，毛利語的意思是「醜陋之神」。要看出為什麼這種昆蟲被稱為難看昆蟲很容易。大多數人一看見這種龐大、移動緩慢的生物都會感到厭惡。

　　「唯它」是夜行性生物；只有天黑之後牠們才會從洞裡出來。大隻「唯它」能成長到超過 3 英寸，且重量多達 1.5 盎司，跳躍可高達兩英尺。牠們有些棲息在樹上，有些棲息在洞內。以昆蟲來說，牠們很長壽，一些成長的「唯它」能活兩年之久。就像牠們的表親蚱蜢和知了一樣，「唯它」會摩擦雙腿或用腿摩擦下半身來「唱歌」。多數人也許不會同情這些瀕臨絕種的生物，但是牠們的確需要保護。行動緩慢、笨拙的「唯它」從恐龍時期起就生長在島上，在老鼠跟著歐洲移民來島上之前，經演化的「唯它」在無天敵的環境中存活下來。由於老鼠喜歡吃「唯它」，島上的老鼠數量對本地的其他物種造成很大的麻煩，更大大威脅到本地「唯它」的生存。

41. From which of the following is the passage **LEAST** likely to be taken?

　　根據本文，哪一項是與本文最無關聯的？

(A) A science magazine.

　　一本科學雜誌。

(B) A travel guide.

　　旅遊指南。

(C) A biology textbook.

　　一本生物學教科書。

(D) A business journal.

　　一本生意雜誌。

解析

從整段文章內容來看，只有 (D) 項的「A business journal.」才是與本文最無關聯的選項。

42. According to the passage, which of the following statements is true?

　　根據本文，下列陳述哪一項為真？

(A) Wetas are unpleasant to the eye.

　　「唯它」長得不好看。

(B) The weta is a newly discovered insect species.

　　「唯它」是一種新發現的昆蟲物種。

(C) The Maoris nicknamed themselves "Wetas".

　　毛利人也把自己稱為「唯它」。

(D) The Europeans brought wetas to New Zealand.

　　歐洲人把「唯它」帶到紐西蘭。

解析

從答題關鍵的「New Zealanders have given it the nickname weta, which is a native Maori word meaning "god of bad looks." It's easy to see why anyone would call this insect a bad-looking bug. Most people feel disgusted at the sight of these bulky, slow-moving creatures.」可看出，(A) 項的「Wetas are unpleasant to the eye.」才是正確選項。

43. Which of the following descriptions of wetas is accurate?

下列哪一項有關「唯它」的描述是正確的？

(A) They are quick in movement

牠們行動快速。

(B) They are very active in the daytime.

牠們在白天很活躍。

(C) They are decreasing in number.

牠們的數量正在減少。

(D) They have a short lifespan for insects.

以昆蟲來看牠們的壽命很短。

解析

從答題關鍵的「Most people probably don't feel sympathy for these endangered creatures,」可看出，(C) 項的「They are decreasing in number.」才是正確選項。

44. Which of the following is the most appropriate interpretation of "**its**" in the last paragraph?

下列哪一項最能解釋最後一段落內容裡的「its」？

(A) The rat's. 老鼠。　　(B) The weta's. 唯它。

(C) The island's. 島。　　(D) The dinosaur's. 恐龍。

解析

從答題關鍵的「Since rats love to hunt and eat wetas, the rat population on the island has grown into a real problem for many of the native species that are unaccustomed to its presence,」可看出，(A) 項的「The rat's.」才是正確選項。

45-48 為題組

The high school prom is the first formal social event for most American teenagers. It has also been a rite of passage for young Americans for nearly a century.

The word "prom" was first used in the 1890s, referring to formal dances in which the guests of a party would display their fashions and dancing skills during the evening's grand march. In the United States, parents and educators have come to regard the prom as an important lesson in social skills. Therefore, proms have been held every year in high schools for students to learn proper social behavior.

The first high school proms were held in the 1920s in America. By the 1930s, proms were common across the country. For many older Americans, the prom was a modest, home-grown affair in the school gymnasium. Prom-goers were well dressed but not fancily dressed up for the occasion: boys wore jackets and ties and girls their Sunday dresses. Couples danced to music provided by a local amateur band or a record player. After the 1960s, and especially since the 1980s, the high school prom in many areas has become a serious exercise in excessive consumption, with boys renting expensive tuxedos and girls wearing designer gowns. Stretch limousines were hired to drive the prom-goers to expensive restaurants or discos for an all-night extravaganza.

Whether simple or lavish, proms have always been more or less traumatic events for adolescents who worry about self-image and fitting in with their peers. Prom night can be a dreadful experience for socially awkward teens or for those who do not secure dates. Since the 1990s, alternative proms have been organized in some areas to meet the needs of particular students. For example, proms organized by and for homeless youth were reported. There were also "couple-free" proms to which all students are welcome.

高中畢業舞會是多數美國青少年第一個正式的社交活動。這也是差不多一個世紀以來年輕美國人的慶祝儀式。

「prom」一字首先是在十九世紀的九〇年代使用，像正式的舞會一樣，在大遊行時與會的貴賓會展示他們的時裝和跳舞技巧。在美國，父母和教育工作者認為「舞會」是一門社交的重要課程。因此，中學校每年都會舉行高中畢業舞會來學習適當的社交行為。

第一個高中畢業舞會是在二十世紀二〇年代的美國舉行。在二十世紀三〇年代，高中畢業舞會普及全國。對很多年長的美國人來說，學校體育館的高中畢業舞會是一種謙虛、國內才有的活動。參加舞會者穿得很正式但不是太花俏：男孩西裝領帶，而女孩則穿前往教堂所穿的服裝。成雙的舞者隨著一個本地業餘樂團或電唱機的音樂跳舞。在二十世紀六〇年代後，特別自八〇年代起，很多地區的高中畢業舞會已經成為一種花大錢的嚴肅活動，男生租昂貴的晚禮服而女生則穿設計師設計的服裝。加長型轎車被租用來載與會者去昂貴餐廳或者狄斯可整晚狂歡。

無論簡單還是浪費，舞會或多或少一直都是青少年擔心形象與同學間之認同與否的心中之痛。舞會當晚可能是不擅社交的青少年，或沒有約會對象者的可怕經歷。從二十世紀九〇年代起，有些地方已有改良型的高中畢業舞會，以符合某些學生的需求。例如，報導說已有專為無家可歸學生所組成的舞會。還有在「不需舞伴」的高中畢業舞會歡迎所有的學生。

45. In what way are high school proms significant to American teenagers?

高中畢業舞會對美國青少年代表的意義是什麼？

(A) They are part of the graduation ceremony.

舞會是畢業典禮的一部分。

(B) They are occasions for teens to show off their limousines.

舞會是青少年炫耀豪華轎車的場合。

(C) They are important events for teenagers to learn social skills.

舞會是青少年學習社交技巧的重要活動。

(D) They are formal events in which teens share their traumatic experiences.

舞會是青少年分享創傷經驗的正式活動。

解析

從答題關鍵的「In the United States, parents and educators have come to regard the prom as an important lesson in social skills.」可看出，(C) 項的「They are important events for teenagers to learn social skills.」才是正確選項。

46. What is the main idea of the third paragraph?

本文第三段的主要意思是什麼？

(A) Proper social behavior must be observed by prom-goers.

舞會參與者必須遵守適當的社會行為。

(B) Proms held in earlier times gave less pressure to teenagers.

早期的舞會給青少年較少壓力。

(C) Proms are regarded as important because everyone dresses up for the occasion.

舞會被認為是重要，因為每人都是盛裝參加。

(D) The prom has changed from a modest event to a glamorous party over the years.

多年來舞會已經從一般的活動轉變成有魅力的聚會。

解析

從答題關鍵的「For many older Americans, the prom was a modest, home-grown affair in the school gymnasium. Prom-goers were well dressed but not fancily dressed up for the occasion: boys wore jackets and ties and girls their Sunday dresses. Couples danced to music provided by a local amateur band or a record player. After the 1960s, and especially since the 1980s, the high school prom in many areas has become a serious exercise in excessive consumption,」可看出，(D) 項的「The prom has changed from a modest event to a glamorous party over the years.」才是正確選項。

47. According to the passage, what gave rise to alternative proms?

根據本文，為什麼會產生改良型的舞會？

(A) Not all students behaved well at the proms.

並非全部學生在舞會都很規矩。

(B) Proms were too serious for young prom-goers.

舞會對年輕的參與者來說太嚴肅了。

(C) Teenagers wanted to attend proms with their dates.

青少年想要與約會對象去參加舞會。

(D) Students with special needs did not enjoy conventional proms.

有特別需要的學生不喜愛傳統的舞會。

解析

從答題關鍵的「Since the 1990s, alternative proms have been organized in some areas to meet the needs of particular students. For example, proms organized by and for homeless youth were reported.」可看出，(D) 項的「Students with special needs did not enjoy conventional proms」才是正確選項。

48. Which of the following statements is true?

下列哪項陳述為真？

(A) Unconventional proms have been organized since the 1960s.

非傳統的舞會從二十世紀六〇年代就已經有了。

(B) In the 1980s, proms were held in local churches for teenagers to attend.

在二十世紀八〇年代，舞會在本地教堂舉辦給青少年參加。

(C) Proms have become a significant event in American high schools since the 1930s.

舞會從二十世紀三〇年代起在美國中學已經成為一種有意義的活動。

(D) In the 1890s, high school proms were all-night social events for some American families.

在十九世紀九〇年代的某些美國家庭來說，高中畢業舞會是整夜的活動。

解析

看完答題關鍵「By the 1930s, proms were common across the country.」後，可看出 (C) 項的「Proms have become a significant event in American high schools since the 1930s.」才是正確選項。

49-52 為題組

No budget for your vacation? Try home exchanges－swapping houses with strangers. Agree to use each other's cars, and you can save bucks on car rentals, too.

Home exchanges are not new. At least one group, Intervac, has been facilitating such an arrangement since 1953. But trading online is gaining popularity these days, with several sites in operation, including HomeExchanges. Founded in 1992, with some 28,000 listings, this company **bills** itself as the world's largest home exchange club, reporting that membership has increased 30% this year.

The annual fee is usually less than US$100. Members can access thousands of listings for apartments, villas, suburban homes and farms around the world. Initial contact is made via e-mail, with subsequent communication usually by phone. Before a match is made, potential swappers tend to discuss a lot.

However, the concept may sound risky to some people. What about theft? Damage? These are reasonable causes for concern, but equally unlikely. As one swapper puts it, "Nobody is going to fly across the ocean or drive 600 miles to come steal your TV. Besides, at the same time they're staying in your home, you are staying in their home."

Exchange sites recommend that swappers discuss such matters ahead of time. They may fill out an agreement spelling out who shoulders which responsibilities if a problem arises. It does not matter if the agreement would hold up in court, but it does give the exchangers a little satisfaction.

　　Generally, the biggest complaint among home exchangers has to do with different standards of cleanliness. Swappers are supposed to make sure their home is in order before they depart, but one person's idea of "clean" may be more forgiving than another's. Some owners say if they come back to a less-than-sparkling kitchen, it may be inconvenient but would not sour them on future exchanges.

　　你的渡假沒有預算嗎？試試住屋交換──與陌生人換房子住。同意使用彼此的汽車，並且你在租車部分也可省錢。住屋交換不是新事務，至少有一個組織，Intervac，從 1953 年起一直都有這樣的安排。但線上交易最近才開始普及，有幾個網站在營運中，包括「住屋交換」在 1992 年成立，有了大約 28,000 個會員，這公司在廣告中聲稱是世界上最大的換屋俱樂部，並報告說會員數已增加了 30%。

　　年費通常少於 100 美元。成員能造訪網上的數千間公寓、別墅、全世界的郊區和農家。一開始的接觸是透過電子郵件，有進一步的通訊則用電話聯絡。在撮合談成之前，準交換者之間的討論是多方面的。

　　不過，對某些人來說，概念可能聽起來有點風險。偷竊怎麼辦？這些是合理擔心的理由，但是同樣也是不太可能。一個交換者這麼說，「沒人會飛越海洋或開六百英里車去偷你的電視機。」此外，在同一時間，他們住在你們家、你們住在他們家。

　　換屋網站建議這類事情換屋者要事先討論。他們可能寫一份協議書，詳細說明一旦有事發生由誰負責。協議書是否送到法院並不重要，但如果有送，會使換屋者放心一些。

　　通常，在換屋者之間的最大抱怨，與清潔標準的不同認定有關。在出發之前，換屋者應該將房子保持井然有序，但是每個人對「乾淨」的看法不一樣。一些房屋所有人說，如果他們回來看到廚房不乾淨，也許這樣不太舒服，但是不會使他們排斥將來的換屋計畫。

49. What is the second paragraph mainly about?

　　第二個段落主要大意是什麼？

(A) How to exchange homes.

　　怎樣進行住屋交換。

(B) How home exchange is becoming popular.

　　為什麼住屋交換變得受歡迎？

(C) The biggest home exchange agency.

　　最大的住屋交換代理商。

(D) A contrast between Intervac and HomeExchange.

　　在 Intervac 和 HomeExchange 之間的一種差別。

解析
從本段落文章內容來看，都是在敘述交換住屋之事，所以 (B) 項的「How home exchange is becoming popular.」才是本段文章的主題。

50. Which of the following is closest in meaning to "**bills**" in the second paragraph?

在第二個段落裡的「bills」是指何意？

(A) advertises 做廣告　(B) dedicates 奉獻　(C) replaces 替換　(D) participates 參加

解析
Bill 另有「張貼廣告」之意，只有(A)項的「advertises」才是意思最接近的正確選項。

51. How do home exchangers normally begin their communication?

住屋交換者通常怎樣開始通訊？

(A) By phone. 用電話。　(B) By e-mail. 透過電子郵件。　(C) Via a matchmaker. 透過媒介者。　(D) Via a face-to-face meeting. 透過面對面的方法。

解析
從答題關鍵的「Initial contact is made via e-mail,」可看出，(B) 項的「By e-mail.」才是正確選項。

52. What is recommended in the passage to deal with theft and damage concerns?

有關偷竊和損害部分本文如何建議？

(A) One can file a lawsuit in court.

　　提出訴訟。

(B) Both parties can trade online.

　　雙方在線上交易。

(C) Both parties can sign an agreement beforehand.

　　雙方能事先簽署一項協議。

(D) One can damage the home of the other party in return.

　　一個人可以損壞對方的房子做報復。

解析
從答題關鍵的「Exchange sites recommend that swappers discuss such matters ahead of time. They may fill out an agreement spelling out who shoulders which responsibilities if a problem arises. It does not matter if the agreement would hold up in court, but it does give the exchangers a little satisfaction.」可看出，(C) 項的「Both parties can sign an agreement beforehand.」才是正確選項。

53-56 為題組

　　Bekoji is a small town of farmers and herders in the Ethiopian highlands. There, time almost stands still, and horse-drawn carts outnumber motor vehicles. Yet, it has consistently yielded many of the world's best distance runners.

It's tempting, when breathing the thin air of Bekoji, to focus on the special conditions of the place. The town sits on the side of a volcano nearly 10,000 feet above sea level, making daily life a kind of high-altitude training. Children in this region often start running at an early age, covering great distances to fetch water and firewood or to reach the nearest school. Added to this early training is a physical trait shared by people there—disproportionately long legs, which is advantageous for distance runners.

A strong desire burns inside Bekoji's young runners. Take the case of Million Abate. Forced to quit school in fifth grade after his father died, Abate worked as a shoe-shine boy for years. He saw a hope in running and joined Santayehu Eshetu's training program. This 18-year-old sprinted to the finish of a 12-mile run with his bare feet bleeding. The coach took off his own Nikes and handed them to him. To help Abate continue running, the coach arranged a motel job for him, which pays $9 a month.

Most families in Bekoji live from hand to mouth, and distance running offers the younger generation a way out. Bekoji's legend Derartu Tulu, who won the 10,000-meter Olympic gold medals in 1992 and 2000, is a national hero. As a reward, the government gave her a house. She also won millions of dollars in the races. They crowd the classrooms at Bekoji Elementary School, where Eshetu works as a physical-education instructor.

Motivated by such signs of success, thousands of kids from the villages surrounding Bekoji have moved into town. All these kids share the same dream: Some day they could become another Derartu Tulu.

Bekoji 是衣索比亞高地的農牧小鎮。那裡，時間幾乎不用，而且馬車數量多於機動車輛。然而，這個地方產生了多位世界最好的長跑選手。

這是很吸引人的，當呼吸 Bekoji 的稀薄空氣時，就必須專注於這個地方的特別條件。該鎮在近火山的海拔 10,000 呎之處，日常生活就是一種高海拔訓練。這個地區小孩很小就開始跑步，要跑很遠的地方去取水、撿木頭或是去上學。這種早期訓練使當地人有了共同的軀體特徵——不成比例的長腿，這對長跑選手特別有利。

一種強烈的願望在 Bekoji 的年輕賽跑者體內燃燒。以 Million Abate 案為例，在父親死後的五年級時被迫輟學，當擦鞋童多年。他看到長跑的希望並參加 Santayehu Eshetu 的培養訓練計畫。這位十八歲選手跑到 12 英里的終點時，光腳上都流了血。教練脫下自己的耐吉跑鞋交給他穿。為了幫助 Abate 繼續練跑，教練幫他安排一個汽車旅館的工作，每月薪資 9 美元。

在 Bekoji 裡多數家庭生活拮据，而長跑比賽提供年輕人一個出路。Bekoji 的傳奇人物 Derartu Tulu 在 1992 和 2000 年贏得 10,000 米的奧林匹克金牌，是一名國家英雄。作為一份獎勵，政府給她一所房子。她也在比賽中贏得數百萬美元。

受成功信念的驅使，Bekoji 鎮附近的數千個小孩都搬進鎮內。他們擠在 Bekoji 國小教室裡，在那裡 Eshetu 擔任體育教練。所有的孩子分享一個相同的夢想：有一天他們也能成為另外一個 Derartu Tulu。

53. Which of the following is NOT mentioned as a factor for the excellence of distance runners in Ethiopia?

　　有關衣索比亞的長跑運動員特佳原因，下列哪一項沒被提及？

　　(A) Well-known coaches.

　　　　著名的教練。

　　(B) Thin air in the highlands.

　　　　在高地的稀薄空氣。

　　(C) Extraordinarily long legs.

　　　　非常長的腿。

　　(D) Long distance running in daily life

　　　　日常生活中的長距離跑步。

解析

整段文章中都沒提到有關教練之事，所以 (A) 項的「Well-known coaches.」才是正確選項。

54. Which of the following is true about Bekoji?

　　關於 Bekoji 下列哪項為真？

　　(A) It's the capital of Ethiopia.

　　　　它是衣索比亞的首都。

　　(B) It has changed a lot over the years.

　　　　事過多年它已經改變了很多。

　　(C) It's located near a volcano.

　　　　它位於一座火山的附近。

　　(D) It has trouble handling car accidents.

　　　　它處理交通事故有困難。

解析

從答題關鍵的「The town sits on the side of a volcano nearly 10,000 feet above sea level,」可看出，(C) 項的「It's located near a volcano.」才是正確選項。

55. What is the goal of Bekoji's school kids?

　　Bekoji 的學校孩子的目標是什麼？

　　(A) To work as motel managers.

　　　　做汽車旅館經理。

　　(B) To win in international competitions.

　　　　在國際比賽中獲勝。

　　(C) To become PE teachers.

　　　　成為體育老師。

(D) To perform well academically at school.

　　在學校學業成績要好。

解析

從答題關鍵的「Motivated by such signs of success, thousands of kids from the villages surrounding Bekoji have moved into town.」可看出，(B) 項的「To win in international competitions」才是正確選項。

56. What can be inferred from this passage?

　　從本文可以推斷出什麼？

(A) More distance runners may emerge from Bekoji.

　　更多的長跑運動員可能來自 Bekoji。

(B) Nike will sponsor the young distance runners in Bekoji.

　　耐吉運動鞋將贊助在 Bekoji 的長跑運動員。

(C) Bekoji will host an international long-distance competition.

　　Bekoji 將舉辦國際長跑比賽。

(D) The Ethiopian government has spared no efforts in promoting running.

　　衣索比亞政府從未努力推廣跑步運動。

解析

從答題關鍵的「Motivated by such signs of success, thousands of kids from the villages surrounding Bekoji have moved into town.」可看出，(A) 項的「More distance runners may emerge from Bekoji.」才是正確選項。

第貳部分：非選擇題（28分）

一、翻譯題（8分）

説明：1. 請將以下兩題中文譯成正確而通順達意的英文，並將答案寫在「答案卷」上。
　　　2. 請依序作答，並標明題號。每題 4 分，共 8 分。

1. 在過去，腳踏車主要是作爲一種交通工具。

解析

先將與題句內容相關字詞與中譯寫出：

在過去 in the past　腳踏車 bicycle　主要是 mainly　作爲 used for　交通工具 transportation（本身已有運輸工具之意，其後不必畫蛇添足加上 tools）

整句英譯

In the past, bicycles are used mainly as one of the transportation.

說明

(1)在談到「以前如何如何」時，可用「in the past」這個說法。如果是說「過去三年來」或「這三年來」，英文就有「for the last three years」或「in the past three years」等說法。

2. 然而，騎腳踏車現在已經成爲一種熱門的休閒活動。

解析

(1)先將與題句內容相關字詞與中譯寫出：

然而 However　騎腳踏車 bicycling　已經成爲 has become　熱門的 popular　休閒活動 recreation
當今 nowadays

(2)bicycling 一字，現已成爲「腳踏車運動」的專有名詞。

整句英譯

However, bicycling has become a popular recreation nowadays.

二、英文作文（20分）

說明：1. 依提示在「答案卷」上寫一篇英文作文。
　　　2. 文長至少 120 個單詞（words）。

提示：請仔細觀察以下三幅連環圖片的內容，並想像第四幅圖片可能的發展，寫出一個涵蓋連環圖片內容並有完整結局的故事。

解析

(1)這種看圖說故事的作文很容易發揮，它並沒有固定的格式要求考生怎麼寫，只要寫出來的文章，不離圖意太遠、加上語句通順、文語法不要錯，也不要寫中式英文，都可得高分。

(2)圖①的麵攤老闆娘與小男孩是什麼關係不重要，由考生隨意寫，寫成母子、姑姪……都可以。

甚至幫圖中人物取名字都可以，男孩叫 Tom，母親叫做 Sue，丟錢的人叫作 Jack 等等。

(3)接著把各圖裡的每一景象，用英文把它寫出來：

圖①：there is a noodle stand 有一個麵攤

there is also a pricelist on the wall 牆上有個價目表

a woman is busy cooking something 有一位婦女在忙著煮東西

her boy is writing his homework 她兒子正在寫功課

a man with glasses is eating his noodle 一個戴眼鏡的男子在吃麵

圖②：the man has gone

the boy and his mother open the bag

they found there was much money in the bag

圖③：the man is now at the Hsin-chu train station

he suddenly realizes that he has lost the bag somewhere

he is so worried ,that's why he is perspiring a lot

圖④：留下一個大問號，就是要考生再自由發揮，把你想要的結果寫出來，你可以說：那位男子立刻搭計程車回去麵攤去要回大包包

the man returned immediately to the noodle stand by taxi

也可以說母子二人在男子到麵攤前，已把大包包送去警察局

mother and son had turned in the bag to the police before the man came back to the stand.

也可以說，那些錢是該男子早上剛剛借來的

the man has just borrowed the money for his mother's hospital bill.

結尾：像以上的例句，考生要看到圖裡有什麼就寫什麼，這樣湊成幾十句之後，再把幾十個字句有意義的組合起來。成為以下的標準答案：

There is a noodle stand in the street corner. It has also a nice looking price-list on the wall. One day, I saw a boy writing his homework at the stand. Later, a man with glasses came to the stand and ordered a bowl of soup noodle and something else. I saw the woman still busy cooking something while the man was eating the noodle. The man left a big bag on the stool between he and the boy. The man seemed enjoy eating the noodle, he finished the noodle and paid the money and left. However, the woman and her son found that the man had left a bag behind, obviously he forgot to take the bag alone when he left.

By the time the man got to Hsin-chu Railway Station, he suddenly realized that he left the bag somewhere, it could possibily be at the noodle stand. He was worried so much about the bag because there was a lot of money in it, that was the money he borrowed this morning from the bank, it was supposed to be the money for his mother's hospital bill. He hurried to the noodle stand, but the woman told him that she had turned in the bag to the police just before he returned to her stand.

However, the woman was so kind to help the man to claim his bag and money at the police station without any trouble.

100 年學測（學科能力測驗）

第壹部分：單選題（72分）

一、詞彙（15分）

1. All the new students were given one minute to ＿＿＿＿＿ introduce themselves to the whole class.

   所有學生有一分鐘 ＿＿＿＿＿ 向全班做自我介紹。

   (A) briefly 簡短地　(B) famously 著名地　(C) gradually 漸漸地　(D) obviously 顯然地

   解析
   (1)答題關鍵在題目空格左、右方的 ＿＿＿＿＿「一分鐘」與「自我介紹」
   (2)四個選項中，只有選(A)項的「簡短地」，才可有意義連成「一分鐘簡短地自我介紹」。

2. His dark brown jacket had holes in the elbows and had ＿＿＿＿＿ to light brown, but he continued to wear it.

   他棕色夾克手肘有破洞也已 ＿＿＿＿＿ 至淺棕色，但他還是照樣穿。

   (A) cycled 回收　(B) faded 褪色　(C) loosened 鬆脫　(D) divided 已分離

   解析
   (1)答題關鍵在題目空格右方的「至淺棕色」。
   (2)四個選項中，只有選(B)項的「褪色」，才可有意義連成「已褪至淺棕色」。

3. Everyone in our company enjoys working with Jason. He's got all the qualities that make a ＿＿＿＿＿ partner.

   公司所有人都想與傑生共事。他具有 ＿＿＿＿＿ 伙伴的所有條件。

   (A) desirable 令人滿意的　(B) comfortable 舒適的　(C) frequent 時常的　(D) hostile 敵方的

   解析
   (1)答題關鍵在題目空格右方的「伙伴」。
   (2)四個選項中，只有選(A)項的「令人滿意的」，才可有意義連成「具有令人滿意伙伴的所有條件」。

4. Eyes are sensitive to light. Looking at the sun _____ could damage our eyes.

　　眼睛對亮光很敏感 _____ 注視陽光會傷害到眼睛。

　　(A) hardly 幾乎不　(B) specially 特別是　(C) totally 全部地　(D) directly 直接地

解析

(1)答題關鍵在題目空格左、右方的「注視陽光」與「傷眼睛」。

(2)四個選項中，只有(D)選項的「直接地」，才可有意義連成「直接注視陽光會傷眼睛」。

5. We were forced to _____ our plan for the weekend picnic because of the bad weather.

　　由於壞天氣我們被迫 _____ 我們週末野餐的計畫。

　　(A) maintain 維持　(B) record 記錄　(C) propose 提議　(D) cancel 取消

解析

(1)答題關鍵在題目空格左、右方的「被迫」與「我們……計畫」。

(2)四個選項中，只有選(D)項的「取消」，才可有意義連成「被迫取消……計畫」。

6. Three people are running for mayor. All three _____ seem confident that they will be elected, but we won't know until the outcome of the election is announced.

　　有三人競選市長。三個 _____ 似乎都有信心會當選，但選舉結果未公布前誰也不知道。

　　(A) particles 分子　(B) receivers 收件者　(C) candidates 候選人　(D) containers 容器

解析

(1)答題關鍵在題目空格左方的「競選市長」。

(2)四個選項中，只有選(C)項的「候選人」，才可有意義連成「三個候選人似乎都有信心」。

7. If you _____ a traffic law, such as drinking and driving, you may not drive for some time.

　　如果你 _____ 交通法規像是酒駕，你就會有一陣子不能開車。

　　(A) destroy 毀損　(B) violate 違反　(C) attack 攻擊　(D) invade 侵略

解析

(1)答題關鍵在題目空格右方的「交通法規」。

(2)四個選項中，只有選(B)項的「違反」，才可有意義連成「如果你違反交通法規」。

8. Applying to college means sending in applications, writing study plans, and so on. It's a long _____ , and it makes students nervous.

　　向大學申請是指寄申請書寫就學計畫等。這個過程很長，學生也會緊張。

　　(A) errand 差事　(B) operation 操作　(C) process 過程　(D) display 展示

解析

(1)答題關鍵在題目空格左方的「很長的」。

(2)四個選項中，只有選(C)項的「過程」，才可有意義連成「向大學申請……這個過程很長」。

9. Dr. Chu's speech on the new energy source attracted great ＿＿＿＿＿＿ from the audience at the conference.

朱博士的演講引起參加會議聽眾很大的 ＿＿＿＿＿＿ 。

(A) attention 注意　(B) fortune 財富　(C) solution 解決方法　(D) influence 影響

解析

(1)答題關鍵在題目空格左方的「引起很大的」。

(2)四個選項中，只有選(A)項的「注意」，才可有意義連成「引起（聽眾）很大的注意」。

10. Everyone in the office must attend the meeting tomorrow. There are no ＿＿＿＿＿＿ allowed.

公司每人都要參加明天的會議。不允許有 ＿＿＿＿＿＿

(A) exceptions 例外　(B) additions 附加　(C) divisions 分開　(D) measures 測量

解析

(1)答題關鍵在題目空格左、右方的「無」與「允許」。

(2)四個選項中，只有選(A)項的「例外」，才可有意義連成「不允許有例外」。

11. To make fresh lemonade, cut the lemon in half, ＿＿＿＿＿＿ the juice into a bowl, and then add as much water and sugar as you like.

要做新鮮檸檬水，將之切一半，把果汁 ＿＿＿＿＿＿ 進大碗內，加些糖水即可。

(A) decrease 減少　(B) squeeze 擠壓　(C) freeze 冰凍　(D) cease 停止

解析

(1)答題關鍵在題目空格右方的「果汁」與「進大碗內」。

(2)四個選項中，只有選(B)項的「擠壓」，才可有意義連成「把果汁擠進大碗內」。

12. Buddhism is the ＿＿＿＿＿＿ religion in Thailand, with 90% of the total population identified as Buddhists.

在泰國佛教是 ＿＿＿＿＿＿ ，有九成的人口是佛教徒。

(A) racial 種族的　(B) competitive 競爭的　(C) modest 謙虛　(D) dominant 占首位的、統治的

解析

(1)答題關鍵在題目空格右方的「宗教」。

(2)四個選項中，只有選(D)項的「占首位的」，才可有意義連成「在泰國它是占首位的」。

13. When I open a book, I look first at the table of ＿＿＿＿＿＿ to get a general idea of the book and to see which chapters I might be interested in reading.

打開一本書時，我先看它的 ＿＿＿＿＿＿ 初步了解書中內容或是要讀哪些章節。

(A) contracts 合約　(B) contents 目錄　(C) contests 比賽　(D) contacts 接觸

解析

(1)答題關鍵在題目空格左方的「table of」。

(2)四個選項中，只有選(B)項的「目錄」，才可有意義連成「書中目錄」。

14. The children were so ＿＿＿＿＿＿ to see the clown appear on stage that they laughed, screamed, and clapped their hands happily.

孩子們很高興看到臺上的小丑，大笑大叫也高興地拍手。

(A) admirable 令人欽佩的　(B) fearful 可怕的　(C) delighted 高興的　(D) intense 劇烈的

解析

(1)答題關鍵在題目空格左、右方的「孩子們」與「看到」。

(2)四個選項中，只有選(C)項的「高興的」，才可有意義連成「孩子們很高興看到臺上的……」。

15. Typhoon Maggie brought to I-lan County a huge amount of rainfall, much greater than the ＿＿＿＿＿＿ rainfall of the season in the area.

瑪姬颱風帶給宜蘭大量雨水，比該區整季的 ＿＿＿＿＿ 降雨量還多。

(A) average 平均　(B) considerate 體諒　(C) promising 有希望的　(D) enjoyable 快樂的

解析

(1)答題關鍵在題目空格右方的「降雨量」。

(2)四個選項中，只有選(A)項的「平均的」，才可有意義連成「比該區整季的平均降雨量還多」。

二、綜合測驗（15分）

説明：第16題至第30題，每題一個空格，請依文意選出最適當的一個答案，畫記在答案卡之「選擇題答案區」。各題答對得1分；未作答、答錯、或畫記多於一個選項者，該題以零分計算。

　　When it comes to Egypt, people think of pyramids and mummies, both of which are closely related to Egyptian religious beliefs. The ancient Egyptians believed firmly in life ＿＿16＿＿ death. When a person died, his or her soul was thought to travel to an underworld, where it ＿＿17＿＿ a series of judgments before it could progress to a better life in the next world. For the soul to travel smoothly, the body had to ＿＿18＿＿ unharmed. Thus, they learned how to preserve the body by drying it out, oiling and then ＿＿19＿＿ the body in linen, before placing it in the coffin. Egyptians also built pyramids as ＿＿20＿＿ for their kings, or pharaohs. The pyramid housed the pharaoh's body together with priceless treasure, which would accompany him into the next world.

　　當談論到埃及時，人們想起金字塔和木乃伊等，這兩者都與埃及宗教信仰密切相關。古埃及堅信人死 ＿＿16＿＿ 的生命。當一個人死時，他或她的靈魂被認為會旅行到地獄，在那裡它會 ＿＿17＿＿ 一系列的評判，來決定是否能前往下一個世界過

好的生活。為了讓靈魂能順利旅行，屍體必須 _____18_____ 完整無傷。因此，埃及人學習怎樣使屍體先弄乾、上油然後用亞麻布 _____19_____ 屍體，之後才放進棺材。埃及人也為他們的國王或法老建造金字塔當作 _____20_____ 。他們會將無價之寶與法老一同放進金字塔，那些陪葬物將會伴隨法老進入下一個世界。

**16. 題句：The ancient Egyptians believed firmly in life _____16_____ death.

古埃及堅信人死 _____16_____ 的生命。

選項：(A) for 為…… 　(B) by 被…… 　(C) after 之後 　(D) into 之內

解析

依題意只有選(C)項的「之後」才是正確選項。

17. 題句：where it _____17_____ a series of judgments before it could progress to a better life in the next world.

在那裡它會 _____17_____ 一系列的評判。

選項：(A) went through 經歷過 　(B) made up 編造 　(C) changed into 變換 　(D) turned out 成為

解析

依題意只有選(A)項的「經歷過」才是正確選項。

18. 題句：For the soul to travel smoothly, the body had to _____18_____ unharmed.

為了讓靈魂能順利旅行，屍體必須 _____18_____ 完整無傷。

選項：(A) remain 保留 　(B) remind 提醒 　(C) repair 修理 　(D) replace 取代

解析

依題意只有選(A)項的「保留」才是正確選項。

**19. 題句：to preserve the body by drying it out, oiling and then _____19_____ the body in linen,

然後用亞麻布 _____19_____ 屍體。

選項：(A) wrapped 包裹（過去式）　(B) wrapping（分詞片語）　(C) to wrap（不定詞）　(D) being wrapped（被動語態）

解析

依題意只有選(B)項的「wrapping」才是正確選項。

20. 題句：Egyptians also built pyramids as _____20_____ for their kings, or pharaohs.

埃及人也為他們的國王或法老建造金字塔當作 _____20_____ 。

選項：(A) galleries 畫廊 　(B) landmarks 地標 　(C) companies 公司 　(D) tombs 墳墓

解析

依題意只有選(D)項的「墳墓」才是正確選項。

On March 23, 1999, the musical MAMMA MIA! made its first public appearance in London. It _____21_____ the kind of welcome it has been getting ever since. The audience went wild. They were literally out of their seats and singing and dancing in the aisles.

MAMMA MIA! has become a _____22_____ entertainment phenomenon. More than 30 million people all over the world have fallen in love with the characters, the story and the music. The musical has been performed in more than nine languages, with more productions than any _____23_____ musical. Its worldwide popularity is mainly due to its theme music, which showcases ABBA's timeless songs in a fresh and vital way _____24_____ retains the essence of both pop music and good musical theater. It has _____25_____ so many people that a film version was also made. To no one's surprise, it has enjoyed similar popularity.

在 1999 年 3 月 23 日，媽媽米亞音樂劇在倫敦首次公開露面。它 _____21_____ 的歡迎就像以前一樣。觀眾變得瘋狂。觀眾簡直無法在他們的座位上而是在走道又唱又跳。媽媽米亞已經成為一個 _____22_____ 的娛樂現象。超過三千萬人已經愛上劇中人物、劇情與音樂。這個音樂劇已被九種以上的語言唱過，比任何 _____23_____ 音樂劇有更多的相關產品問世。它以清新與充滿活力的方式，展現出 ABBA 劇團之隨時流行的歌曲，_____24_____ 保留流行音樂與好劇院的本質。它也 _____25_____ 世人，也製作了電影版本。沒有意外地，電影版本也同樣的流行。

**21. 題句：It _____21_____ the kind of welcome it has been getting ever since.
　　　　它 _____21_____ 的歡迎就像以前一樣。
　　選項：(A) is given 被給　(B) was given（過去式）　(C) has given（現在完成式）　(D) had given（過去完成式）

解析

依題意只有選(B)項的「被給予的」（也就是「所受到的歡迎」之意）才是正確選項。內容敘述發生時間為 1999 年，故應選 it was given ... 意指那時候被給予……。

22. 題句：MAMMA MIA! has become a _____22_____ entertainment phenomenon.
　　　　媽媽米亞已經成為一個 _____22_____ 的娛樂現象。
　　選項：(A) worthy 值得　(B) global 全球的　(C) sticky 黏的　(D) physical 軀體的

解析

依題意只有選(B)項的「全球的」才是正確選項。

**23. 題句：with more productions than any _____23_____ musical.
　　　　比任何 _____23_____ 音樂劇有更多的相關產品問世。
　　選項：(A) one 一　(B) thing 事物　(C) other 其他　(D) else 另外

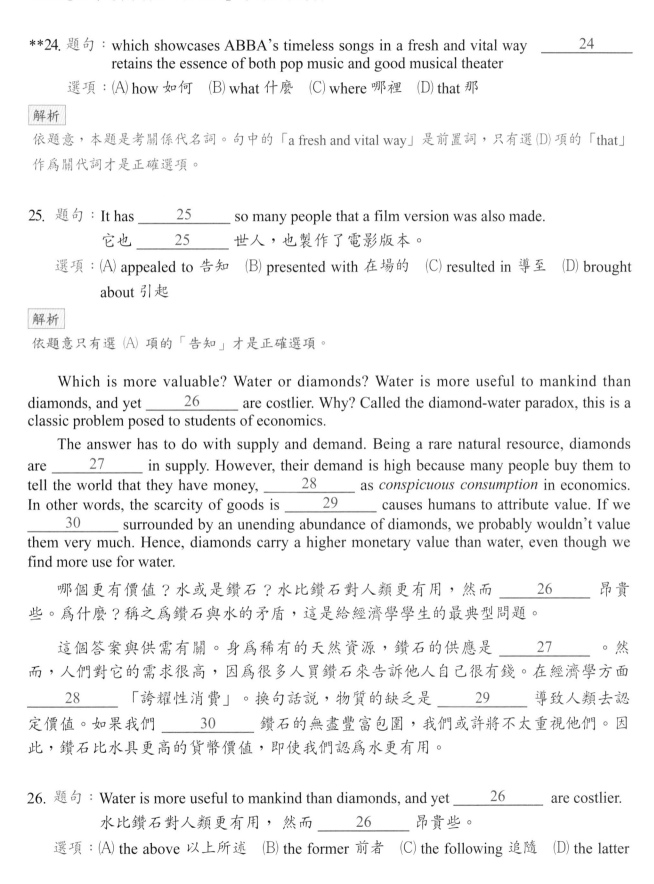

解析

依題意只有選(C)項的「其他的」才是正確選項。

**24. 題句：which showcases ABBA's timeless songs in a fresh and vital way ＿＿＿24＿＿＿
retains the essence of both pop music and good musical theater

選項：(A) how 如何　(B) what 什麼　(C) where 哪裡　(D) that 那

解析

依題意，本題是考關係代名詞。句中的「a fresh and vital way」是前置詞，只有選(D)項的「that」
作為關代詞才是正確選項。

25. 題句：It has ＿＿＿25＿＿＿ so many people that a film version was also made.
它也 ＿＿＿25＿＿＿ 世人，也製作了電影版本。

選項：(A) appealed to 告知　(B) presented with 在場的　(C) resulted in 導至　(D) brought
about 引起

解析

依題意只有選 (A) 項的「告知」才是正確選項。

Which is more valuable? Water or diamonds? Water is more useful to mankind than
diamonds, and yet ＿＿＿26＿＿＿ are costlier. Why? Called the diamond-water paradox, this is a
classic problem posed to students of economics.

The answer has to do with supply and demand. Being a rare natural resource, diamonds
are ＿＿＿27＿＿＿ in supply. However, their demand is high because many people buy them to
tell the world that they have money, ＿＿＿28＿＿＿ as *conspicuous consumption* in economics.
In other words, the scarcity of goods is ＿＿＿29＿＿＿ causes humans to attribute value. If we
＿＿＿30＿＿＿ surrounded by an unending abundance of diamonds, we probably wouldn't value
them very much. Hence, diamonds carry a higher monetary value than water, even though we
find more use for water.

哪個更有價值？水或是鑽石？水比鑽石對人類更有用，然而 ＿＿＿26＿＿＿ 昂貴
些。為什麼？稱之為鑽石與水的矛盾，這是給經濟學學生的最典型問題。

這個答案與供需有關。身為稀有的天然資源，鑽石的供應是 ＿＿＿27＿＿＿ 。然
而，人們對它的需求很高，因為很多人買鑽石來告訴他人自己很有錢。在經濟學方面
＿＿＿28＿＿＿ 「誇耀性消費」。換句話說，物質的缺乏是 ＿＿＿29＿＿＿ 導致人類去認
定價值。如果我們 ＿＿＿30＿＿＿ 鑽石的無盡豐富包圍，我們或許將不太重視他們。因
此，鑽石比水具更高的貨幣價值，即使我們認為水更有用。

26. 題句：Water is more useful to mankind than diamonds, and yet ＿＿＿26＿＿＿ are costlier.
水比鑽石對人類更有用，然而 ＿＿＿26＿＿＿ 昂貴些。

選項：(A) the above 以上所述　(B) the former 前者　(C) the following 追隨　(D) the latter

後者

解析

依題意只有選(D)項的「後者」才是正確選項。

27. 題句：Being a rare natural resource, diamonds are _____27_____ in supply.

身為稀有的天然資源，鑽石的供應是 _____27_____ 。

選項：(A) traded 交易的　(B) weakened 削弱　(C) limited 受限制的　(D) noticed 注意的

解析

依題意只有選(C)項的「受限制的」才是正確選項。

**28. 題句：many people buy them to tell the world that they have money, _____28_____ as conspicuous consumption in economics

在經濟學方面 _____28_____ 「誇耀性消費」。

選項：(A) term 稱為　(B) termed （過去式）　(C) terms （三單現在式）　(D) was termed （被動過去式）

解析

依題意只有選(B)項的「稱為」才是正確選項。termed as 為「被稱為」之意，不能選(D)項的 was termed，除非它之前有 which。

**29. 題句：In other words, the scarcity of goods is _____29_____ causes humans to attribute value.

換句話說，物質的缺乏是 _____29_____ 導致人類去認定價值。

選項：(A) what 什麼　(B) which 哪一　(C) why 為什麼　(D) how 為何

解析

依題意，空格後的 causes 是動詞，所以放入空格的必須是「主詞」。(A)項的「what」在此是代名詞，可當主詞用，才是正確選項。

**30. 題句：If we _____30_____ surrounded by an unending abundance of diamonds,

如果我們 _____30_____ 鑽石的無盡豐富包圍。

選項：(A) be （原形動詞）　(B) being （現在分詞）　(C) to be （不定詞）　(D) were （過去式）

解析

(1)依題意只有選(D)項的「were」才是正確選項。

(2)在 if 之後的 be 動詞，其主詞不論人稱或單複數，皆須選 were。

三、文意選填（10分）

說明：第 31 題至第 40 題，每題一個空格，請依文意在文章後所提供的 (A) 到 (J) 選項中分別選出最適當者，並將其英文字母代號畫記在答案卡之「選擇題答案區」。各題答對得 1 分；未作答、答錯、或畫記多於一個選項者，該題以零分計算。

Popcorn is one of the snacks that rarely fail to make watching a movie more fun. However, the modern way of preparing this _____31_____ snack may carry an unhappy secret. Research by the U.S. government now reports that microwave popcorn may contain substances that can cause health _____32_____ .

Researchers found that commercial popcorn companies often coat their microwave popcorn bags with a _____33_____ called perfluorooctanoic acid (PFOA) which has been found to cause both cancer and lung disease in laboratory animals. Making matters worse, the artificial butter substitute that generally _____34_____ with microwavable popcorn contains a common food-flavoring substance. This substance, according to health scientists, is _____35_____ for some serious lung diseases.

For an easy and _____36_____ alternative, nutritionists suggest that we pop our own popcorn. All that is _____37_____ a large, high pot, about four tablespoons of vegetable oil and a small handful of organic popcorn kernels. When the kernels start _____38_____ , shake the pot to let the steam escape and to let the unpopped kernels fall to the bottom. As soon as the popping slows down, _____39_____ the pot from the stove. Then pour the popcorn into a bowl and season with a small _____40_____ of real butter or olive oil and natural salt. And the healthy and fun snack is ready to serve.

爆米花是使看電影更爲有趣的點心之一。不過，準備這份 _____31_____ 點心的現代做法可能有一個不愉快的祕密。美國政府的研究做出報告，微波爆米花可能含有引起健康 _____32_____ 的物質。研究人員發現商業的爆米花公司經常給他們的微波爆米花袋塗上 _____33_____ 叫 perfluorooctanoic 酸的（PFOA），而這物質已被發現是引起實驗室動物得癌症和肺病。更糟的是，人造奶油替代品通常 _____34_____ 可微波爆米花而來，包含一種普通食品口味的物質。這種物質，根據健康科學家所言，要對一些嚴重的肺疾病 _____35_____ 。

對一個簡單與 _____36_____ 的選擇來說，營養學家建議我們自己做爆米花。 所 _____37_____ 的只是一個大些高些的鍋，大約要四大匙植物油和一小把有機的玉米花果仁。當果仁開始 _____38_____ 的時候，搖晃鍋子讓蒸汽跑出走並且讓未爆果仁掉至底部。當砰爆聲緩慢下來時，把鍋子 _____39_____ 。然後把爆米花倒進一只大碗再用少 _____40_____ 眞正的奶油或者橄欖油和自然的鹽作調味。健康和有趣的點心就完成了。

(A) chemical 化學物質　　(B) amount 數量　　(C) popping 突出、爆出

(D) popular 受歡迎的　　(E) comes 來　　(F) healthy 健康

(G) needed 有需要　　(H) responsible 負責　　(I) remove 移開　　(J) problems 問題

31. 題句：準備這份 ＿＿＿31＿＿＿ 點心的現代做法可能有一個不愉快的祕密。

解析

依題意只有選(D)項的「受歡迎的」才是正確選項。

32. 題句：微波爆米花可能含有引起健康 ＿＿＿32＿＿＿ 的物質。

解析

依題意只有選(J)項的「問題」才是正確選項。

33. 題句：爆米花公司經常給他們的微波爆米花袋塗上 ＿＿＿33＿＿＿ 叫 perfluorooctanoic 酸的（PFOA）。

解析

依題意只有選(A)項的「化學物質」才是正確選項。

34. 題句：the artificial butter substitute that generally ＿＿＿34＿＿＿ with microwavable popcorn ....

　　　　　人造奶油替代品通常 ＿＿＿34＿＿＿ 可微波爆米花而來。

解析

依題意只有選(E)項的「comes」才是正確選項。 come with 指「伴隨而來」之意。

35. 題句：根據健康科學家所言，要對一些嚴重的肺疾病 ＿＿＿35＿＿＿ 。

解析

⑴依題意只有選(H)項的「responsible」才是正確選項。

⑵be responsible for 是「為……負責」之意，也就是「為某事的起因」。

36. 題句：對一個簡單與 ＿＿＿36＿＿＿ 的選擇來說。

解析

依題意只有選(F)項的「健康的」才是正確選項。

37. 題句：所 ＿＿＿37＿＿＿ 的只是一個大些高些的鍋。

解析

依題意只有選(G)項的「needed」才是正確選項。 Is needed 為「所需的」之意。

38. 題句：當果仁開始 ＿＿＿38＿＿＿ 的時候。

解析

依題意只有選(C)項的「爆出」才是正確選項。

39. 題句：當砰爆聲緩慢下來時，把鍋子＿＿＿＿39＿＿＿＿。

解析

依題意只有選(I)項的「移開」才是正確選項。

40. 題句：然後把爆米花倒進一只大碗再用少＿＿＿＿40＿＿＿＿真正的奶油。

解析

依題意只有選(B)項的「量」才是正確選項。

四、閱讀測驗（32分）

說明：第 41 題至第 56 題，每題 4 個選項，請分別根據各篇文章之文意選出最適當的一個答案，畫記在答案卡之「選擇題答案區」。各題答對得 2 分；未作答、答錯、或畫記多於一個選項者，該題以零分計算。

41-44 題組

There is a long-held belief that when meeting someone, the more eye contact we have with the person, the better. The result is an unfortunate tendency for people making initial contact—in a job interview, for example—to stare fixedly at the other individual. However, this behavior is likely to make the interviewer feel very uncomfortable. Most of us are comfortable with eye contact lasting a few seconds. But eye contact which persists longer than that can make us nervous.

Another widely accepted belief is that powerful people in a society—often men—show their dominance over others by touching them in a variety of ways. In fact, research shows that in almost all cases, lower–status people initiate touch. Women also initiate touch more often than men do.

The belief that rapid speech and lying go together is also widespread and enduring. We react strongly—and suspiciously—to fast talk. However, the opposite is a greater cause for suspicion. Speech that is slow, because it is laced with pauses or errors, is a more reliable indicator of lying than the opposite.

很久以來就有人相信，當你與人見面時，越能注視對方的眼睛越好。在求職時的第一次面談時，這種結果是不利的。舉例來說，固定的凝視對方，不管怎樣，這種凝視對方的舉動可能使對方感到不舒服。我們多數人對幾秒鐘的眼光接觸不會感到不舒服，但是長於幾秒鐘的眼光接觸會使我們緊張。

另一種說法是，社會上有權勢的人，用各種不同的接觸方式來顯示自己的優越。實際上，研究顯示幾乎在所有情況下，位階低者先起動接觸。婦女比男性更會先啟動接觸。

相信「說話快速和說謊常相隨而來」的人很普遍，對說話快速部分，我們反應強烈——也表示懷疑。不過，對方才是存疑的原因。說話慢是因為其中有暫停或錯誤，是對方說謊的更確實指標。

41. Which of the following statements is true according to the passage?

根據本文，下列哪項為真？

(A) Rapid speech without mistakes is a reliable sign of intelligence.

沒有錯誤的快速說話是智力的可靠訊息。

(B) Women often play a more dominant role than men in a community.

在社區裡，婦女經常比男性更有支配欲。

(C) Speaking slowly is more often a sign of lying than speaking quickly.

講話慢比講話快才是說謊的表徵。

(D) Touching tends to be initiated first by people of higher social positions.

社會地位低的人比地位高的人會首先起動接觸。

解析

從答題關鍵的「Speech that is slow, because it is laced with pauses or errors, is a more reliable indicator of lying than the opposite.」可看出，(C) 項的「Speaking slowly is more often a sign of lying than speaking quickly.」才是正確選項。

42. What is true about fixing your eyes on a person when you first meet him/her?

有關用眼睛凝視第一次會見的人，下列陳述哪項為真？

(A) Fixing your eyes on the person will make him/her feel at ease.

凝視他人會使對方很舒服。

(B) It is more polite to fix your eyes on him/her as long as you can.

凝視對方越久越有禮貌。

(C) Most people feel uneasy to have eye contact for over a few seconds.

多於幾秒鐘的凝視他人會使人感到不安。

(D) It doesn't make a difference whether you fix your eyes on him/her or not.

你是否凝視對方沒有差別。

解析

從答題關鍵的「However, this behavior is likely to make the interviewer feel very uncomfortable.」可看出，(C) 項的「Most people feel uneasy to have eye contact for over a few seconds.」才是正確選項。

43. Which of the following is **NOT** discussed in the passage?

下列哪一項本文並未提及？

(A) Facial expressions. 臉部表情。

(B) Physical contact. 肢體接觸。

(C) Rate of speech. 講話速度。

(D) Eye contact. 眼光接觸。

從整段文章並未提及臉部表情一事，所以 (A) 項的「Facial expressions.」才是未被提及的正確選項。

44. What is the main idea of the passage?

　　本文的大意是什麼？

(A) People have an instinct for interpreting non-verbal communication.

　　人們有詮釋非語言溝通的本能。

(B) We should not judge the intention of a person by his body language.

　　我們不應依他人的肢體語言去斷定一個人的意圖。

(C) A good knowledge of body language is essential for successful communication.

　　良好的肢體語言知識對成功的溝通是必要的。

(D) Common beliefs about verbal and non-verbal communication are not always correct.

　　一般關於語言或非語言溝通說法不是完全正確。

解析

從整段文章內容判斷，(D) 項的「Common beliefs about verbal and non-verbal communication are not always correct.」才是正確選項。

45-48 為題組

It is easy for us to tell our friends from our enemies. But can other animals do the same? Elephants can! They can use their sense of vision and smell to tell the difference between people who pose a threat and those who do not.

In Kenya, researchers found that elephants react differently to clothing worn by men of the Maasai and Kamba ethnic groups. Young Maasai men spear animals and thus pose a threat to elephants; Kamba men are mainly farmers and are not a danger to elephants.

In an experiment conducted by animal scientists, elephants were first presented with clean clothing or clothing that had been worn for five days by either a Maasai or a Kamba man. When the elephants detected the smell of clothing worn by a Maasai man, they moved away from the smell faster and took longer to relax than when they detected the smells of either clothing worn by Kamba men or clothing that had not been worn at all.

Garment color also plays a role, though in a different way. In the same study, when the elephants saw red clothing not worn before, they reacted angrily, as red is typically worn by Maasai men. Rather than running away as they did with the smell, the elephants acted aggressively toward the red clothing.

The researchers believe that the elephants' emotional reactions are due to their different interpretations of the smells and the sights. Smelling a potential danger means that a threat is nearby and the best thing to do is run away and hide. Seeing a potential threat without its smell means that risk is low. Therefore, instead of showing fear and running away, the elephants express their anger and become aggressive.

　　區分我們的朋友或敵人不難。但其他動物能這樣做嗎？大象能！他們能利用視覺和氣味去區別對他們有過威脅的人。

　　在肯亞，研究人員發現大象對馬賽族與堪巴族的穿著反應不同。年輕的馬賽人用矛刺動物，對大象有威脅；堪巴族主要是農人，對大象沒有危險。

　　在動物科學家負責的實驗中，大象之前放著乾淨的衣服，或者該二族人穿過五天的衣服。當大象偵測到馬賽人穿過衣服的氣味時，他們迅速地不再聞了。但需稍長的時間才恢復平靜。

　　服裝顏色也有關係，雖然以不同模式做測試。在相同的研究裡，大象看到沒穿過的紅色衣服時，反應很憤怒，紅色通常是馬賽人的衣服顏色。大象向紅色衣服反應很具侵略性，而不是之前用聞的那樣。

　　研究人員相信大象的感情反應是來自對嗅覺與視覺有所不同。聞出潛在危險表示威脅就在附近，最好趕快逃走並且躲起來。看到而非聞到的潛在威脅表示危險很低。因此，大象表示了他們的憤怒並變得有侵略性而不是害怕地逃走。

45. According to the passage, which of the following statements is true about Kamba and Maasai people?

　　根據本文，下列陳述哪一項關於堪巴人和馬賽人的為真？

　　(A) Maasai people are a threat to elephants.

　　　　馬賽人對象有威脅。

　　(B) Kamba people raise elephants for farming.

　　　　堪巴人飼養大象。

　　(C) Both Kamba and Maasai people are elephant hunters.

　　　　堪巴人和馬賽人都是獵象人。

　　(D) Both Kamba and Maasai people traditionally wear red clothing.

　　　　堪巴人和馬賽人傳統上穿紅色衣服。

解析

從答題關鍵的「從第一段內容『年輕的馬賽人用矛刺動物，對大象有威脅。』」可看出，(A) 項的「Maasai people are a threat to elephants.」才是正確選項。

46. How did the elephants react to smell in the study?

　　上項研究中，大象的嗅覺有何反應？

　　(A) They attacked a man with the smell of new clothing.

　　　　牠們攻擊有新衣服氣味的人。

　　(B) They needed time to relax when smelling something unfamiliar.

　　　　當聞出不熟悉之物，牠們需要時間恢復情緒。

(C) They became anxious when they smelled Kamba-scented clothing.

當聞到有堪巴人味道的衣服時，牠們變得焦慮不安。

(D) They were frightened and ran away when they smelled their enemies.

當牠們聞到敵人的味道時，牠們被嚇住並離開。

解析

從答題關鍵的「第五段內容：『Smelling a potential danger means ... run away and hide』」可看出，

(D) 項的「They were frightened and ran away when they smelled their enemies.」才是正確選項。

47. What is the main idea of this passage?

本文的大意是什麼？

(A) Elephants use sight and smell to detect danger.

大象利用視覺與嗅覺偵測危險。

(B) Elephants attack people who wear red clothing.

大象攻擊穿紅衣服的人。

(C) Scientists are now able to control elephants' emotions.

科學家目前能夠控制大象的情感。

(D) Some Kenyan tribes understand elephants' emotions very well.

某些肯亞部落很能了解大象的情感。

解析

從整段內容可看出，(A) 項的「Elephants use sight and smell to detect danger.」才是正確選項。

48. What can be inferred about the elephant's behavior from this passage?

從本文內容可以推論出何種大象行為？

(A) Elephants learn from their experiences.

大象從經驗中學習。

(B) Elephants have sharper sense of smell than sight.

大象的嗅覺比視覺敏銳。

(C) Elephants are more intelligent than other animals.

大象比其他動物聰明。

(D) Elephants tend to attack rather than escape when in danger.

處於險境時，大象傾向於攻擊而不是逃走。

解析

從整段文章內容可看出，(A) 項的「Elephants learn from their experiences.」才是正確選項。

49-52 為題組

It was something she had dreamed of since she was five. Finally, after years of training and intensive workouts, Deborah Duffey was going to compete in her first high school basketball game. The goals of becoming an outstanding player and playing college ball were never far from Deborah's mind.

The game was against Mills High School. With 1: 42 minutes left in the game, Deborah's team led by one point. A player of Mills had possession of the ball, and Deborah ran to guard against her. As Deborah shuffled sideways to block the player, her knee went out and she collapsed on the court in burning pain. Just like that, Deborah's season was over.

After suffering the bad injury, Deborah found that, for the first time in her life, she was in a situation beyond her control. Game after game, she could do nothing but sit on the sidelines watching others play the game that she loved so much.

Injuries limited Deborah's time on the court as she hurt her knees three more times in the next five years. She had to spend countless hours in a physical therapy clinic to receive treatment. Her frequent visits there gave her a passion and respect for the profession. And Deborah began to see a new light in her life.

Currently a senior in college, Deborah focuses on pursuing a degree in physical therapy. After she graduates, Deborah plans to use her knowledge to educate people how to best take care of their bodies and cope with the feelings of hopelessness that she remembers so well.

那是她五歲至今一直夢想的事。最後，在多年的密集訓練後，黛博拉・達菲將要參加她的第一次中學籃球比賽。黛博拉一心一意只想成為傑出的運動員及參加大學校隊。那是與米爾中學的比賽。

在比賽剩下 1 分 42 秒時，黛博拉的球隊領先 1 分。一名米爾隊球員擁有控球權，而黛博拉跑去防範她。當黛博拉側面拖行以阻止該運動員，她的膝伸出時跌了一跤，當場疼痛萬分。就那樣，黛博拉的時機結束了。

在嚴重受傷之後，黛博拉發現有生以來的第一次，她無法控制自己。一場又一場的比賽，她除了在旁參觀別人打她最喜歡的比賽外，什麼也不能做。

在受傷後的五年內，她的膝蓋又受了三次傷，使她在球場比賽的時間大受限制。她必須接受很長時間的物理治療。她的頻繁進出門診中心使她對中心產生熱情並尊重他們的專業。黛博拉開始看到她生命中的一線曙光。

黛博拉目前是大學的高年級生，專心追求物理療法學位。在她畢業之後，黛博拉計畫用她的學識專長，教育人們怎樣最能照顧身體，並處理她不會忘懷的失落感問題。

49. What is the best title for this passage?

這段文章最佳主題是什麼？

(A) A Painful Mistake.

一個痛苦的錯誤。

(B) A Great Adventure.

　　大的冒險。

(C) A Lifelong Punishment.

　　一次終身處罰。

(D) A New Direction in Life.

　　在生命裡的新方向。

解析

從整段文章內容可看出，(D) 項的「A New Direction in Life.」才是正確選項。

50. How did Deborah feel when she first hurt her knee?

　　當她第一次受傷時，黛博拉感到怎樣？

(A) Excited. 令人激動。　　(B) Confused. 干擾。　　(C) Ashamed. 慚愧。　　(D) Disappointed. 失望。

解析

從答題關鍵的「從文章第三段內容『在嚴重受傷之後，除了看人比賽之外，什麼也不能做』」可看出，(D) 項的「Disappointed.」才是正確選項。

51. What is true about Deborah Duffey?

　　關於黛博拉・達菲哪一項為真？

(A) She didn't play on the court after the initial injury.

　　她在初次受傷後就沒再上球場打球。

(B) She injured her knee when she was trying to block her opponent.

　　她是在試圖阻止她的對手時，膝蓋受了傷。

(C) She knew that she couldn't be a basketball player when she was a child.

　　從小她就知道，她不會成為籃球選手。

(D) She refused to seek professional assistance to help her recover from her injuries.

　　她拒絕尋找專業協助來幫她從傷中恢復。

解析

從文章第二段內容可看出，(B) 項的「She injured her knee when she was trying to block her opponent.」才是正確選項。

52. What was the new light that Deborah saw in her life?

　　黛博拉在她的生命中看到的新曙光是什麼？

(A) To help people take care of their bodies.

　　幫助人們照顧自己的身體。

(B) To become a teacher of Physical Education.

成為一名體育教師。

(C) To become an outstanding basketball player.

成為一名傑出的籃球選手。

(D) To receive treatment in a physical therapy office.

接受物理療法部門的治療。

解析

從文章第五段內容可看出，(A) 項的「To help people take care of their bodies.」才是正確選項。

53-56 為題組

Redwood trees are the tallest plants on the earth, reaching heights of up to 100 meters. They are also known for their longevity, typically 500 to 1000 years, but sometimes more than 2000 years. A hundred million years ago, in the age of dinosaurs, redwoods were common in the forests of a much more moist and tropical North America. As the climate became drier and colder, they retreated to a narrow strip along the Pacific coast of Northern California.

The trunk of redwood trees is very stout and usually forms a single straight column. It is covered with a beautiful soft, spongy bark. This bark can be pretty thick, well over two feet in the more mature trees. It gives the older trees a certain kind of protection from insects, but the main benefit is that it keeps the center of the tree intact from moderate forest fires because of its thickness. This fire resistant quality explains why the giant redwood grows to live that long. While most other types of trees are destroyed by forest fires, the giant redwood actually prospers because of them. Moderate fires will clear the ground of competing plant life, and the rising heat dries and opens the ripe cones of the redwood, releasing many thousands of seeds onto the ground below.

New trees are often produced from sprouts, little baby trees, which form at the base of the trunk. These sprouts grow slowly, nourished by the root system of the "mother" tree. When the main tree dies, the sprouts are then free to grow as full trees, forming a **"fairy ring"** of trees around the initial tree. These trees, in turn, may give rise to more sprouts, and the cycle continues.

紅杉樹是在地球上最高的植物，最高可長到一百公尺的高度。它們也以長壽聞名，通常會有五百年到一千年，也有些會超過兩千年。一億年以前的恐龍時期，紅杉在比較潮濕和北美洲的熱帶林裡很普遍。當氣候變得乾冷時，它們沿著北加州的太平洋沿岸形成狹窄的帶狀。

紅杉樹的樹幹非常堅固且通常形成一根筆直的柱子。它外層為美麗柔軟的海綿狀樹皮所覆蓋。這塊樹皮可能相當厚，成樹的樹皮都會有兩英尺以上的厚度。 樹皮的厚度可保護老樹免受昆蟲傷害，主要好處是，發生一般森林火災時，樹皮的厚度可使樹中心部位完好無傷。這種防火的品質就是紅杉木能長那麼高的原因。多數的其他樹種都被森林火災摧毀時，巨大的紅杉樹反而因他樹毀損而長得更好。一般的火災會燒光其他植物，而且升高的熱度會烤乾並打開紅杉的圓錐形毬果，把數以千計的種子散播在地上。

新樹經常長自於嫩芽、小樹、成為樹幹的基礎。這些嫩芽成長緩慢，由母樹的樹

根系統提供養分。當主樹死亡時，這些樹芽就可獨立成長為全樹，形成環繞母樹的「仙女環」。這些樹，可能長出更多的樹芽，它的生命週期會循環下去。

53. Why were redwood trees more prominent in the forests of North America millions of years ago?

百萬年前在北美洲森林的紅杉樹為什麼更突出？

(A) The trees were taller and stronger.

樹更大更強壯。

(B) The soil was softer for seeds to sprout.

土壤更柔軟容易長出樹芽。

(C) The climate was warmer and more humid.

氣候更溫暖和更潮濕。

(D) The temperature was lower along the Pacific coast.

太平洋沿岸的溫度更低。

解析

從文章第一段內容「紅杉在比較潮濕和熱帶雨林很普遍」可看出，(C) 項的「The climate was warmer and more humid.」才是正確選項。

54. What does a "**fairy ring**" in the last paragraph refer to?

最後一段文章所提的「仙女環」是指什麼？

(A) Circled tree trunks.

環繞的樹幹。

(B) Connected root systems.

連結樹根系統。

(C) Insect holes around an old tree.

古樹周圍的昆蟲洞。

(D) Young trees surrounding a mature tree.

幼樹圍繞成樹。

解析

從文章末段內容「樹芽就可獨立成長……形成環繞母樹的仙女環」可看出，(D) 項的「Young trees surrounding a mature tree.」才是正確選項。

55. Which of the following is a function of the tree bark as mentioned in the passage?

下列內容哪項描述樹皮的功能？

(A) It allows redwood trees to bear seeds.

它讓紅杉樹生出種子。

(B) It prevents redwood trees from attack by insects.

　它防止昆蟲攻擊紅杉樹。

(C) It helps redwood trees absorb moisture in the air.

　它幫助紅杉樹吸收空氣中的水分。

(D) It makes redwood trees more beautiful and appealing.

　它使紅杉樹更美麗、更動人。

解析

從文章第二段內容「樹皮的厚度可保護老樹免受蟲害」可看出，(B) 項的「It prevents redwood trees from attack by insects.」才是正確選項。

56. Why do redwood trees grow to live that long according to the passage?

　根據本文紅杉樹為什麼會活那麼久？

(A) They have heavy and straight tree trunks.

　它們有強壯和筆直的樹幹。

(B) They are properly watered and nourished.

　它們接受正確地澆水與養分。

(C) They are more resistant to fire damage than other trees.

　它們比其他樹種對火更有抵抗力。

(D) They produce many young trees to sustain their life cycle.

　它們長出很多幼樹支援它們的生命週期。

解析

從文章第二段內容「這種防火的品質就是紅杉能長那麼高的原因」可看出，(C) 項的「They are more resistant to fire damage than other trees.」才是正確選項。

第貳部分：非選擇題（28分）

一、中譯英（8分）

說明：1. 請將以下中文句子譯成正確、通順、達意的英文，並將答案寫在「答案卷」上。

　　　2. 請依序作答，並標明題號。每題 4 分，共 8 分。

1. 臺灣的夜市早已被認為足以代表我們的在地文化。

解析

先將題句內相關字詞寫出中譯：

臺灣的夜市 night markets in Taiwan　被認為 is thought to be　足以代表 to represent　我們的在地文化 our local culture

整句英譯

The night markets in Taiwan are thought to be to represent our local culture.

2. 每年它們都吸引了成千上萬來自不同國家的觀光客。

解析

先將題句內相關字詞寫出中譯：

每年 every year　它們都吸引了 the night markets attract　成千上萬 hundreds of thousands　來自不同國家的觀光客 tourists from all over the world

整句英譯

Night markets in Taiwan attract hundreds of thousands tourists from all over the world.

二、英文作文（20分）

> 說明：1. 依提示在「答案卷」上寫一篇英文作文。
> 2. 文長約 100 至 120 個單詞（words）。

提示：請仔細觀察以下三幅連環圖片的內容，並想像第四幅圖片可能的發展，寫出一個涵蓋連環圖片內容並有完整結局的故事。

解析

⑴這種看圖說故事的作文很容易發揮，它並沒有固定的格式要求考生怎麼寫，只要寫出來的文章，不離圖意太遠、加上語句通順、文語法不要錯，都可得高分。

⑵接下來把每一幅圖畫的細節寫出來：

圖①：那是一場化妝舞會 a boy and a girl were in a costume party

　　　男生帶著眼罩　　the boy ware a blindfold

　　　女生化妝成選美女王 the girl was playing a role of beauty queen

　　　丘比特愛心之箭射向女生 Cupid's arrow was shooting toward the girl

　　　酒杯裡還剩有酒　　there was still some wine left in the glass

圖②：圖中有星星月亮 表示是晚上 it was a night time scene

　　　男生在女生住家外面的樹旁 the boy was playing a guitar and singing outside the girl's residence

　　　要唱給那位女生聽　　the boy was doing it for the girl

圖③：不久就有人開窗出來抗議 there were some people complaining about the loud noise

　　　三樓的那位還是滿臉狐疑，不知發生什麼事 the man on the third floor was wondering what was going on

圖④：這時考生就可以開始自己編繼續下去的情節：

　　　這個男生向大家抱歉 the boy apologized for the loud music

　　　在這個尷尬的時刻，那位女生也跑出來 at this embarrassing moment, the girl came out

　　　兩人一起散步到附近的小公園繼續純聊天 the boy and the girl both walked to the park nearby and made a happy ending

　　There were a boy and a girl attended a costume party one evening, the boy could not see anything because he was wearing a blindfold while the girl was playing a role of beauty queen. The boy's Cupid's arrow was shooting toward the girl, means he had a crush on the girl. Next evening the boy stood outside the girl's house, and was playing a guitar and singing a song at the same time, he was doing it for the girl. Before long, there were some people complaining about the loud music. the man on the third floor was wondering what was going on. Finally, the boy apologized for the loud noise.However, at this embarrassing moment, the girl came out she didn't even bother to say "Hello" to her neighbors, took the boy to the park nearby and made a happy ending on this passage.（約153字）

101年指考（指定考試）

第壹部分：選擇題（72分）

一、詞彙詞題（10分）

1. Since it hasn't rained for months, there is a water _____ in many parts of the country.
   (A) resource　(B) deposit　(C) shortage　(D) formula

2. The problem with Larry is that he doesn't know his limitations; he just _____ he can do everything.
   (A) convinces　(B) disguises　(C) assumes　(D) evaluates

3. Agnes seems to have a _____ personality. Almost everyone is immediately attracted to her when they first see her.
   (A) clumsy　(B) durable　(C) furious　(D) magnetic

4. Jason always _____ in finishing a task no matter how difficult it may be. He hates to quit halfway in anything he does.
   (A) persists　(B) motivates　(C) fascinates　(D) sacrifices

5. Poor _____ has caused millions of deaths in developing countries where there is only a limited amount of food.
   (A) reputation　(B) nutrition　(C) construction　(D) stimulation

6. The helicopters _____ over the sea, looking for the divers who had been missing for more than 30 hours.
   (A) tackled　(B) rustled　(C) strolled　(D) hovered

7. One of the tourist attractions in Japan is its hot spring _____, where guests can enjoy relaxing baths and beautiful views.
   (A) resorts　(B) hermits　(C) galleries　(D) faculties

8. When a young child goes out and commits a crime, it is usually the parents who should be held _____ for the child's conduct.

　(A) eligible　(B) dispensable　(C) credible　(D) accountable

9. Since you have not decided on the topic of your composition, it's still _____ to talk about how to write your conclusion.

　(A) preventive　(B) premature　(C) productive　(D) progressive

10. Human rights are fundamental rights to which a person is _____ entitled, that is, rights that she or he is born with.

　(A) inherently　(B) imperatively　(C) authentically　(D) alternatively

二、綜合測驗（占10分）

說明：第11題至第20題，每題一個空格，請依文意選出最適當的一個選項，請畫記在答案卡之「選擇題答案區」。各題答對者，得1分；答錯、未作答或畫記多於一個選項者，該題以零分計算。

第 11 至 15 題為題組

　　The Nobel Peace Center is located in an old train station building close to the Oslo City Hall and overlooking the harbor. It was officially opened on June 11, 2005 as part of the celebrations to ____11____

　　Norway's centenary as an independent country. It is a center where you can experience and learn about the various Nobel Peace Prize Laureates and their activities ____12____ the remarkable history of Alfred Nobel, the founder of the Nobel Prize. In addition, it serves as a meeting place where exhibits, discussions, and reflections ____13____ to war, peace, and conflict resolution are in focus. The Center combines exhibits and films with digital communication and interactive installations and has already received attention for its use of state-of-the-art technology. Visitors are welcome to experience the Center ____14____ or join a guided tour. Since its opening, the Nobel Peace Center has been educating, inspiring and entertaining its visitors ____15____ exhibitions, activities, lectures, and cultural events. The Center is financed by private and public institutions.

11. (A) help　(B) solve　(C) take　(D) mark

12. (A) so much as　(B) as well as　(C) in spite of　(D) on behalf of

13. (A) related　(B) limited　(C) addicted　(D) contributed

14. (A) in this regard　(B) one on one　(C) on their own　(D) by and large

15. (A) among　(B) regarding　(C) including　(D) through

第 16 至 20 題為題組

　　In 1985, a riot at a Brussels soccer match occurred, in which many fans lost their lives. The ____16____ began 45 minutes before the start of the European Cup final. The British team was scheduled to ____17____ the Italian team in the game. Noisy British fans, after setting off some rockets and fireworks to cheer for _____18_____ team, broke through a thin wire fence and started to attack the Italian fans. The Italians, in panic, _____19_____ the main exit in their section when a six-foot concrete wall collapsed. By the end of the night, 38 soccer fans had died and 437 were injured. The majority of the deaths resulted from people _____20_____ trampled underfoot or crushed against barriers in the stadium. As a result of this 1985 soccer incident, security measures have since been tightened at major sports competitions to prevent similar events from happening.

16. (A) circumstance   (B) sequence   (C) tragedy   (D) phenomenon
17. (A) oppose to   (B) fight over   (C) battle for   (D) compete against
18. (A) a   (B) that   (C) each   (D) their
19. (A) headed for   (B) backed up   (C) called out   (D) passed on
20. (A) be   (B) been   (C) being   (D) to be

三、文意選填（占10分）

說明：第21題至第30題，每題一個空格，請依文意在文章後所提供的(A)到(L)選項中分別選出最適當者，並將其英文字母代號畫記在答案卡之「選擇題答案區」。各題答對者，得1分；答錯、未作答或畫記多於一個選項者，該題以零分計算。

第 21 至 30 題為題組

The Taiwanese puppet show ("Budaixi") is a distinguished form of performing arts in Taiwan. Although basically hand puppets, the _____21_____ appear as complete forms, with hands and feet, on an elaborately decorated stage.

The puppet performance is typically _____22_____ by a small orchestra. The backstage music is directed by the drum player. The drummer needs to pay attention to what is going on in the plot and follow the rhythm of the characters. He also uses the drum to _____23_____ the other musicians. There are generally around four to five musicians who perform the backstage music. The form of music used is often associated with various performance _____24_____, including acrobatics and skills like window-jumping, stage movement, and fighting. Sometimes unusual animal puppets also appear on stage for extra _____25_____, especially for children in the audience.

In general, a show needs two performers. The main performer is generally the chief or _____26_____ of the troupe. He is the one in charge of the whole show, manipulating the main puppets, singing, and narrating. The _____27_____ performer manipulates the puppets to coordinate with the main performer. He also changes the costumes of the puppets, and takes care of the stage. The relationship between the main performer and his partner is one of master and apprentice. Frequently, the master trains his sons to eventually _____28_____ him as puppet masters.

Budaixi troupes are often hired to perform at processions and festivals held in honor of local gods, and on happy _____29_____ such as weddings, births, and promotions. The main purpose of Budaixi is to _____30_____ and offer thanks to the deities. The shows also serve as a popular means of folk entertainment.

(A) attracted   (B) appeal   (C) accompanied   (D) conduct   (E) director   (F) figures

(G) occasions   (H) succeed   (I) transparent   (J) supporting   (K) techniques   (L) worship

四、篇章結構（占10分）

說明：第31題至第35題，每題一個空格。請依文意在文章後所提供的(A)到(F)選項中分別選出最適當者，填入空格中，使篇章結構清晰有條理，並將其英文字母代號畫記在答案卡之「選擇題答案區」。各題答對者，得2分；答錯、未作答或畫記多於一個選項者，該題以零分計算。

第 31 至 35 題為題組

All advertising includes an attempt to persuade. ___31___ Even if an advertisement claims to be purely informational, it still has persuasion at its core. The ad informs the consumers with one purpose: to get the consumer to like the brand and, on that basis, to eventually buy the brand. Without this persuasive intent, communication about a product might be news, but it would not be advertising.

Advertising can be persuasive communication not only about a product but also an idea or a person.

___32___ Although political ads are supposed to be concerned with the public welfare, they are paid for and they all have a persuasive intent. ___33___ A Bush campaign ad, for instance, did not ask anyone to buy anything, yet it attempted to persuade American citizens to view George Bush favorably. ___34___ Critics of President Clinton's health care plan used advertising to influence lawmakers and defeat the government's plan.

___35___ For instance, the international organization Greenpeace uses advertising to get their message out. In the ads, they warn people about serious pollution problems and the urgency of protecting the environment. They, too, are selling something and trying to make a point.

(A) Political advertising is one example.

(B) To put it another way, ads are communication designed to get someone to do something.

(C) Advertising can be the most important source of income for the media through which it is conducted.

(D) They differ from commercial ads in that political ads "sell" candidates rather than commercial goods.

(E) Aside from campaign advertising, political advertising is also used to persuade people to support or oppose proposals.

(F) In addition to political parties, environmental groups and human rights organizations also buy advertising to persuade people to accept their way of thinking.

五、閱讀測驗（占32分）

說明：第36題至第51題，每題請分別根據各篇文章之文意選出最適當的一個選項，請畫記在答案卡之「選擇題答案區」。各題答對者，得2分；答錯、未作答或畫記多於一個選項者，該題以零分計算。

第 36 至 39 題為題組

A sense of humor is something highly valued. A person who has a great sense of humor is often considered to be happy and socially confident. However, humor is a double-edged sword. It can forge better relationships and help you cope with life, but sometimes it can also damage self-esteem and antagonize others.

People who use bonding humor tell jokes and generally lighten the mood. They're perceived as being good at reducing the tension in uncomfortable situations. They often make fun of their common experiences, and sometimes they may even laugh off their own misfortunes. The basic message they deliver is: We're all alike, we find the same things funny, and we're all in this together.

Put-down humor, on the other hand, is an aggressive type of humor used to criticize and manipulate others through teasing. When it's aimed against politicians, as it often is, it's hilarious and mostly harmless. But in the real world, it may have a harmful impact. An example of such humor is telling friends an embarrassing story about another friend. When challenged about their teasing, the put-down jokers might claim that they are "just kidding," thus allowing themselves to avoid responsibility. This type of humor, though considered by some people to be socially acceptable, may hurt the feelings of the one being teased and thus take a toll on personal relationships.

Finally, in hate-me humor, the joker is the target of the joke for the amusement of others. This type of humor was used by comedians John Belushi and Chris Farley-both of whom suffered for their success in show business. A small dose of such humor is charming, but routinely offering oneself up to be humiliated erodes one's self-respect, and fosters depression and anxiety.

So it seems that being funny isn't necessarily an indicator of good social skills and well-being. In certain cases, it may actually have a negative impact on interpersonal relationships.

36. According to the passage, which group is among the common targets of put-down humor?

   (A) Comedians.

   (B) People who tell jokes.

   (C) Politicians.

   (D) People who are friendly to others.

37. How can people create a relaxing atmosphere through bonding humor?

   (A) By laughing at other people's misfortunes.

   (B) By joking about experiences that they all have.

   (C) By revealing their own personal relationships.

   (D) By making fun of unique experiences of their friends.

38. According to the passage, which of the following is true about John Belushi and Chris Farley?

(A) They suffered from over-dosage of anxiety pills.

(B) They often humiliated other people on the stage.

(C) They were successful in their careers as comedians.

(D) They managed to rebuild their self-respect from their shows.

39. What is the message that the author is trying to convey?

(A) Humor deserves to be studied carefully.

(B) Humor has both its bright side and dark side.

(C) Humor is a highly valued personality trait.

(D) Humor can be learned in many different ways.

第 40 至 43 題為題組

On June 23, 2010, a Sunny Airlines captain with 32 years of experience stopped his flight from departing. He was deeply concerned about a balky power component that might eliminate all electrical power on his trans-Pacific flight. Despite his valid concerns, Sunny Airlines' management pressured him to fly the airplane, over the ocean, at night. When he refused to jeopardize the safety of his passengers, Sunny Airlines' security escorted him out of the airport, and threatened to arrest his crew if they did not cooperate.

Besides that, five more Sunny Airlines pilots also refused to fly the aircraft, citing their own concerns about the safety of the plane. It turned out the pilots were right: the power component was faulty and the plane was removed from service and, finally, fixed. Eventually a third crew operated the flight, hours later. In this whole process, Sunny Airlines pressured their highly experienced pilots to ignore their safety concerns and fly passengers over the Pacific Ocean at night in a plane that needed maintenance. Fortunately for all of us, these pilots stood strong and would not be intimidated.

Don't just take our word that this happened. Please research this yourself and learn the facts. Here's a starting point: www.SunnyAirlinePilot.org. Once you review this shocking information, please keep in mind that while their use of Corporate Security to remove a pilot from the airport is a new procedure, the intimidation of flight crews is becoming commonplace at Sunny Airlines, with documented events occurring on a weekly basis.

The flying public deserves the highest levels of safety. No airlines should maximize their revenues by pushing their employees to move their airplanes regardless of the potential human cost. Sunny Airlines' pilots are committed to resisting any practices that compromise your safety for economic gain. We've been trying to fix these problems behind the scenes for quite some time; now we need your help. Go to www.SunnyAirlinePilot.org to get more information and find out what you can do.

40. According to the passage, what happened to the captain after he refused to fly the aircraft?

(A) He was asked to find another pilot to replace his position.

(B) He was forced to leave the airport by security staff of Sunny Airlines.

(C) He was made to help the Airlines find out what was wrong with the plane.

(D) He was fired for refusing to fly the plane and abandoning the passengers.

41. What is the main purpose of the passage?

(A) To maximize Sunny Airlines' revenues.

(B) To introduce Sunny Airlines' pilot training programs.

(C) To review plans for improving Sunny Airlines' service.

(D) To expose problems with Sunny Airlines' security practices.

42. What happened to the aircraft after the pilots refused to operate the flight?

(A) It was found to be too old for any more flight service.

(B) Its mechanical problem was detected and finally repaired.

(C) It was removed from the airport for a week-long checkup.

(D) Its power component problem remained and no crew would operate the flight.

43. By whom was the passage most likely written?

(A) Sunny Airlines security guards.

(B) Sunny Airlines personnel manager.

(C) Members of Sunny Airlines pilot organization.

(D) One of the passengers of the Sunny Airlines flight.

第 44 至 47 題為題組

Angry Birds is a video game developed by Finnish computer game developer Rovio Mobile. Inspired primarily by a sketch of stylized wingless birds, the game was first released for Apple's mobile operating system in December 2009. Since then, over 12 million copies of the game have been purchased from Apple's App Store.

With its fast-growing popularity worldwide, the game and its characters-angry birds and their enemy pigs-have been referenced in television programs throughout the world. The Israeli comedy

A Wonderful Country, one of the nation's most popular TV programs, satirized recent failed Israeli-Palestinian peace attempts by featuring the Angry Birds in peace negotiations with the pigs. Clips of the segment went *viral*, getting viewers from all around the world. American television hosts Conan O'Brien, Jon Stewart, and Daniel Tosh have referenced the game in comedy sketches on their respective series, *Conan, The Daily Show*, and *Tosh.0*. Some of the game's more notable fans include Prime Minister David Cameron of the United Kingdom, who plays the iPad version of the game, and author Salman Rushdie, who is believed to be "something of a master at *Angry Birds*."

Angry Birds and its characters have also been featured in advertisements in different forms. In March 2011, the characters began appearing in a series of advertisements for Microsoft's Bing search engine. In the same year, Nokia projected an advertisement in Austin, Texas that included the game's characters on a downtown building for its new handset. Later, a T-Mobile advertisement filmed in Spain included a real-life mock-up of the game in a city plaza. Nokia also used the game in Malaysia to promote an attempt to set a world record for the largest number of people playing a single mobile game.

Angry Birds has even inspired works of philosophical analogy. A five-part essay entitled "Angry Birds Yoga-How to Eliminate the Green Pigs in Your Life" was written by Giridhari Dasar in Brazil, utilizing the characters and gameplay mechanics to interpret various concepts of yoga philosophy. The piece attracted much media attention for its unique method of philosophical presentation.

44. What is the purpose of the passage?

　(A) To explain how the video game *Angry Birds* was devised.

　(B) To investigate why *Angry Birds* has quickly become well-liked.

　(C) To introduce *Angry Birds* characters in TV programs and advertisements.

　(D) To report on the spread of *Angry Birds* in different media around the world.

45. Which of the following is closest in meaning to the word "*viral*" in the second paragraph?

　(A) Apparent.　(B) Sarcastic.　(C) Exciting.　(D) Popular.

46. According to the passage, which of the following people is good at playing *Angry Birds*?

　(A) Giridhari Dasar.　(B) Conan O'Brien.　(C) Salman Rushdie.　(D) Daniel Tosh.

47. Which of the following is true about the use of *Angry Birds*, according to the passage?

　(A) It has been cited by UK Prime Minister to illustrate political issues.

　(B) Its characters are used in advertisements mainly for Apple's products.

　(C) Its real-life mock-up has appeared in an advertisement for mobile phones.

　(D) It has been developed into a film about the life of a Brazilian yoga master.

第 48 至 51 題為題組

　　Demolition is the tearing-down of buildings and other structures. You can level a five-story building easily with excavators and wrecking balls, but when you need to bring down a 20-story skyscraper, explosive demolition is the preferred method for safely demolishing the huge structure.

　　In order to demolish a building safely, blasters must map out a careful plan ahead of time. The first step is to examine architectural blueprints of the building to determine how the building is put together. Next, the blaster crew tours the building, jotting down notes about the support structure on each floor. Once they have gathered all the data they need, the blasters devise a plan of attack. They decide what explosives to use, where to position them in the building, and how to time their explosions.

　　Generally speaking, blasters will explode the major support columns on the lower floors first and then on a few upper stories. In a 20-story building, the blasters might blow the columns on the first and second floor, as well as the 12th and 15th floors. In most cases, blowing the support structures on the lower floors is sufficient for collapsing the building, but loading explosives on upper floors helps break the building material into smaller pieces as it falls. This makes for easier cleanup following the blast. The main challenge in bringing a building down is controlling the direction in which it falls. To topple the building towards the north, the blasters set off explosives on the north side of the building first. By controlling the way it collapses, a blasting crew will be able to tumble the building over on one side, into a parking lot or other open area. This sort of blast is the easiest to execute, and it is generally the safest way to go.

48. What do the blasters need to do in preparing for the demolition of a building, according to the passage?

(A) Study the structure of the building.　(B) Hire an experienced tour guide.

(C) Make a miniature of the building.　(D) Consult the original architect.

49. In most cases, where does the explosion start in the building during its destruction?

(A) The topmost layer.　(B) The upper floors.　(C) The lower levels.　(D) The basement.

50. According to the following diagram, which part of the target building should the demolition team explode first to safely bring it down?

(A) The east side.

(B) The west side.

(C) The south side.

(D) The north side.

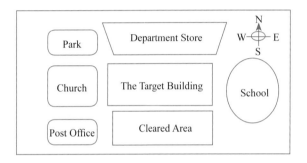

51. What is the passage mainly about?

(A) How to execute demolition at the right time.

(B) How to collapse a building with explosives.

(C) How to use explosives for different purposes.

(D) How to destroy a building with minimum manpower.

第貳部分：非選擇題（占28分）

說明：本部分共有二題，請依各題指示作答，答案必須寫在「答案卷」上，並標明大題號（一、二）。作答務必使用筆尖較粗之黑色墨水的筆書寫，且不得使用鉛筆。

一、中譯英（占8分）

說明：1.請將以下中文句子譯成正確、通順、達意的英文，並將答案寫在「答案卷」上。

2.請依序作答，並標明子題號（1、2）。每題4分，共8分。

1. 有些我們認為安全的包裝食品可能含有對人體有害的成分。

2. 為了我們自身的健康，在購買食物前我們應仔細閱讀包裝上的說明。

二、英文作文（占20分）

> 說明：1. 依提示在「答案卷」上寫一篇英文作文。
> 　　　2. 文長至少120個單詞（words）。

提示：請以運動為主題，寫一篇至少120個單詞的文章，說明你最常從事的運動是什麼。
　　　文分兩段，第一段描述這項運動如何進行（如地點、活動方式、及可能需要的相關用品等），第二段說明你從事這項運動的原因及這項運動對你生活的影響。

101年指考解答

題號	1	2	3	4	5	6	7	8	9	10	11	12	13	14	15	16	17	18	19	20
答案	C	C	D	A	B	D	A	D	B	A	D	B	A	C	D	C	D	D	A	C
題號	21	22	23	24	25	26	27	28	29	30	31	32	33	34	35	36	37	38	39	40
答案	F	C	D	K	B	E	J	H	G	L	B	A	D	E	F	C	B	C	B	B
題號	41	42	43	44	45	46	47	48	49	50	51									
答案	D	B	C	D	D	C	C	A	C	C	B									

101 年學測（學科能力測驗）

第壹部分：單選題（72分）

一、詞彙（占15分）

> 說明：第1題至第15題，每題有4個選項，其中只有一個是正確或最適當的選項，請畫記在答案卡之「選擇題答案區」。各題答對者，得1分；答錯、未作答或畫記多於一個選項者，該題以零分計算。

1. The ending of the movie did not come as a ＿＿＿＿＿ to John because he had already read the novel that the movie was based on.
   (A) vision　(B) focus　(C) surprise　(D) conclusion

2. In order to stay healthy and fit, John exercises ＿＿＿＿＿. He works out twice a week in a gym.
   (A) regularly　(B) directly　(C) hardly　(D) gradually

3. Traveling is a good way for us to ＿＿＿＿＿ different cultures and broaden our horizons.
   (A) assume　(B) explore　(C) occupy　(D) inspire

4. The story about Hou-I shooting down nine suns is a well-known Chinese ＿＿＿＿＿, but it may not be a true historical event.
   (A) figure　(B) rumor　(C) miracle　(D) legend

5. According to recent research, children under the age of 12 are generally not ＿＿＿＿＿ enough to recognize risk and deal with dangerous situations.
   (A) diligent　(B) mature　(C) familiar　(D) sincere

6. Helen let out a sigh of ＿＿＿＿＿ after hearing that her brother was not injured in the accident.
   (A) hesitation　(B) relief　(C) sorrow　(D) triumph

7. Research suggests that people with outgoing personalities tend to be more ＿＿＿＿＿, often expecting that good things will happen.
   (A) efficient　(B) practical　(C) changeable　(D) optimistic

8. No one could beat Paul at running. He has won the running championship ＿＿＿＿＿＿ for three years.

(A) rapidly　(B) urgently　(C) continuously　(D) temporarily

9. If you fly from Taipei to Tokyo, you'll be taking an international, rather than a ＿＿＿＿＿＿ flight.

(A) liberal　(B) domestic　(C) connected　(D) universal

10. Jack is very proud of his fancy new motorcycle. He has been ＿＿＿＿＿＿ to all his friends about how cool it looks and how fast it runs.

(A) boasting　(B) proposing　(C) gossiping　(D) confessing

11. The ideas about family have changed ＿＿＿＿＿＿ in the past twenty years. For example, my grandfather was one of ten children in his family, but I am the only child.

(A) mutually　(B) narrowly　(C) considerably　(D) scarcely

12. The chairperson of the meeting asked everyone to speak up instead of ＿＿＿＿＿＿ their opinions among themselves.

(A) reciting　(B) giggling　(C) murmuring　(D) whistling

13. Although Mr. Chen is rich, he is a very ＿＿＿＿＿＿ person and is never willing to spend any money to help those who are in need.

(A) absolute　(B) precise　(C) economic　(D) stingy

14. If you want to know what your dreams mean, now there are websites you can visit to help you ＿＿＿＿＿＿ them.

(A) overcome　(B) interpret　(C) transfer　(D) revise

15. The memory ＿＿＿＿＿＿ of the new computer has been increased so that more information can be stored.

(A) capacity　(B) occupation　(C) attachment　(D) machinery

二、綜合測驗（占15分）

說明：第16題至第30題，每題一個空格，請依文意選出最適當的一個選項，請畫記在答案卡之「選擇題答案區」。各題答對者，得1分；答錯、未作答或畫記多於一個選項者，該題以零分計算。

　　Kizhi is an island on Lake Onega in Karelia, Russia, with a beautiful collection of wooden churches and houses. It is one of the most popular tourist ＿＿＿16＿＿＿ in Russia and a United Nations Educational, Scientific, and Cultural Organization (UNESCO) World Heritage Site.

　　The island is about 7 km long and 0.5 km wide. It is surrounded by about 5,000 other islands, some of _____17_____ are just rocks sticking out of the ground.

The entire island of Kizhi is, _____18_____, an outdoor museum of wooden architecture created in 1966. It contains many historically significant and beautiful wooden structures, _____19_____ windmills, boathouses, chapels, fish houses, and homes. The jewel of the architecture is the 22-domed Transfiguration Church, built in the early 1700s. It is about 37 m tall, _____20_____ it one of the tallest log structures in the world. The church was built with pine trees brought from the mainland, which was quite common for the 18th century.

16. (A) affairs   (B) fashions   (C) industries   (D) attractions

17. (A) them   (B) that   (C) those   (D) which

18. (A) in fact   (B) once again   (C) as usual   (D) for instance

19. (A) except   (B) besides   (C) including   (D) regarding

20. (A) make   (B) making   (C) made   (D) to make

There was once a time when all human beings were gods. However, they often took their divinity for granted and _____21_____ abused it. Seeing this, Brahma, the chief god, decided to take their divinity away from them and hide it _____22_____ it could never be found.

Brahma called a council of the gods to help him decide on a place to hide the divinity. The gods suggested that they hide it _____23_____ in the earth or take it to the top of the highest mountain. But Brahma thought _____24_____ would do because he believed humans would dig into the earth and climb every mountain, and eventually find it. So, the gods gave up.

Brahma thought for a long time and finally decided to hide their divinity in the center of their own being, for humans would never think to _____25_____ it there. Since that time humans have been going up and down the earth, digging, climbing, and exploring-searching for something already within themselves.

21. (A) yet   (B) even   (C) never   (D) rather

22. (A) though   (B) because   (C) where   (D) when

23. (A) close   (B) apart   (C) deep   (D) hard

24. (A) each   (B) more   (C) any   (D) neither

25. (A) look for   (B) get over   (C) do without   (D) bump into

In the fall of 1973, in an effort to bring attention to the conflict between Egypt and Israel, *World Hello Day* was born. The objective is to promote peace all over the world, and to _____26_____ barriers between every nationality. Since then, *World Hello Day*-November 21st of every year- _____27_____ observed by people in 180 countries.

Taking part couldn't be _____28_____. All one has to do is say hello to 10 people on the day. However, in response to the _____29_____ of this event, the concepts of fostering peace and harmony do not have to be confined to one day a year. We can _____30_____ the spirit going by communicating often and consciously. It is a simple act that anyone can do and it reminds us that communication is more effective than conflict.

26. (A) skip over   (B) come across   (C) look into   (D) break down

27. (A) is   (B) has been   (C) was   (D) had been

28. (A) quicker   (B) sooner   (C) easier   (D) better

29. (A) aim   (B) tone   (C) key   (D) peak
30. (A) push   (B) keep   (C) bring   (D) make

三、文意選填（占10分）

> 說明：第31題至第40題，每題一個空格，請依文意在文章後所提供的 (A) 到 (J) 選項中分
> 別選出最適當者，並將其英文字母代號畫記在答案卡之「選擇題答案區」。各題
> 答對者，得1分；答錯、未作答或畫記多於一個選項者，該題以零分計算。

Generally there are two ways to name typhoons: the number-based convention and the list-based convention. Following the number-based convention, typhoons are coded with ____31____ types of numbers such as a 4-digit or a 6-digit code. For example, the 14th typhoon in 2003 can be labeled either as Typhoon 0314 or Typhoon 200314. The ____32____ of this convention, however, is that a number is hard to remember. The list-based convention, on the other hand, is based on the list of typhoon names compiled in advance by a committee, and is more widely used.

At the very beginning, only ____33____ names were used because at that time typhoons were named after girlfriends or wives of the experts on the committee. In 1979, however, male names were also included because women protested against the original naming ____34____ for reasons of gender equality.

In Asia, Western names were used until 2000 when the committee decided to use Asian names to ____35____ Asians' awareness of typhoons. The names were chosen from a name pool ____36____ of 140 names, 10 each from the 14 members of the committee. Each country has its unique naming preferences. Korea and Japan ____37____ animal names and China likes names of gods such as Longwang (dragon king) and Fengshen (god of the wind).

After the 140 names are all used in order, they will be ____38____. But the names can be changed. If a member country suffers great damage from a certain typhoon, it can ____39____ that the name of the typhoon be deleted from the list at the annual committee meeting. For example, the names of Nabi by South Korea, and Longwang by China were ____40____ with other names in 2007. The deletion of both names was due to the severe damage caused by the typhoons bearing the names.

(A) request   (B) favor   (C) disadvantage   (D) composed   (E) recycled
(F) practice   (G) replaced   (H) raise   (I) various   (J) female

四、閱讀測驗（占32分）

> 說明：第41題至第56題，每題請分別根據各篇文章之文意選出最適當的一個選項，請畫
> 記在答案卡之「選擇題答案區」。各題答對者，得2分；答錯、未作答或畫記多
> 於一個選項者，該題以零分計算。

41-44為題組

The kilt is a skirt traditionally worn by Scottish men. It is a tailored garment that is wrapped around the wearer's body at the waist starting from one side, around the front and back and across the front again to the opposite side. The overlapping layers in front are called "aprons." Usually, the kilt covers the body from the waist down to just above the knees. A properly made kilt should not be so loose that the wearer can easily twist the kilt around the body, nor should it be so tight that it causes bulging of the fabric where it is buckled. Underwear may be worn as one prefers.

One of the most distinctive features of the kilt is the pattern of squares, or sett, it exhibits. The association of particular patterns with individual families can be traced back hundreds of years. Then in the Victorian era (19th century), weaving companies began to systematically record and formalize the system of setts for commercial purposes. Today there are also setts for States and Provinces, schools and universities, and general patterns that anybody can wear.

The kilt can be worn with accessories. On the front apron, there is often a kilt pin, topped with a small decorative family symbol. A small knife can be worn with the kilt too. It typically comes in a very wide variety, from fairly plain to quite elaborate silver- and jewel-ornamented designs. The kilt can also be worn with a sporran, which is the Gaelic word for pouch or purse.

41. What's the proper way of wearing the kilt?

(A) It should be worn with underwear underneath it.

(B) It should loosely fit on the body to be turned around.

(C) It should be long enough to cover the wearer's knees.

(D) It should be wrapped across the front of the body two times.

42. Which of the following is a correct description about setts?

(A) They were once symbols for different Scottish families.

(B) They were established by the government for business purposes.

(C) They represented different States and Provinces in the 19th century.

(D) They used to come in one general pattern for all individuals and institutions.

43. Which of the following items is **NOT** typically worn with the kilt for decoration?

(A) A pin.　(B) A purse.　(C) A ruby apron.　(D) A silver knife.

44. What is the purpose of this passage?

(A) To introduce a Scottish garment.　(B) To advertise a weaving pattern.

(C) To persuade men to wear kilts.　(D) To compare a skirt with a kilt.

45-48為題組

Wesla Whitfield, a famous jazz singer, has a unique style and life story, so I decided to see one of her performances and interview her for my column.

I went to a nightclub in New York and watched the stage lights go up. After the band played an introduction, Wesla Whitfield wheeled herself onstage in a wheelchair. As she sang, Whitfield's voice was so powerful and soulful that everyone in the room forgot the wheelchair was even there.

At 57, Whitfield is small and pretty, witty and humble, persistent and philosophical. Raised in California, Whitfield began performing in public at age 18, when she took a job as a singing waitress at a pizza parlor. After studying classical music in college, she moved to San Francisco and went on to sing with the San Francisco Opera Chorus.

Walking home from rehearsal at age 29, she was caught in the midst of a random shooting that left her paralyzed from the waist down. I asked how she dealt with the realization that she'd never walk again, and she confessed that initially she didn't want to face it. After a year of depression she tried to kill herself. She was then admitted to a hospital for treatment, where she was able to recover.

Whitfield said she came to understand that the only thing she had lost in this misfortunate event was the ability to walk. She still possessed her most valuable asset-her mind. Pointing to her head, she said, "Everything important is in here. The only real disability in life is losing your mind." When I asked if she was angry about what she had lost, she admitted to being frustrated occasionally, "especially when everybody's dancing, because I love to dance. But **when that happens** I just remove myself so I can focus instead on what I can do."

45. In which of the following places has Wesla Whitfield worked?

　(A) A college.　(B) A hospital.　(C) A pizza parlor.　(D) A news agency.

46. What does "**when that happens**" mean in the last paragraph?

　(A) When Wesla is losing her mind.

　(B) When Wesla is singing on the stage.

　(C) When Wesla is going out in her wheelchair.

　(D) When Wesla is watching other people dancing.

47. Which of the following statements is true about Wesla Whitfield's physical disability?

　(A) It was caused by a traffic accident.

　(B) It made her sad and depressed at first.

　(C) It seriously affected her singing career.

　(D) It happened when she was a college student.

48. What advice would Wesla most likely give other disabled people?

　(A) Ignore what you have lost and make the best use of what you have.

　(B) Be modest and hard-working to earn respect from other people.

　(C) Acquire a skill so that you can still be successful and famous.

　(D) Try to sing whenever you feel upset and depressed.

49-52為題組

Forks trace their origins back to the ancient Greeks. Forks at that time were fairly large with two tines that aided in the carving of meat in the kitchen. The tines prevented meat from twisting or moving during carving and allowed food to slide off more easily than it would with a knife.

By the 7th century A.D., royal courts of the Middle East began to use forks at the table for dining. From the 10th through the 13th centuries, forks were fairly common among the wealthy in Byzantium. In the 11th century, a Byzantine wife brought forks to Italy; however, they were not widely adopted there until the 16th century. Then in 1533, forks were brought from Italy to France. The French were also slow to accept forks, for using them was thought to be awkward.

In 1608, forks were brought to England by Thomas Coryate, who saw them during his travels in Italy. The English first ridiculed forks as being unnecessary. "Why should a person need a fork when God had given him hands?" they asked. Slowly, however, forks came to be adopted by the wealthy as a symbol of their social status. They were prized possessions made of expensive materials intended to impress guests. By the mid 1600s, eating with forks was considered fashionable among the wealthy British.

Early table forks were modeled after kitchen forks, but small pieces of food often fell through the two tines or slipped off easily. In late 17th century France, larger forks with four curved tines were developed. The additional tines made diners less likely to drop food, and the curved tines served as a scoop so people did not have to constantly switch to a spoon while eating. By the early 19th century, four-tined forks had also been developed in Germany and England and slowly began to spread to America.

49. What is the passage mainly about?

(A) The different designs of forks.

(B) The spread of fork-aided cooking.

(C) The history of using forks for dining.

(D) The development of fork-related table manners.

50. By which route did the use of forks spread?

(A) Middle East→Greece→England→Italy→France

(B) Greece→Middle East→Italy→France→England

(C) Greece→Middle East→France→Italy→Germany

(D) Middle East→France→England→Italy→Germany

51. How did forks become popular in England?

(A) Wealthy British were impressed by the design of forks.

(B) Wealthy British thought it awkward to use their hands to eat.

(C) Wealthy British gave special forks to the nobles as luxurious gifts.

(D) Wealthy British considered dining with forks a sign of social status.

52. Why were forks made into a curved shape?

(A) They could be used to scoop food as well.

(B) They looked more fashionable in this way.

(C) They were designed in this way for export to the US.

(D) They ensured the meat would not twist while being cut.

53-56為題組

Animals are a favorite subject of many photographers. Cats, dogs, and other pets top the list, followed by zoo animals. However, because it's hard to get them to sit still and "perform on command," some professional photographers refuse to photograph pets.

One way to get an appealing portrait of a cat or dog is to hold a biscuit or treat above the camera. The animal's longing look toward the food will be captured by the camera, but the treat won't appear in the picture because it's out of the camera's range. When you show the picture to your friends afterwards, they'll be impressed by your pet's loving expression.

If you are using fast film, you can take some good, quick shots of a pet by simply snapping a picture right after calling its name. You'll get a different expression from your pet using this technique. Depending on your pet's mood, the picture will capture an interested, curious expression or possibly a look of annoyance, especially if you've awakened it from a nap.

Taking pictures of zoo animals requires a little more patience. After all, you can't wake up a lion! You may have to wait for a while until the animal does something interesting or moves into a position for you to get a good shot. When photographing zoo animals, don't get too close to the cages, and never tap on the glass or throw things between the bars of a cage. Concentrate on shooting some good pictures, and always respect the animals you are photographing.

53. Why do some professional photographers **NOT** like to take pictures of pets?

(A) Pets may not follow orders.

(B) Pets don't want to be bothered.

(C) Pets may not like photographers.

(D) Pets seldom change their expressions.

54. What is the use of a biscuit in taking pictures of a pet?

(A) To capture a cute look.

(B) To create a special atmosphere.

(C) To arouse the appetite of the pet.

(D) To keep the pet from looking at the camera.

55. What is the advantage of calling your pet's name when taking a shot of it?

(A) To help your pet look its best.

(B) To make sure that your pet sits still.

(C) To keep your pet awake for a while.

(D) To catch a different expression of your pet.

56. In what way is photographing zoo animals different from photographing pets?

(A) You need to have fast film.

(B) You need special equipment.

(C) You need to stay close to the animals.

(D) You need more time to watch and wait.

第貳部分：非選擇題（占28分）

一、中譯英（占8分）

> 說明：1.請將以下中文句子譯成正確、通順、達意的英文，並將答案寫在「答案卷」
> 　　　　上。
> 　　　2.請依序作答，並標明題號。每題4分，共8分。

1. 近年來，許多臺灣製作的影片已經受到國際的重視。

2. 拍攝這些電影的地點也成爲熱門的觀光景點。

二、英文作文（占20分）

> 說明：1.依提示在「答案卷」上寫一篇英文作文。
> 　　　2.文長至少120個單詞（words）。

提示：你最好的朋友最近迷上電玩，因此常常熬夜，疏忽課業，並受到父母的責罵。你
　　　（英文名字必須假設爲 Jack 或 Jill）打算寫一封信給他/她（英文名字必須假設爲
　　　Ken或Barbie），適當地給予勸告。

請注意：必須使用上述的Jack或Jill在信末署名，**不得使用自己的眞實中文或英文名字。**

101年學測解答

題號	1	2	3	4	5	6	7	8	9	10	11	12	13	14	15	16	17	18	19	20
答案	C	A	B	D	B	B	D	C	B	A	C	C	D	B	A	D	D	A	C	B
題號	21	22	23	24	25	26	27	28	29	30	31	32	33	34	35	36	37	38	39	40
答案	B	C	C	D	A	D	B	C	A	B	I	C	J	F	H	D	B	E	A	G
題號	41	42	43	44	45	46	47	48	49	50	51	52	53	54	55	56				
答案	D	A	C	A	C	D	B	A	C	B	D	A	A	A	D	D				

附錄一
統測、學測、指考等之重點文法

　　雖然沒有正式統計數據，但幾乎可以說，在臺灣，有爲數不少的人對「英文文法」很排斥。作者教了幾十年英文，每逢有人問起「英文文法重不重要」時，我都會給兩個答案：

1.不參加英文考試時，英文文法不那麼重要。
2.要參加英文考試時，英文文法就會很重要。

　　諷刺的是，很多人排斥英文文法，但它卻是英文考試得分的重要關鍵。因爲，英文文法的所有規定都是死板的、固定的，考生只要記熟這些規定，加上本書中〈重點文法篇〉的「解題技巧」協助，要考高分並不難。

　　相較之下，字彙測驗的範圍就大得多。因爲字彙題的「單字量」是無限寬廣的，不像「英文文法」，尤其是初級、中級的英文文法，其範圍是固定的，準備起來就輕鬆多了。

　　了解「英文文法」的唯一步驟，就應從「英文八大詞類」說起。以下僅就在八大詞類部分，選擇與考試得分有關，也就是「各層級英文考題較常出現的文法項目」舉例說明如下：

名詞

1.不可數名詞的「數量」

中文裡常說「數量」二字，即「數」與「量」的意思。在英文裡，「可數名詞的多寡」是用「數」的多少表示；反之，「不可數名詞的多寡」是用「量」的多少表示。

例句：Can I have two books?（可數名詞）

　　　Can I have two cups of tea / glasses of water ?（不可數名詞）

重點提醒：在不可數名詞前的「計量名詞」，如「cups of」、「glasses of」等，不可漏掉其後的介系詞「of」。

2.人稱所有格，有一種形式→Tom is her friend.

非人稱所有格，有一種形式→The cover of the book.（用「of」來代表所有格）

3.雙重所有格，有兩種形式

　→Tom is a friend of Bob's.（用「of」與「 's」，表示雙重所有格）

　→Tom is a friend of my brother's.（用「of」與「 's」，表示雙重所有格）

代名詞

1.代名詞所有格：共有my、our、your、his、her、its、their等七個，其後必需加名詞。
2.所有代名詞：共有mine、ours、yours、his、hers、its、theirs等七個，其後不可加名

詞。

上述兩項詞稱不同，用法就不同。

前項詞稱是「所有格」，所以其後必加名詞，不可不加。如my car、our school、his friends……等。

後項詞稱是「代名詞」，其後不可加名詞。如a friend of mine、a book of hers、a car of his……等。

3.such a nice ～　　　　It is such a nice book.　They are such nice books.

　　so nice a ～　　　　It is so nice a book..　　　　The books are so nice.

重點提醒：這兩個用法固定，不要混淆。考生要注意的是形容詞（nice）的不同位置。

such as+多個名詞→He enjoys sports, such as swimming, diving and skiing.

重點提醒：such as，中譯為「像是、諸如」之意，其後大多接複數。

4.both 的三種用法

　　⑴(Both A and B) → Both Tom and Mary are from Paris.

　　⑵(Both of them...)→Both of them　　　are from Paris.

　　⑶(They both) →　They both　　　　　are from Paris.

重點提醒：用both的前提，只限在「兩者之間」，三者以上不適用。

5.either兩者任一皆～　Either girl can dance.（兩位女生中的任何一個都會跳舞。）

　　neither兩者任一皆不～　Neither girl can dance.（兩位女生中的任何一個都不會跳舞。）

重點提醒：

⑴neither屬於「否定」字，本身已含否定字義，其後同句內不可有「not、no」等字出現。其他常用否定字有：never、seldom、rarely、hardly、scarcely等。

⑵用either, neither的前提，只限在「兩者之間」，三者以上皆不適用。

⑶請考生注意，either、neither二字，也可當副詞，例如：

　　I like this book, too.（肯定句的「也」用「too」作副詞）

　　I don't like this book, either（否定句的「也」，用「either」作副詞）

6.關係代名詞：who、which、what等三字，位於句中時稱為「關係代名詞」，例句：

　　Tom is the student who called yesterday.

　　Tom is the student whom I met yesterday.

　　Tom is the student whose father is a doctor.

重點提醒：題目空格處要選who、whom或whose，取決於空格右方的字，該字是「動詞」時，需選主格的who；該字是「人稱主格」（如Tom、Mary、you、I、they）時，選受格的whom；該字是「一般名詞」時，選所有格的whose。

7.關係副詞：when、where、why、how等四字位於句中時，稱為「關係副詞」，例句：

　　Last Tuesday was the day when he returned to Taipei.

　　Hualien is the place where his parents live.

Financial problem is the reason <u>why</u> he stole the money.

Going by metro is the way <u>how</u> he goes to work.

重點提醒：考題空格內要選擇哪一個關係副詞，取決於空格前的先行詞，代表「時間」的用when，代表「地方」的用where，代表「原因」的用why，代表「方法」的用how。

8.不能省略的介系詞──有些片語組內的介系詞，在關係代名詞的使用不能省略。例句：

Tom was the person whom <u>I talked with</u> yesterday.

=Tom was the person <u>with whom</u> I <u>talked</u> yesterday.

This is issue <u>of which</u> they <u>spoke</u> a week ago.

This is issue which they <u>spoke of</u> a week ago.

重點提醒：片語的末字為介系詞，用在關係代名詞或關係副詞時，介系詞不可省略。

9.連接詞用法：

位於兩個子句中的七個疑問詞都是連接詞。另外，最常用的連接詞還有who、which、what、when、where、why、how、that、before、after、because、whether、if、unless、in case、 as soon as、as long as……等。

重點提醒：

⑴連接詞後的「從屬子句」，不可倒裝。例句：

(○) I know <u>who you are</u>.

(x) I know who are you.

⑵連接詞後的「從屬子句」，不用否定句。例句：

(○) I <u>don't think</u> he is coming.

(x) I think he is not coming.

形容詞

1.形容詞的後位形容：

名詞＋現在分詞片語 The man <u>sitting by the tree</u> came from New York..

                = The man <u>who is sitting by the tree</u> came from New York.

名詞＋過去分詞片語 This is the book <u>published by ABC Co.</u> last week.

           =This is the book <u>which was published by ABC Co.</u> last week.

重點提醒：名詞後加現在分詞片語或過去分詞片語，在許多考題上常出現。它等於關係代名詞後的「形容詞片語」。換言之，是上述例句內的「sitting by the tree = who is sitting by the tree」。

2.形容詞三級

級別	原級	比較級	最高級
單音節時	tall	taller	tallest
多音節	expensive	more expensive	most expensive

⑴單音節的「比較級」，是在原級字後加「er」；「最高級」，是在原級字後加「est」。

⑵多音節的「比較級」，是在原級字前加「more」；「最高級」，是在原級字前加「most」。

⑶不論單音節或多音節的最高級，都需在字前加「the」，如the tallest、the most expensive。

[動詞]

1. 英文動詞分「有限類動詞」與「非限類動詞」兩大類。

⑴有限類動詞：包括「普通動詞」與「特別動詞」兩種。

⑵英文動詞字後未加s、es、ed、ing等，統稱為「普通動詞」。

⑶特別動詞只有六組（24個）（請參閱P.191「英文動詞字群（表一）」）。24個特別動詞外的成千上萬個動詞，都稱為「普通動詞」。

⑷不論特別動詞或普通動詞，一定是句子中的第一個動詞。而24個特別動詞，在句中的位階都比普通動詞高。

例句：He goes to school every day.

He did not go to school yesterday.

He will go to school tomorrow.

（第一句為「現在式」，句中第一個動詞goes，因為不在24個特別動詞內，所以是普通動詞。第二句為「未來式」，因文法公式，在原句第一個動詞goes前加入will。此時will才是句中第一個動詞，原有的goes變成句中第二個動詞。既然不再是第一個動詞，所以它只好恢復原形，成為「原形動詞」。）

2. 一個英文句子如果有兩個以上的動詞時，特別動詞之後可接哪些動詞，依表二規定（見P.191表二）。

⑴99%的普通動詞之後加「不定詞」。例句：

I want to go home to study English and to take a shower.

⑵1%的普通詞詞之後加「動名詞」。例句：

I enjoy reading.

Keep talking.

Don't stop singing.

換言之，

⑴其後需加動名詞的這1%普通動詞，有mind、enjoy、avoid、finish、keep、stop、deny、quit、resent、delay、admit、consider、begin……。

⑵其後需加動名詞的，還有兩個形容詞busy、worth。

⑶其後需加動名詞的，還有片語組 be sued to、be accustomed to、look forward to、according to、be up to、be capable of、feel like、have fun、it's no use、end up等的所

　　有介系詞之後。

3. 簡單過去式與現在完成式的差別在於：

簡單過去式（有明顯的過去時間副詞）→Tom bought a new car last week.

現在完成式（不可有明顯的過去時間副詞）→Tom has bought a new car.

4. 現在完成式與現在完成進行式的差別在於：

現在完成式，指「至今為止的狀態」　He has been sick for two days.

　　　　　　　　　　　　　　　　I have just finished my homework.

現在完成進行式，指「持續的動作」　He has been playing the game for two hours.

　　　　　　　　　　　　　　　　He has been standing there all morning.

5. 過去進行式與過去完成式的差別在於：

過去進行式：主要子句用「was, were +Ving + 連接詞 + 從屬子句用過去式動詞」

I　　　　was reading a report　　　　　when　　　　　Peter came in..

= When Peter came in , I was reading a report.

過去完成式：主要子句用「had + pp（過去分詞） + 連接詞 + 從屬子句用過去式動
　　　　　　詞」

I　　　　had finished the tet　　　　　before　　　　　I left school.

The manager had left　　　　when　　　　　I arrived at his office.

6. 時間或條件子句時，從屬句用現在式動詞　Give this letter to Joe when he comes.

從屬子句作受詞時，用未來式動詞　　　　I don't know when he will come

7. 附帶問句用法：

⑴ 肯定句用否定附帶 He is nice, isn't he ?

　　　　　　　　　He has been here before, hasn't he ?

⑵ 否定句用肯定附帶 She always comes early, doesn't she ?

　　　　　　　　　She was late yesterday, didn't she ?

重點提醒：

⑴ 這種句子的應答技巧，在於句中第一個動詞。前句是用哪一個特別動詞，附帶句就用同一
　 個特別動詞答回去。

⑵ 前句的第一個動詞如果是用普通動詞說，附帶句就只能用 do 組的 do、does、did 的某一個
　 答回去。

⑶ 此外，考生還要注意：不管上述否定附帶或肯定附帶，它的前半句與後半句都是相反的。

8. 原形動詞的省略：

want to, hope to, like to, try to,　　Do you want to go ?　　　No, I don't want to.

have to, be going to,　　　　　　　Do you have to write it ?　　Yes, I have to.

9. 原形動詞的位置：

⑴ 在下列 14 個特別動詞之後 do, does, did, can, could, may, might, shall, should, will,
　 would, must, need, dare

Do you want...? Does she like...? Did they say...? Can you sing ...? May I speak...? Shall we go...? Will you be....? Would you like...? He must go. You need not go. He dare not say that.

(2) 在感官動詞see, hear之後

I hear her sing every morning.

I see her sell watches every day.

(3) 在下列使役動詞或成語之後 make, let, have, had better, would rather, do nothing but, can not but,

Don't make me laugh

Let's go

You had better leave before I change my mind.

10. 常用聯結動詞有三組，後加原級形容詞

(1) be 動詞組 am, are, is, was, were　　　She is beautiful.

(2) 感官動詞組feel, look, smell, sound, taste　The hat looks nice on you.

(3) 其他組 become, get, grow, seem, keep,　The culture remain strong.
　　　　　Appear, remain

11. 分詞構句

Judging from ～ 由～判斷　　　　Judging from his accent, he must be English.

Speaking of ～ 說到～　　　　　Speaking of the devil, here comes Tom..

Generally speaking 一般而言　Generally speaking, he is a good person.

12. 現在分詞與過去分詞作為形容詞

The baby is sleeping

The wounded soldier needs help.

13. 試題四選項裡怎應選 Ved 或 Ving？

The movie is embarrassing　還是 This movie is embarrassed?

I am / feel bored.　　　　　還是 I am / feel boring.

重點提醒：embarrassing 與 embarrassed 都當形容詞。要看句中主詞來決定用哪一個。

(1) 主詞為事或物時，用 embarrassing 只形容該事或物如何如何。

(2) 主詞為人時，用 embarrassed 來說明主詞這個人的「感覺」如何如何。

14. have +人時，後接原形動詞 I will have Tom mail the letter.

　　have +物時，後接過去分詞　　I had my house painted last week.

重點提醒：have 後面是人 Tom，所以接原形動詞 mail

　　　　　had 之後是物 house，所以接過去分詞 painte

used to + 原形動詞　　　　My friend Bob used to come here every week.

be used to 名詞 / 動名詞　　I am used to my wife's nagging.

get used to　　　　　　　You'd better get used to his bad temper if you want this high salary.

重點提醒：

⑴ 空格右邊是動詞 come，所以空格內選 used to。

⑵ 空格右邊是名詞 my wife's，所以空格內選 be used to。

⑶ 空格右邊是名詞 his bad temper，所以空格內選 get used to。

15. if 之後如果選 be 動詞，只能選 were I wouldn't say that if I were you.

He talks as if he were the manager of the department

16. 倒裝題的解題

試題開頭，如果有 never, hardly, only, no 等相關字（no sooner, on no account...等），選項要倒裝：

Not only did we lost the money, but we also got lost.

Only if you have a visa can you enter the country.

英文動詞字群（表一）

第一類動詞：一定是句子中第一個動詞，字形隨主詞作變化。
1. 特別動詞　24 個
2. 普通動詞　N 個（24 個特別動詞外的所有動詞原式）
說明：
(1) 特別動詞後接的動詞，應依（表二）規定
(2) 普通動詞後接的動詞，規定如下：
① 99%普通動詞 + 不定詞
② 1%普通動詞 + 動名詞
第二類動詞：不可做為句子中第一個動詞，字形不隨主詞作變化。
1. 原形動詞：不加 s、es、ed、ing 等動詞原形。如 come、go 等。
2. 不定詞：原形動詞前加 to 者，如 to come、to go 等。
3. 動名詞：原形動詞後加 ing 者，如 coming、going 等。
4. 現在分詞：原形動詞後加 ing 者，如 coming、going 等。
5. 過去分詞：規則變化時，原形後加 ed；不規則時，字形不定。

特別動詞 + 第二類動詞（表二）

組別	特限類動詞	非限類動詞	
Be	Am　Are　Is　Was　Were	+現在分詞 = 進行式 +過去分詞 = 被動語態 +不定詞　 = 表目的	例句1 例句2 例句3
Have	Have Has　　Had	+過去分詞 = 完成式 +不定詞　 = 表必須	例句4 例句5

Do	Do Doe Did		例句6
Can	Can May Could Might	＋原型動詞	例句7
Shall	Shall Will Should Would		例句8
Must	Must Need Dare		例句9
Ought	Used	＋不定詞	例句10

1. They <u>are having</u> a meeting at the moment.

2. All students <u>are told to stand</u> in line at the ticket counter.

3. We <u>are to study</u> European history today.

4. She <u>has passed</u> her final exam at school.

5. You don't <u>have to take</u> this job if you don't want to.

6. <u>Do</u> you <u>want</u> me to wake you up in the morning ?

7. <u>Can</u> I <u>use</u> the pay-phone there ?

8. I <u>will call</u> you sometime tomorrow.

9. You <u>mustn't leave</u> now, we are in the middle of the meeting

10. You <u>ought to do</u> what your mother says.

    They <u>used to come</u> here every week.

附錄二
重要片語、俚語之補充
（學測、指考、統測）

A

a stone's throw/cast　短距離

annoyed at　惱怒

at a premium　高價

at a snail's pace　緩慢

at all cost　不計代價

at any rate　無論如何

at finger's ends　精通

at issue　爭論中

at length　最後 詳細的

at sixes and sevens　七嘴八舌

at the risk of　冒險

aware of　知道

B

be opposed to　相對立

behind time　過期

blame for　責備

bound for　開往

break out　爆發

bring about　引起

by fours and fives　三五成群

by means of　用～方法

by no means　決沒有

by virture of　由於

C

carry on　繼續

carry out　進行

charge with　控訴

comparable with　可比較

correspond with　符合

count on / rely on　倚賴

crucial for　至關重要

D

deal with　處理

deprive of　剝奪

derive from　從～得到

devote to　奉獻

different from　不同於

distant from　遠的

distinct from　與不同

distinguish from　辨別

divided into　分開

donkey's years　很長時間

F

famous for　因～出名

free from　沒有

G

get away with　僥倖做到

give in　屈服

give up　放棄

H

hear from　到～訊息

hinder from　妨礙

I

identify with　認同

in care of　由～轉交

in case of　如果

in charge of　負責

in lieu of 代替
in the lion's paws 處於險境
inquire into 查究
interfere with 干擾 妨礙

K
keep house 管理家務

L
live a dog's life 過悲慘生活

M
meet the demand 滿足需求
mistaken for 誤為

N
not a dog's chance 毫無機會

O
on a razor's edge 處險境
on account of 因為
on all fours 吻合 爬行
on behalf of 代表
one's hearts' content 心滿意足
out of order 故障
out of question 毫無疑問

P
persuade of 說服
prevent from 防止
provide with 提供
put off 延遲

R
remind of 提醒
responsible for 對～負責
result from 起因於
result in 導致

S
separate from 與～分開
set about 開始
set in 開始
show off 炫耀
show up 出現
six of one and half a dozen 差不多
stir up a hornet's nest 自找麻煩
straight from the horse's mouth 來自可靠消息
substitute for 代替

T
take for 認為
take off 起飛 脫下
take on 呈現
ten to one 十之八九
to one's advantage 對～有利
to sum up 總之
turn out 變成
turn out 變成
turn up 出現
two by four 微不足道的
twos and threes 三三兩兩

U
under the circumstances 在此情況下

W
with a view to 為了～

附錄三
重要字彙補充
（學測、指考、統測）

A

accuracy　準確
achievement　成就
administration　管理
aggressive　積極
agriculture　農業
alternative　選擇
amateur　業餘
ambitious　有雄心
analyze　分析
anniversary　週年日
announcement　公告
anxious　焦慮不安
applause　掌聲
appliance　器具
appropriate　合適
aquarium　水族館
architecture　建築
artificial　人造
assassinate　暗殺
athelete　運動員
atmosphere　氣氛
attractive　有吸引力
autobiography　自傳

B

bacteria　細菌
bankrupt　破產
bargain　講價
behavior　行為
beneficial　受益
budget　預算
bulletin board　佈告牌

C

campaign　活動
candidate　候選人
canyon　峽谷
capacity　能力
casualty　傷亡
celebrate　慶祝
ceremony　典禮
certificate　證明書
characteristic　特性
circulation　流通
civilization　文明
classify　分類
climax　高潮
clumsy　笨拙
coincidence　巧合
collapse　瓦解
colleague　同事
combination　結合
comfortable　舒適
commission　委托
communication　通訊
community　社區
competitor　競爭者
complicated　複雜
comprehension　理解
concentrate　集中
conference　會議
confidence　信任
congratulate　祝賀
connection　連接
consequence　後果
conservative　保守

constitution　憲法
construction　建設
consumer products　消費產品
contemporary　當代
continental　大陸
contribution　貢獻
convenience　便利
convention　傳統
convince　使確信
courtesy　禮貌
crash　碰撞
creature　動物
criminal　犯罪
criticize　批評
cultivate　培養
curiosity　好奇
cyclist　騎車者

D

deadline　期限
decade　十年
declaration　宣告
decoration　裝飾
defend　防衛
definition　定義
delegate　代表
democracy　民主
demonstration　遊行示威
depression　沮喪
describe　描述
deserve　應得的
destination　目的地
destroy　破壞
destructive　有破壞性
determination　決心
development　發展
device　小設備
devote　奉獻
digestion　消化
digital　數據化

disappointed　失望
disaster　災難
discipline　紀律
disguise　偽裝
disgust　厭惡
domestic　國內
dominate　支配
drawbacks　缺點
dynamic　動力

E

editorial　社論
efficiency　效率
elementary　初步
eliminate　消除
emphasize　強調
energetic　充滿活力
enlarge　擴大
entertainer　演員
enthusiasm　熱情
entitle　有資格
environment　環境
equipment　設備
escalator　電扶梯
essential　必要的
establish　建立
estimate　估計
evaluate　評價
eventually　終於
evidence　證據
exaggerate　誇大
excellent　極好
excursion　旅行
executive　執行
exhaust　筋疲力盡
exhibition　展覽會
experiment　實驗
extreme　極端

F

facility 能力

faithful 忠實

familiar with 熟悉

farewell party 惜別會

fatal 致命

feedback 回饋

financial 金融

forecast weather 預報天氣

fortunately 幸好

frequenly 經常

frightened 嚇住

frustrate 受挫

function 起作用

G

genuine 真實

gigantic 龐大

glorious 光榮

gradually 逐漸

greenhouse 溫室

grocery 雜貨店

guarantee 保證

guardian 守護人

H

habitual 習慣

hairdresser 理髮師

handicap 障礙

hardship 艱難

harmony 和諧

harvest 收成

headquaters 總部

hesitate 猶豫

hijack 劫持

historical 歷史

horizon 地平線

humanity 人類

humidity 濕度

hurricane 颶風

hydrogen 氫

I

identification 鑑定

identity 身分

ignore 忽視

imagination 想像

immediately 立即

impact 影響

impression 印象

increasing 增加

independent 獨立於

inevitable 不可避免

inflation 通貨膨脹

informal 非正式

ingredient 成分

inhabitant 居民

injection 注射

injured 使受傷

innocence 清白

inquiry 詢問

inspector 檢查員

inspire 鼓舞

institution 機構 學院

intellectual 智慧

intensify 加強

interact 相互作用

interfere 干涉

internal 內部

interpret 解釋

intruder 入侵者

invade 侵入

invention 發明

investment 投資

invisible 看不見

J

journey 旅行

K

kidnap　拐走

knowledge　知識

L

landmark　地標

landscape　風景

landslide　山崩

language barrier　語言障礙

latitude　緯度

launch　發動　開始～

lavatory　洗手間

league　聯盟

lecture　演講

legendary　傳奇

leisure　休閒

liberate　解放

literature　文學

loyalty　忠實

luxurious　豪華

M

magnet　磁鐵

majority　多數

manageable　可管理

manufacture　製造

marathon　馬拉松

margin profit　最低利潤

mature　成熟

measurement　測量

memorandum　備忘錄

mineral　礦物質

ministry　部會

minority　少數

miracle　奇跡

miserable　痛苦

moderate　適度

moisture　水分

monument　紀念碑

mortgage　抵押

motivation　動機

multiple　倍數

mystery　神祕

N

negotiate　談判

novelist　小説家

nuclear　核子

numerous　許多

nutrition　營養

O

obedient　服從

observe　觀察

obviously　顯而易見

occasion　場合

occupy　佔用

offensive　冒犯

opposition　反對

oral　口頭

orchestra　管弦樂隊

organic　有機

orphanage　育幼院

outstanding　傑出

overcome　克服

overthrow　推翻

oxygen　氧

P

panic　恐慌

paragraph　段落

parliament　議會

participate　參加

particular　特別

partnership　合夥

patriotic　愛國

peculiar　獨特

penalty　懲罰

penguin　企鵝

performance　表現

perfume　香水

pernanent　永久

persist　堅持

persuade　說服

phenomenon　現象

philosopher　哲學家

physical　物理

pilgrim　朝拜者

pioneer　開發者

pirate　海盜

poetry　詩

poisonous　有毒

politics　政治

portable　可攜帶

portrait　肖像

postpone　延遲

potential　潛能

practical　實際

predict　預言

preferable　更好

pregnant　懷孕

presentation　說明會

prevent　防止

previous　之前

primary　主要

privacy　隱私

privilege　特權

procedure　程序

profitable　有利潤

progressive　進步

prohibit　禁止

promote　推廣

prompt　迅速

proper　適當

proportion　比例

proposal　提議

prosperous　繁榮

protective　保護

psychology　心理學

publicity　宣傳

punctual　準時

pursuit　追逐

Q

qualification　資格

quantity　數量

quotation　報價

R

racial　種族

radiation　輻射

rank　職級

reaction　反應

realistic　實際

recession　衰退

recognize　認出

recommend　推薦

recreation　娛樂

reduction　減少

reference　參考

reflection　反射

refugee　難民

registration　登記

rehearsal　排練

relative　有關

relax　放鬆

reliable　可靠

relief　舒緩疼痛

religion　宗教

remarkable　驚人

remind　提醒

reputation　名聲

requirement　要求

research　研究

resemble　相像

reservation　預定

resignation　辭職

S

sacrifice　犧牲

sanctions　國際制裁

satellite　衛星

satisfy　滿足

scenery　風景

scheme　計畫

scholarship　獎學金

scold　訓斥

scratch　抓癢

sculpture　雕刻品

security　安全

seize　抓住

sensitive　敏感

settlement　解決

sexual　性

significance　意義

similarity　相似

skyscraper　摩天大廈

slighly　稍微

sociable　愛交際

sorrow　悲哀

specific　具體　明確

spiritual　精神

splendid　壯觀

sportsmanship　運動員風格

squeeze　擠壓

stadium　體育場

starve　飢餓

stimulate　刺激

strategy　策略

structor　指導者

structure　架構

stubborn　頑固

substance　物質

suburbs　市郊

suffer　遭受

sufficient　足夠

suicide　自殺

summarize　總結

superior　優良

supervisor　監督人

supreme court　最高法院

survival　生存

suspect　懷疑

suspend　中止

suspicious　疑心

symbolize　象徵性

sympathy　同情

symphony　交響樂

symptom　症狀

T

talent　才能

technical　技術

temporary　暫時

terminal　終端

territory　領土

tolerate　容忍

tornado　龍捲風

tortoise　烏龜

tragedy　悲劇

transform　改變

tremendous　驚人地

typical　典型

U

unconscious　無意識

underweight　重量不足

unfortunately　令人遺憾

urge　呼籲

urgent　緊急

V

vacant　空位空房

vegetarian　素食者

victom　受害者

vigor　活力

visual　視覺

vital　至關重要

voluntary　自願

voyage　航行

W

wages　工資

wander　徘徊

welfare　福利

widespread　廣泛

worthwhile　值得

國家圖書館出版品預行編目資料

97～101年英文科指考・學測等歷屆試題解
析應考破題技巧大公開／黃惠政著. ――二
版.――臺北市：文字復興，2013.01
　面；　公分
ISBN 978-957-11-6936-1（平裝）
1.英語　2.問題集　3.中等教育　4.技職教育
524.38　　　　　　　　　101015721

WX06　　升大學05

97～101年英文科指考・學測等歷屆試題解析
應考破題技巧大公開

作　　者— 黃惠政（302.5）

發 行 人— 楊榮川

總 編 輯— 王翠華

主　　編— 黃惠娟

責任編輯— 盧羿珊

封面設計— 黃聖文

出 版 者— 文字復興有限公司

地　　址：106台北市大安區和平東路二段339號4樓

電　　話：(02)2705-5066　　傳　　真：(02)2706-6100

網　　址：http://www.wunan.com.tw

電子郵件：wunan@wunan.com.tw

劃撥帳號：01068953

戶　　名：文字復興有限公司

台中市駐區辦公室/台中市中區中山路6號

電　　話：(04)2223-0891　　傳　　真：(04)2223-3549

高雄市駐區辦公室/高雄市新興區中山一路290號

電　　話：(07)2358-702　　傳　　真：(07)2350-236

法律顧問　元貞聯合法律事務所　張澤平律師

出版日期　2013年 1 月二版一刷

定　　價　新臺幣250元